# Religion and Law in Serbia

# Religion and Law in Serbia

**Second Edition**

**Marko Nikolić**
**Vladimir Davidović†**
**Darko Tanasković**
**Mileta Radojević†**

This book was originally published as a monograph in the International Encyclopaedia of Laws/Religion Law.

Founding Editor: Roger Blanpain
General Editor: Frank Hendrickx
Volume Editor: Wouter Druwé

Wolters Kluwer

*Published by:*
Kluwer Law International B.V.
PO Box 316
2400 AH Alphen aan den Rijn
The Netherlands
E-mail: lrs-sales@wolterskluwer.com
Website: www.wolterskluwer.com/en/solutions/kluwerlawinternational

*Sold and distributed by:*
Wolters Kluwer Legal & Regulatory U.S.
920 Links Avenue
Landisville, PA 17538
United States of America
E-mail: customer.service@wolterskluwer.com



ISBN 978-94-035-1698-1

e-Book: ISBN 978-94-035-1708-7
web-PDF: ISBN 978-94-035-1718-6

# The Authors

Dr Marko Nikolić was born in Belgrade on 28 February 1975. He holds a Master's in International Relations from the Faculties of Political Science in Belgrade and Rome (La Sapienza), with the topics NATO Expansion to the East (1998) and European Union Foreign Policy and Security (2003). He defended his doctoral dissertation entitled *Ecumenism and the Relationship Between the Roman Catholic and Serbian Orthodox Churches after the Second Vatican Council* at the Faculty of Philosophy in Belgrade in 2010. His book *Ecumenical Relations of Serbian Orthodox and Roman Catholic Church 1962–2000* (Official Gazette of RS, Belgrade, 2011) was suggested by Vienna's Foundation *Pro Oriente* to be translated into English and German.

Dr Marko Nikolić has been a Research Fellow at the Institute of International Politics and Economics (IIPE) in Belgrade (2001–2015), Editor-in-Chief of its Scientific Journal *Review of International Affairs* (RIA, 2013–2015) and Coordinator of the Institute's Ambassadors' Forum (2011–2015). By the decision of the Government of the Republic of Serbia, he was appointed Assistant Director of the Administration for Cooperation with Churches and Religious Communities of the Ministry of Justice, in the position of Head of the Sector for Relations with Churches and Religious Communities in December 2015.

His scientific area and research have focused on European (NATO, European Union (EU) foreign and security policy, political groups in the EU) and migration issues (migration within the EU and the Western Balkans, re-admission), and since 2006, research on interreligious cooperation, ecumenism, interchurch relations and the relationship between the state and the church in the context of the Vatican's contemporary policy in Southeast Europe. He has participated in numerous international and interreligious scientific conferences in the region and Europe during 2008–2015 and published several books and over thirty scientific papers, articles and presentations. Marko Nikolić speaks English, Italian, French and Russian.

## The Authors

Dr Vladimir Davidović (deceased 2020) was born in 1955 in Smederevo, Serbia. He graduated from the Faculty of Law of the University of Belgrade in 1978. He is an expert in the protection of human rights, legal aspects of the fight against money laundering and the financing of terrorism, organized crime and corruption. During his career, he worked as the Secretary of the Serbian Academy of Sciences and Arts, Deputy Minister of Science of the Republic of Serbia, Director of the Information Directorate in the Ministry of Foreign Affairs and Assistant Minister of Justice of the Republic of Serbia. He has published more than twenty books, mostly in the field of history.

Prof. Dr Darko Tanasković was born in Zagreb in 1948. He graduated from the Faculty of Philology in Belgrade with a Bachelor's in Oriental Philology (1970), a Master's (1972) and a Doctorate (1979) with a dissertation entitled 'Arabic Language in Modern Tunisia – Diclosia and Bilingualism'.

He was a lecturer at the Department of Oriental Studies of the Faculty of Philology (1972–2018) in several subjects in the fields of Arabic, Turkish and Islam Studies and Oriental Philology. Dr Tanasković has been a guest lecturer at numerous faculties in Serbia and abroad. He has published over eight hundred scientific and professional papers in the field of oriental studies and is the recipient of numerous awards and recognitions. From 1995 to 2018, Darko Tanasković served as ambassador to Turkey and Azerbaijan, the Holy See, Knights of Malta and as Permanent Representative of the Republic of Serbia to UNESCO in Paris. Darko Tanasković speaks English, French, Italian, Arabic, Turkish and Russian.

Mileta Radojević (deceased 2021) was born on 17 December 1955. He defended his Master's thesis entitled 'Production Management – Development Management' at the Faculty of Agriculture in Belgrade in 2007 and his doctoral dissertation entitled 'Macroeconomic changes as a factor of effectiveness and efficiency of companies' at the Faculty of Economics, University 'Megatrend' in Belgrade in 2012. In the field of development management, he has authored numerous monographs and scientific papers. Mileta Radojević was the Director of the Office for Cooperation with Churches and Religious Communities of the Government of the Republic of Serbia during 2012–2014, and during 2014–2020, he was the Director of the Administration for Cooperation with Churches and Religious Communities of the Ministry of Justice.

# Table of Contents

The Authors 3

List of Abbreviations 9

Highlights 11

General Introduction 13

§1. General Background of the Country 13

§2. Social Facts about Religion 16

§3. Historical Background 25

Part I. Legal Framework and Sources 27

Chapter 1. Constitutional Position of Religion 27

Chapter 2. Other Legislation with Regard to Religion 33

Chapter 3. Typology of the System 50

Part II. Religious Freedom in General 53

Chapter 1. Individual Religious Freedom 55

Chapter 2. Collective Religious Freedom 61

Chapter 3. Organizational Religious Freedom 64

Part III. Legal Status of Religious Communities 67

Chapter 1. Formal Status of Religious Communities 67

Chapter 2. Autonomy of Religious Communities 69

Chapter 3. Fundamental Rights and Religious Communities 70

Chapter 4. Contractual Religious Freedom 72

Part IV. International, Transnational and Regional Effects on Religious Communities 75

Chapter 1. International Law Effects on Religious Communities 75

Chapter 2. Transnational Law Effects on Religious Communities in Serbia 81

Chapter 3. Regional Law Effects on Religious Communities 83

Part V. Religion and Politics 97

Chapter 1. Religion's Influence in Politics 97

Chapter 2. Political Influence in Religion 106

Chapter 3. Interaction Between Religion and State on a Political and Legal Level 110

Part VI. Labour Law within Religious Communities 115

Chapter 1. Scope of Application of Labour Law 115

Chapter 2. Religious Ministers and Labour Law 117

Chapter 3. Other Church Officials and Labour Law 119

Part VII. Religious Communities and Protections of the Individual 121

Chapter 1. Protecting Privacy 122

Chapter 2. Freedom to Marry (The Right to a Family) 129

Chapter 3. Freedom of Expression 131

Chapter 4. Professional Secrecy 134

Chapter 5. Medical Deontology 136

Chapter 6. Prohibition of Discrimination 139

Chapter 7. Criminal Law and Religion 140

Part VIII. Church Financing 141

Chapter 1. Direct Financing of Religious Communities 141

Chapter 2. Indirect Financing of Religious Communities 150

Part IX. Education 153

Chapter 1. Religious Education in Public and Private Schools 155

Chapter 2. Religious Schools in Serbia 159

Part X. Matrimonial and Family Law 163

Chapter 1. The Legal Position of Religious Marriage 164

Chapter 2. Legal Position of Religious Family Law 165

Part XI. Religion and Culture 169

Chapter 1. Religion and Art 174

Chapter 2. Religion and Media 176

Chapter 3. Religion and Civil Society 178

Chapter 4. Religion and Public Debate 179

Selected Bibliography 181

Index 191

**Table of Contents**

# List of Abbreviations

| | |
|---|---|
| BiH | Bosnia and Herzegovina |
| CC | Criminal Code |
| CG | Montenegro |
| CoE | Council of Europe |
| DFRY | Democratic Federal Republic of Yugoslavia |
| EU | European Union |
| FPRY | Federal People's Republic of Yugoslavia |
| FRY | Federal Republic of Yugoslavia |
| GCC | Greek Catholic Church |
| GPA | Grade Point Average |
| ICinS | Islamic Community *in* Serbia |
| ICofS | Islamic Community *of* Serbia |
| JC | Jewish Community |
| JCS | Jewish Community of Serbia |
| KiM | Kosovo and Metohija |
| Kingdom of SCS | Serbs, Croats, and Slovenes |
| MIA | Ministry of Internal Affairs |
| MOC | 'Macedonian Orthodox Church' |
| NATO | North Atlantic Treaty Organization |
| OSCE | Organization for Security and Co-operation in Europe |
| OTF | Orthodox Theological Faculty, University of Belgrade |
| PIO | Pension and Disability Insurance |
| RCC | Roman Catholic Church |
| ROC | Romanian Orthodox Church |
| RS | Republic of Serbia |
| RTS | Serbian Broadcasting Corporation |
| RTV | Radio Television of Vojvodina |

**List of Abbreviations**

| | |
|---|---|
| SAA with the EU | Stabilisation and Association Agreement with the European Union |
| SECAV | Slovak Evangelical Church a.v. |
| SFRY | Socialist Federal Republic of Yugoslavia |
| SIV | Federal Executive Council |
| SOC | Serbian Orthodox Church |
| State Union of SCG | State Union of Serbia and Montenegro |
| UN | United Nations |
| UNESCO | UN Organization for Education, Science and Culture |
| VAT | Value Added Tax |

# Highlights

The monograph *Religious Law in the Republic of Serbia* aims to acquaint the professional and general public with the nature of the law-related religious system in Serbia, a candidate for EU membership.

In accordance with Kluwer's outline, its authors covered, after the *General Introduction*, the following topics: *Legal Framework; Religious Freedom; Legal Status of Religious Communities; International, Transnational and Regional Influences on Religious Communities; Religion and Politics; Labour Law within Religious Communities; Religious Communities and the Protection of the Individual; Church Financing; Education; Matrimonial and Family Law;* and *Religion and Culture*. In the end, a Bibliography and Index of Terms are listed. Each part is divided into several (two to eight) chapters. Depending on the subject to which they are dedicated, the chapters are of unequal scope, the longer and more detailed ones being those that refer in an in-depth sense to legal and legislative matters. On that basis, the reader has been offered extensive data related to various aspects of religious life in the Republic of Serbia.

Concise and practical, this book is a valuable source of data and a comprehensive and useful guide for all academics, researchers and the general public who are interested in religious issues. *Its content embodies the personal and professional views of the First Author, not the official views of the institution of the Republic of Serbia in which he is employed.*

## Highlights

# General Introduction

## §1. General Background of the Country

*1.* The Republic of Serbia is located in Southeast Europe, in the central part of the Balkan Peninsula, at the crossroads of the most important roads connecting Europe and Asia. It covers an area of 88,361 km$^2$.[1] The northern part of the country is predominantly flat, while the central and southern parts are hilly and mountainous. Serbia has 55% of arable land, and 27% is under forests. Fertile plains are in the Pannonian lowland and its peripheral regions (Mačva, Posavina, Pomoravlje, Stig and Negotin). The length of the state border is 2,619.2 km. In the east, Serbia borders with the Republic of Bulgaria, in the northeast with the Republic of Romania, in the north with the Republic of Hungary, in the west with the Republics of Croatia and Bosnia and Herzegovina (BiH), in the southwest with the Republic of Montenegro, and in the south with the Republics of Albania and Northern Macedonia.[2]

*2.* The Constitution of the Republic of Serbia, adopted in 2006, states that it is based on the *state tradition of the Serbian people and equality of all citizens and ethnic communities*, as well as the fact that Kosovo and Metohija (KiM) is an integral part of Serbia.[3] The Republic of Serbia is defined as a *state of the Serbian people and all citizens living in it*, based on the rule of law and social justice, principles of civil democracy, human and minority rights and freedoms, and commitment to European principles and values.[4]

*3.* The legal system of the Republic of Serbia is *unique*,[5] and its territory is *inseparable,* indivisible *and decentralized.*[6]

### Horizontal and Vertical Organization of Government

*4.* The bearer of *legislative power* in the Republic of Serbia is the *National Assembly*, which consists of 250 deputies elected in direct elections, by secret ballot

1. *Statistical Yearbook of the Republic of Serbia 2018*, Statistical Office, www.stat.gov.rs, 21 Jan. 2019.
2. Ministry of Foreign Affairs of RS, http://www.mfa.gov.rs/lat/republika-srbija, 5 Mar. 2024.
3. Preamble, indent 3 of the Constitution of the Republic of Serbia, Official Gazette of RS, no. 98/2006.
4. Constitution of the Republic of Serbia from 2006, Official Gazette of RS, no. 98/2006, Art. 1.
5. Constitution of the Republic of Serbia from 2006, *supra* n. 4, Art. 4, para. 1.
6. Constitution of the Republic of Serbia from 2006, *supra* n. 4, Art. 8, para. 1 and Art. 176.

in accordance with the law.[7] It guarantees and ensures *equality and representation of national minorities* and the *use of minority languages.*[8] *The Law on the Election of Members of Parliament*[9] stipulates that political parties of national minorities and their coalitions *participate in the distribution of mandates even when they receive less than the required threshold of 5% of the total number of voters in the elections*, with the aim of representing the interests of national minorities and protecting and improving the rights of their members in accordance with international legal standards.[10] The bearer of *executive power* in Serbia is the *Government* which establishes and conducts state policy, executes laws and other general acts of the National Assembly, adopts regulations and other general acts for the purpose of law enforcement, proposes laws and other general acts to the National Assembly and gives its opinion on them, directs and adjusts the work of public administration bodies.[11] *The Unity of State of the Republic of Serbia* is personified by the *President of the Republic* who represents the state in the country and abroad, promulgates laws by decree, proposes candidates for Prime Minister to the National Assembly after considering the views of representatives of elected lists of candidates, receives letters of credit and revocable letters of foreign diplomatic representatives, grants amnesties and awards honours, commands the Serbian Army and appoints, promotes and relieve its officers.[12]

*5.* The Republic of Serbia has two *autonomous provinces* (AP) – *KiM and Vojvodina.* The Constitution provided for the possibility of establishing new provinces, as well as revoking or merging the existing ones according to the procedure envisaged for changing the Constitution. Following the North Atlantic Treaty Organization (NATO) aggression on the Federal Republic of Yugoslavia (FRY) from March to June 1999, United Nations (UN) Security Council (UN) Resolution no. 1244[13] established the *UN Provisional Administration (UNMIK)* in the Autonomous Province of KiM, which will remain in place until its *essential autonomy is ensured and implemented within the Republic of Serbia.*[14] Autonomy shall be regulated when conditions are created by a special law which shall be passed in accordance with the proceedings envisaged for amending the Constitution.

*6. The* competence *of the autonomous provinces* in the Republic of Serbia refers to issues of urban planning and development; agriculture, water management, forestry, hunting, fishery, tourism, catering, environmental protection, industry and craftsmanship, road, river and railway transport and road repairs, organizing fairs

7. Constitution of the Republic of Serbia from 2006, *supra* n. 4, Art. 100, para. 1.
8. Constitution of the Republic of Serbia from 2006, *supra* n. 4, Art. 100, para. 2.
9. Law on the Election of Members of Parliament, Official Gazette of RS, nos 101/2005, 104/2009, 36/2011, 68/2020.
10. *Ibid.*, Art. 81, paras 2 and 3.
11. Constitution of the Republic of Serbia from 2006, *supra* n. 4, Art. 123.
12. Constitution of the Republic of Serbia from 2006, *supra* n. 4, Art. 112.
13. UN Security Council Resolution 1244 of 10 Jun. 1999, https://unmik.unmissions.org/sr/rezolucija-ujedinjenih-nacija-1244, 5 Mar. 2024.
14. Constitution of the Republic of Serbia from 2006, *supra* n. 4, Art. 182, paras 2 and 3.

and other economic events; education, sports, culture, health care and social welfare, public informing at the provincial level; *exercising human and minority rights* in accordance with the law; and to establish the symbols of the province and the manner in which they are used.[15] The state may also entrust certain issues within its competence to the autonomous provinces of the state of Serbia. Provinces manage *provincial property* in accordance with the law,[16] have *direct revenues, provide resources for local self-government units* for performing entrusted tasks and adopt *their budget* and *annual balance sheets.*[17] Their highest legal act is the *statute,*[18] which is adopted by the Provincial Assembly based on the consent of the National Assembly of the Republic of Serbia. The bodies of AP Vojvodina are the Assembly, the Executive Council, and the administrative bodies. Since it is *inhabited by a population with a mixed ethnic composition, a proportional representation of national minorities is enabled in its assemblies.*[19]

*7. Units of local self-government* in the Republic of Serbia are *municipalities, cities, and the City of* Belgrade. *Competencies of cities and municipalities*[20] are determined by law.[21] Municipalities are engaged in the performance and development of *municipal activities*; regulating, providing and using *urban construction sites and business premises*; construction, reconstruction and maintenance of *local roads, streets and other public facilities* of municipal importance and provision of local transport; meeting the needs of citizens in the *field of education, culture, health care and social welfare, child welfare, sports and physical culture*; by promoting *tourism, craftsmanship, catering and commerce*; *environment protection, from natural and other disasters* and the protection of *cultural heritage* of importance to the municipality; as well as the protection, improvement and use of *agricultural land.* In accordance with the law, the municipality *independently adopts its budget and balance sheet, urban plan, and development programme* and determines its *symbols* and the manner of their use. It also takes care of the *realization, protection, and promotion of human and minority rights*, as well as *public information* in its territory.[22]

## Human and Minority Rights in Serbia – Basic Principles

*8.* Human and minority rights represent the *values* on which, among others, the Republic of Serbia is founded.[23] The entire second part of its Constitution is dedicated to them. The basic principles of human and minority rights include the *direct application of guaranteed rights, the constitutional regulation of the purpose of*

15. Constitution of the Republic of Serbia from 2006, *supra* n. 4, Art. 183.
16. Constitution of the Republic of Serbia from 2006, *supra* n. 4, Art. 178, para. 1.
17. Constitution of the Republic of Serbia from 2006, *supra* n. 4, Art. 183, para. 6.
18. Constitution of the Republic of Serbia from 2006, *supra* n. 4, Art. 185.
19. Constitution of the Republic of Serbia from 2006, *supra* n. 4, Art. 180, para. 4 and Law on Establishing the Competencies of the Autonomous Province of Vojvodina, Official Gazette of RS, nos 99/2009 and 67/2012 – Decision US.
20. Law on Local Self-Government, Official Gazette of RS, nos 129/2007, 83/2014, 101/2016, and 47/2018.
21. Constitution of the Republic of Serbia from 2006, *supra* n. 4, Art. 177.
22. Constitution of the Republic of Serbia from 2006, *supra* n. 4, Art. 190.
23. Constitution of the Republic of Serbia from 2006, *supra* n. 4, Art. 1.

*constitutional guarantees, the regulation of restrictions on human and minority rights, the prohibition of discrimination* and *their protection.*

*9.* The direct application of guaranteed rights is provided for in Article 18, paragraph 2 of the Constitution, which stipulates that human and minority rights guaranteed by generally accepted rules of international law and ratified international treaties are guaranteed by this Constitution and as such are *directly implemented.* Only if the Constitution explicitly provides for that, the Law may prescribe the manner of exercising certain human rights, whereby it must not influence the substance of the guaranteed right. In accordance with the applicable international standards of human and minority rights, as well as the practice of international institutions that monitor their implementation, the provisions of the Constitution on human and minority rights are interpreted to the benefit of *promoting values of a democratic society.*[24] The Constitution guarantees inalienable human and minority rights, which *preserve human dignity* and *exercise the full freedom and equality of each individual* in a just, open and democratic society based on the principle of the *rule of law.*[25] Human and minority rights in Serbia guaranteed by the Constitution *may be restricted by the law to the extent necessary* to meet the constitutional purpose of restriction in a democratic society and without encroaching upon the substance of the relevant guaranteed right.[26] Before the Constitution and the law, *all citizens are equal,* and *any direct or indirect discrimination is explicitly prohibited* on any grounds.[27] *Everyone has the right to judicial protection* if their human or minority rights, as guaranteed by the Constitution, have been violated or denied, and a citizen h*as the right to address international institutions* in order to protect their freedoms and rights guaranteed by the Constitution of the Republic of Serbia.[28]

## §2. Social Facts about Religion

*10.* Religions did not participate significantly in social life in Yugoslavia during 1945–1990.[29] The authorities at the time knew they had significant cohesion and 'integrative' potential, especially in the conditions of existing antagonized interethnic and interfaith relations after the Second World War. As part of the policy of 'brotherhood and unity', the Yugoslav authorities sought to 'channel' and exploit the mentioned potentials of religious entities with the aim of interethnic and interfaith reconciliation (primarily between the Serbian and Croatian people and their churches), but to the extent that would not endanger the ruling system. The premises of the mentioned policy were various types of ethnocultural research, assessments and projections, which, among other things, concerned religious issues. *Data on religion* was collected in all three Yugoslavias after the Second World War

24. Constitution of the Republic of Serbia from 2006, *supra* n. 4, Art. 18, para. 3.
25. Constitution of the Republic of Serbia from 2006, *supra* n. 4, Art. 19.
26. Constitution of the Republic of Serbia from 2006, *supra* n. 4, Art. 20.
27. Constitution of the Republic of Serbia from 2006, *supra* n. 4, Art. 21.
28. Constitution of the Republic of Serbia from 2006, *supra* n. 4, Art. 22.
29. Materials for the session of the Federal Commission for Religious Affairs, confidential, number 558, 25 Nov. 1963, Archives of Yugoslavia, fund 144, folder 67, 1963.

(Democratic Federal Republic of Yugoslavia (DFRY), Socialist Federal Republic of Yugoslavia (SFRY) and FRY), within 1953, 1991 and 2002 censuses. In the independent Republic of Serbia (since 2006), their successor, the first and thus far only census was held in 2011. The Republic of Serbia has rich statistical material on the religious structure not only of today's Serbia but also of the newly formed states from the former Yugoslavia.

*11.* Today, from a historical distance of thirty years, the results of a comparative analysis of then and now religious, national, linguistic and other data and facts from the entire former Yugoslavia best demystify the real intentions and goals of geopolitical and religious 'long-term processes' whose 'engineering' culminated in Southeast Europe in the late twentieth and early twenty-first centuries. The war conflicts and migrations in the former Yugoslavia (1991–1999) resulted in a noticeable *qualitative change in the religious representation* in this area. Figures show that the largest part of the Orthodox Serb population was expelled from the territory of today's Republic of Croatia,[30] or due to various types of pressure converted to Roman Catholicism.[31] The largest part of the Muslim population, especially in today's BiH, but also in Croatia, Montenegro, Northern Macedonia, Slovenia and Serbia, are members of the newly formed Bosniak nation. It should be borne in mind that the Muslim corps declared themselves as 'Muslims' in the censuses of communist Yugoslavia, even though they belonged to different nationalities (Serbs, Croats, Macedonians, etc.). In today's Republic of Serbia, compared to the period when it was a Yugoslav republic, the number of Muslims and Roman Catholics has not been reduced nearly as drastically as the number of Orthodox believers in the independent Republics of Croatia and BiH.[32] According to the official data of the Croatian Bureau of Statistics, the number of Serbs in this republic in 1971 was 14.2%, in 1981 11.6%, and in 1991 12.2%. Censuses results in Croatia in 2001 and 2011 showed that Serbs participated with 4.5% and 4.4% in its population, which is a decrease of nearly 8% in comparison with 1991 (395 thousand persons).[33] Also, there were 1.366 million Orthodox Serbs in BiH in 1991 and 1.087 million in 2013 (280 thousand people less). On the other side, which can be seen in Table 1, there were 496 thousand Catholics in Serbia in 1991 and 410 thousand in 2012 (eighty-five thousand people less). During 1991–2012, the number of Muslims increased in Serbia from 224 to 240 thousand.[34]

30. In the 1991 census, Orthodox Serbs made up *over 12%* of the Croatian population, and according to its constitution were a constituent people. In independent Croatia there are about 4% Orthodox Serbs and this decrease is due to the fact that between 220 and 250 thousand people were expelled in the military and police operations 'Flash' and 'Storm' of the Croatian Army in May and August 1995. Detailed information on this topic can be found on the Internet page of the non-governmental and non-partisan organization Veritas, http://www.veritas.org.rs/, 20 Feb. 2020.
31. According to Veritas, about 40,000 Orthodox Serbs converted to Catholicism in Croatia in the last decade of the twentieth century.
32. *See* Table 1.
33. Population by Ethnicity, 1971–2011 Censuses, in: Census of Population, Households and Dwellings 2011, Population by Citizenship, Ethnicity, Religion and Mother Tongue, Croatian Bureau of Statistics, Zagreb, 2013, https://www.dzs.hr/, pp. 13–16.
34. http://www.statistika.ba/?lang=en.

*12.* The offered methodological framework and the nature of the questions that the respondents were asked during the last four censuses in Serbia (1953–2011), about religion, ranged from a clearly ideological to a factual profile. During the 1953 census, respondents declared themselves on a principled 'attitude towards religion', which in the then conditions resulted in the existence of many 'religiously undecided' (atheists) or those 'without answers' responses. The most represented religious communities were the three Christian denominations (Orthodox, Roman Catholic and Protestant), along with Islamic and Jewish faiths. In the 1991 census, few Jews declared themselves as members of the 'Judaic faith'. For the first time, members of 'pro-oriental cults' and 'religion not listed' are also mentioned. Even then, there were numerous 'believers who do not belong to any religion'.[35] Starting from the provisions of the then valid constitutions,[36] the 2002 and 2011 censuses offered citizens the right *not to declare themselves at all on the issue of religion*, with the term 'agnostic' being used for the first time in the 2011 census.[37] This indicates a tendency of gradual 'legalization' and establishment of various forms of secular orientation of citizens, and the processes of diversification, 'fragmentation', transformation and deinstitutionalization of their religiosity, in the context of 'global democratization' and growth of 'supply in the market of religions' in the late twentieth century. The data from the 1991 census do not contain information relating to the religion of the citizens in the Autonomous Province of KiM because that census was boycotted by the local Albanian population even then. The conditions for its implementation did not exist on the territory of the province in 2002 and 2011 either.

*Table 1 Population by Religion in Serbia as per Censuses in 1953, 1991, 2002 and 2011*

| | *1953* | *1991* | *2002* | *2011* |
|---|---|---|---|---|
| ***Total*** | **6,979,154** | **7,759,571** | **7,498,001** | **7,186,862** |
| ***Christian*** | 5,374,634 | 6,931,527 | 6,876,279 | 6,555,931 |
| *Orthodox* | 4,595,336 | 6,347,026 | 6,371,584 | 6,079,396 |
| *Catholic* | 634,349 | 496,226 | 410,976 | 356,957 |
| *Protestant* | 111,637 | 86,894 | 78,646 | 71,284 |
| *Other Christian* | 33,312 | 1,381 | 2,191 | 3,211 |
| ***Islam*** | 699,839 | 224,120 | 239,658 | 222,828 |
| ***Judaism*** | 1,089 | 740 | 785 | 578 |
| ***Eastern religions*** | – | – | 240 | 1,237 |
| ***Other*** | 1,991 | 13,982 | 6,649 | 1,776 |

35. *Source*: Republic Bureau of Statistics of the Republic of Serbia.
36. Constitution of the FRY 1992, Art. 43, https://data.globalcit.eu/NationalDB/docs/MON%20FRY%20ustav%20srj%201992.pdf, 5 Mar. 2024; Constitution of the Republic of Serbia from 2006, Official Gazette of RS, no. 98/2006, Art. 43.
37. *Source*: Republic Statistical Office of Serbia.

| | *1953* | *1991* | *2002* | *2011* |
|---|---|---|---|---|
| ***Agnostics*** | – | – | – | 4,010 |
| ***Non-believers (atheists)*** | 890,031 | 159,642 | 40,068 | 80,053 |
| ***Did not declare*** | – | – | 197,031 | 220,735 |
| ***Unknown*** | 11,570 | 429,560 | 137,291 | 99,714 |

*Source*: Population – religion, mother tongue and ethnicity – data by municipalities and cities, Republic Statistical Office of the Republic of Serbia, Belgrade, 2013. The publication can be found at https://www.stat.gov.rs/sr-latn/oblasti/popis/popis-2011/.

## Traditional Religiosity in Serbia at the Beginning of the Twenty-First Century

*13.* At the beginning of the twenty-first century, in the conditions of 'universalist transition', the traditional *society* in Serbia also underwent the revitalization of religious influence. Despite decades of ideological indoctrination, the 'traditionally religious' soul of citizens survived in the depths of their individual and collective consciousness. Statistical data from 2010 shows that in Serbia, 78% of respondents from a representative sample of 1,220 people from all over the country (excluding those from the AP KiM) consider themselves religious persons.[38] As the basis of their religiosity, they indicated primarily 'love of God' (29%) and 'aversion to God's punishment' (17%).[39] Of them, 63% belonged to the younger generation (20–50 years).

*14.* The nature of today's religiosity in Serbia (Orthodox, Roman Catholic, Protestant, Muslim and Jewish) can be defined as 'religious traditionalism'. It represents the 'valuable' framework and the basis of the *process of revitalization of religiosity among the atheized population* in the twenty-first century. This thesis is confirmed by statistical data, according to which 39% of the surveyed citizens considered themselves 'traditional believers' who *respect customs* but do not *actively and regularly participate in the life* of their religious community. The following 16% are 'religious' but do not accept *all the teachings* of their faith. It is very important to know that 35% of the surveyed citizens of Serbia in 2010 pointed out that they go to religious ceremonies (excluding weddings, funerals and baptisms) only on *major religious holidays*, that is to say, four to five times a year (mostly on Christmas and Easter). Of them, 20% stated that they attend religious services 'even less often', 20% never, and 7% once a year. Finally, 46% of them do not take communion at all.[40]

38. That year, a research project was conducted entitled 'Research on the religiosity of Serbian citizens and their attitude towards the EU integration process', organized by the Christian Cultural Centre from Belgrade, the Konrad Adenauer Foundation and the Centre for European Studies in Brussels.
39. Nikolić Marko & Ana Jović Lazić, *'Religious Transition' and/or 'Transition of Religiosity' in Serbia*, in: *Religiosity in Serbia 2010*, Christian Cultural Centre, Konrad Adenauer, Centre for European Studies, Belgrade, Brussels, 2010, 114–115.
40. *Ibid.*, 115.

*15.* During the *2011* census, on the issue of religious affiliation, citizens in the Republic of Serbia declared themselves as follows (*see* Table 2).

*Table 2 Population by Religion in Serbia as per 2011 Census*

| *Religion* | *Number* | *%* |
|---|---|---|
| Orthodox | 6,079,396 | 85.124 |
| Roman Catholic | 356,957 | 4.998 |
| Protestant | 71,284 | 0.998 |
| Other Christian | 3,211 | 0.045 |
| Islam | 222,828 | 3.120 |
| Judaism | 578 | 0.008 |
| Eastern religions | 1,237 | 0.018 |
| Agnostic | 4,010 | 0.056 |
| Atheist | 80,053 | 1.121 |
| Did not declare | 220,735 | 3.091 |
| Other | 101,490 | 1.421 |
| **Total:** | **7,141,779** | **100.00** |

*Source*: Republic Statistical Office of the Republic of Serbia.

## The Relationship Between the Religious and the National

*16.* The religious and national were closely connected and intertwined throughout the entire history of the Serbian people and their state. The relationship between these two terms can be defined as *distinctly interdependent*, with the *necessary and essential distinction and demarcation.*[41] This is confirmed by the results of the mentioned survey from 2010, according to which 43% of citizens thought that the relationship between religion and nation was 'mutual'. Of them, 58% pointed out that 'belonging to both is important', but 57% of them emphasized that 'national affiliation does not necessarily determine religion'.[42] Citizens of Serbia have not only an awareness of the essential difference in content but also the necessary interdependence of religion and national. This represents a significant peace-making, democratic and security potential not only for Serbia but also for the entire area of Southeast Europe in the turbulent circumstances of the beginning of the twenty-first century.

41. More in: *Sarajevo transcript of the Laws of St. Sava from the 14th century* – translation, Published by the SOC Metropolitanate of Dabar and Bosnia, Dabar, 2018.
42. Nikolić Marko & Ana Jović Lazić, *supra* n. 39, 119.

*Table 3 Population by Ethnicity and Religion in Serbia According to the 2011 Census*

| | *Christian* | | | | | *Islam* | *Jewish* | *Eastern* | *Other* | *Agnostic* | *Atheist* | *Did not Declare* | *Unknown* |
|---|---|---|---|---|---|---|---|---|---|---|---|---|---|
| | *Total* | *Orthodox* | *Catholic* | *Protestant* | *Other* | | | | | | | | |
| Republic of Serbia | **6,555,931** | **6,079,396** | **356,957** | **71,284** | **3,211** | **222,828** | **578** | **1,237** | **1,776** | **4,010** | **80,053** | **220,735** | **99,714** |
| Serbian | 5,850,571 | 5,794,537 | 10,434 | 5,061 | 1,498 | 2,686 | 102 | 410 | 1,053 | 2,609 | 52,748 | 61,352 | 16,619 |
| Albanian | 1,142 | 151 | 978 | 2 | 4 | 4,128 | – | 4 | 2 | 1 | 92 | 280 | 160 |
| Ashkali | 1 | 1 | – | – | – | 970 | – | – | – | – | – | 11 | 15 |
| Bosniak | 59 | 52 | 6 | 0 | 0 | 144,569 | – | – | 2 | 12 | 196 | 196 | 244 |
| Bulgarian | 17,859 | 16,854 | 733 | 17 | 10 | 26 | – | 3 | 3 | 6 | 186 | 409 | 51 |
| Bunjevak | 15,742 | 311 | 15,304 | 47 | 8 | – | – | 1 | 6 | 12 | 383 | 527 | 35 |
| Vlach | 34,712 | 34,468 | 4 | 50 | 27 | 1 | – | 3 | 4 | 7 | 83 | 353 | 167 |
| Gorani | 83 | 81 | 2 | – | – | 7,053 | – | 2 | 1 | – | 39 | 469 | 120 |
| Greek | 681 | 661 | 11 | 2 | 1 | 1 | – | – | 1 | – | 21 | 18 | 3 |
| Egyptian | 68 | 53 | 4 | 7 | – | 1,749 | – | 2 | – | – | 2 | 7 | 6 |
| Jewish | 72 | 48 | 17 | 2 | – | 1 | 392 | – | 1 | 15 | 165 | 121 | 20 |
| Armenian | 211 | 191 | 6 | – | – | 1 | – | – | 1 | – | 7 | 1 | 1 |
| Yugoslav | 11,736 | 6,597 | 4,434 | 263 | 26 | 468 | 7 | 46 | 66 | 294 | 6,147 | 3,904 | 635 |
| Hungarian | 244,118 | 2,923 | 224,291 | 15,861 | 388 | 14 | 24 | 21 | 89 | 34 | 1,893 | 6,660 | 1,046 |
| Macedonian | 21,372 | 21,071 | 55 | 82 | 26 | 242 | 1 | 6 | 5 | 19 | 430 | 579 | 101 |
| Muslim | 345 | 282 | 42 | 2 | 6 | 20,692 | – | – | – | 5 | 271 | 801 | 187 |
| German | 3,515 | 397 | 2,708 | 346 | 7 | 12 | 1 | 4 | 6 | 7 | 171 | 304 | 44 |
| Roma | 92,610 | 82,454 | 4,865 | 2,966 | 690 | 36,591 | – | 13 | 19 | 7 | 1,094 | 12,553 | 4,717 |
| Romanian | 27,737 | 24,614 | 2,253 | 619 | 87 | 4 | – | – | 7 | 9 | 163 | 1,055 | 357 |
| Russian | 3,016 | 2,911 | 50 | 9 | 6 | 12 | 2 | 3 | 2 | 6 | 87 | 95 | 24 |

| | Christian | | | | | Islam | Jewish | Eastern | Other | Agnostic | Atheist | Did not Declare | Unknown |
|---|---|---|---|---|---|---|---|---|---|---|---|---|---|
| | Total | Orthodox | Catholic | Protestant | Other | | | | | | | | |
| Rutherian | 13,521 | 2,640 | 10,746 | 100 | 4 | – | – | 3 | 8 | 3 | 152 | 513 | 46 |
| Slovak | 48,393 | 1,127 | 3,523 | 43,452 | 64 | 2 | 3 | 4 | 15 | 21 | 570 | 3,490 | 252 |
| Slovenian | 3,064 | 440 | 2,515 | 58 | 1 | – | 1 | 1 | 3 | 20 | 460 | 427 | 57 |
| Turkish | 52 | 45 | 3 | – | 1 | 509 | – | 1 | 1 | 3 | 24 | 39 | 18 |
| Ukrainian | 4,646 | 2,822 | 1,772 | 28 | 4 | 1 | – | – | 3 | 2 | 41 | 201 | 9 |
| Croatian | 52,670 | 1,434 | 50,717 | 244 | 40 | 7 | – | 7 | 11 | 133 | 2,116 | 2,664 | 292 |
| Cincar | 214 | 211 | – | – | – | 1 | – | – | 1 | 3 | 11 | 10 | 3 |
| Montenegrin | 34,165 | 33,771 | 215 | 54 | 7 | 196 | 2 | 8 | 14 | 90 | 2,278 | 1,581 | 193 |
| Czech | 1,552 | 183 | 1,268 | 81 | 1 | 1 | – | 1 | – | 2 | 106 | 134 | 28 |
| Sokci | 557 | 44 | 511 | 1 | – | – | – | – | 2 | 1 | 16 | 29 | 2 |
| Sopi | 134 | 131 | 1 | – | – | 2 | – | 1 | – | – | – | 4 | 1 |
| Other | 8,501 | 5,385 | 2,323 | 403 | 25 | 816 | 19 | 555 | 283 | 177 | 1,512 | 1,979 | 1,000 |
| Undeclared, nor determined acc. to Article 47 of the Constitution of RS | 36,642 | 23,848 | 10,945 | 870 | 220 | 1,298 | 15 | 71 | 86 | 273 | 5,024 | 115,537 | 1,400 |
| Declared according to regional belonging | 22,190 | 15,388 | 5,755 | 563 | 14 | 477 | 6 | 54 | 65 | 204 | 3,190 | 4,147 | 438 |
| Unknown | 3,980 | 3,270 | 466 | 94 | 46 | 298 | 3 | 13 | 16 | 35 | 375 | 285 | 71,423 |

*Source*: Republic Statistical Office of the Republic of Serbia.

## Territorial Representation of Religion in Serbia

*17.* The Orthodox population is evenly distributed and represents the absolute and dominant majority in the entire Republic of Serbia (85% of the total population). Exceptions are some municipalities and cities in the north and southeast of the country.

*18.* In the north of AP Vojvodina – in the North Bačka and North Banat administrative districts, in the municipalities of Subotica, Senta, Kanjiža and Ada – the majority of the population is *Roman Catholic*. In the municipalities of Bačka Topola, Mali Idjoš and Bečej, they also represent the largest religious community, but their percentage is below 50%.[43]

*19.* In the southeast of the Republic of Serbia, in the Zlatibor and Raška administrative districts,[44] in the cities and municipalities of Sjenica, Tutin and Novi Pazar, the *Muslim population* makes up the majority of citizens.

*20.* Most members of *Protestant communities* (Slovak Evangelical Church and Reformed Christian Church) in the Republic of Serbia are concentrated in two municipalities – Bački Petrovac in the South Bačka District, where they represent the majority, and Kovačica[45] in the South Banat District, where they constitute under 50% of the population.

*21.* The small *Jewish population* in the Republic of Serbia[46] is concentrated in large cities and trading centres, primarily in Belgrade, Novi Sad, Subotica and Pančevo.

43. *See* Figure 1.
44. Most Muslims in Serbia call this area *Sandžak*, which is a term that meant the administrative area in the Ottoman Empire. The territory of *Sandžak* according to Muslims includes some parts of the Republic of Montenegro and BiH.
45. This municipality is known worldwide for its naive painters, mostly Protestant Slovaks.
46. The Jewish Community had a total of 578 members in the 2011 census.

*Figure 1 Territorial Representation of Religion in Serbia*

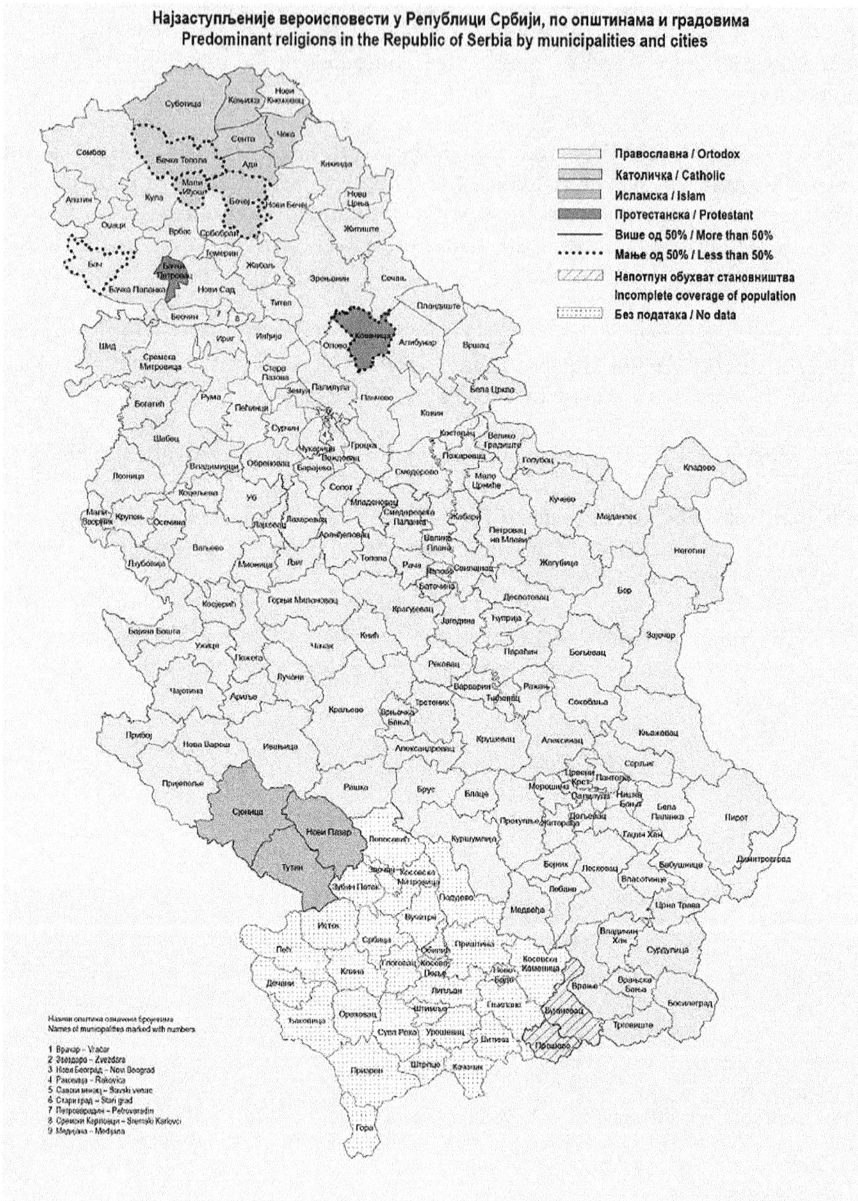


*Source*: Republic Statistical Office of Serbia, https://publikacije.stat.gov.rs/G2013/Pdf/G201318004.pdf, 5 March 2024.

## §3. Historical Background

*22.* Serbia is an old European state that emerged as completely independent due to the activities of the Serbian *ruling dynasty Nemanjić* in the Middle Ages. Its founder was Stefan Nemanja,[47] who united all the then-Serbian lands and gained independence from the Byzantine Empire at the end of the twelfth century.[48] Serbia became a kingdom in 1217 and an empire in 1346.[49] Concurrently with the process of political independence of the state, Nemanja's youngest son Rastko, as monk Sava, managed to achieve independence (autocephaly) of the Serbian Church from the Byzantine emperor in 1219.[50] Sava was its founder and first archbishop.[51]

*23.* The Ottoman Empire conquered the entire Balkan Peninsula in the fourteenth and fifteenth centuries, and Serbia lost its independence in 1459. It was under Turkish rule until the *First Serbian Uprising* in 1804, which represented a kind of *social revolution* and the beginning of the construction and development of the modern Serbian state. Serbia became an *autonomous principality* within the Turkish Empire after the *Second Serbian Uprising* in 1815, which was confirmed by the Hatt-i Sharif, and the Charters of 1830 and 1833.[52] Serbia obtained its independence from the Ottoman Empire after the *Serbian-Turkish Wars (1876–1878),* whose results were confirmed at the *Berlin Congress in 1878.*

*24.* After the *First World War* (1918), Montenegro and Vojvodina joined the independent *Kingdom of Serbia.* The Kingdom of Serbia was the backbone for the creation of the *Kingdom of Serbs, Croats, and Slovenes* (SCS) on 1 December 1918, which was renamed the *Kingdom of Yugoslavia* in 1929. After the Second World War, this state creation became the DFRY in 1946 and later the SFRY in 1961. In these countries, the Socialist Republic of Serbia was one of the federal units for a full four decades. After the secession of the Republic of Slovenia and Croatia from SFRY in 1991, the republics that wanted to remain in Yugoslavia (Serbia and Montenegro) created the FRY in April 1992. By reorganizing their relationship, the State Union of Serbia and Montenegro (State Union of SCG) was created in 2003. In referendums in May and October 2006, the people of Montenegro and Serbia decided for their republics to become independent states. In the same year, the current Constitution of Serbia was adopted, and she remained the *legal successor* of all the mentioned countries that preceded it.

---

47. Later monk and Saint Simeon the Myrrh-Gusher.
48. More in: Stefan Nemanja, Sveti Simeon Mirotočivi & Istorija i predanje (Jovanka Kalić ed.). *Odeljenje istorijskih nauka*, knjiga 26, Srpska akademija nauka i umetnosti (SANU), Beograd, 2000.
49. During the reign of Emperor Dušan the Mighty (*Dušan Silni*).
50. More in: Sava Nemanjić, Sveti Sava & Istorija i predanje (Akademik Vojislav Djurić ed.) *Predsedništvo*, knjiga 1, Srpska akademija nauka i umetnosti (SANU), Beograd, 1979.
51. The Serbian Orthodox people perceive this Saint not only as an imperishable spiritual leader and patron in the Kingdom of God for a full eight centuries but also as its greatest educator in the cultural and civilizational sense.
52. *Source*: *Istorija Srpskog naroda – Od prvog ustanka do Belinskog kongresa 1804–1878*, 5, knjiga, drugo izdanje, Sprska književna zadruga, Beograd, 1994.

# Part I. Legal Framework and Sources

## Chapter 1. Constitutional Position of Religion

*25.* Religious issues have been present in the constitutional history and tradition of Serbia since the adoption of the *Constitution of the Kingdom of Serbia in 1903*. It proclaimed the 'Eastern Orthodox faith' as the state religion.[53] It accepted the 'God-man institution' of the mentioned faith, the 'Serbian Autocephalous Church', as *independent*, in the sense that 'it does not depend on any foreign Church', but with the conclusion that it is inextricably linked in a spiritual and dogmatic sense with the Ecumenical Orthodox Church ('Eastern Orthodox Church'). Unlike all the latter ones in the twentieth and early twenty-first century, this Constitution attached greater importance to religious issues, respecting to a large extent dogmatic-ecclesiological tenets and principles of the Orthodox Church and other religious entities in the country. It gave the right to 'the Synod of Bishops for the internal administration of the Eastern Orthodox Church' and of the other religions to 'their spiritual authorities'. However, it also prescribed that all spiritual authorities 'are under the supervision of the Minister of Church Affairs'[54] while in practice the state did not interfere in internal church issues. This Constitution also provided that the issue of *theological education* of the Orthodox Church (status and position of theological schools) be regulated by law, based on an 'agreement between the Minister and the Council of Bishops'.[55] It gave the church authorities the right to 'try priests for misconduct while performing priestly duties', except for those 'punishable under the Criminal Code'. In addition, clergy and church institutions were 'subject to the laws of the land' in terms of 'civil relations and property'.[56] The 'Minister of Church Affairs' had important powers – he received 'complaints against abuses of church authorities and all religions in the country' and gave 'approvals' for the establishment of cooperation of the spiritual authorities of the Serbian Orthodox Church (SOC) with foreign church authorities (Councils and Synods), after 'investigation and approval' of official correspondence.[57] Finally, the

53. Constitution of the Kingdom of Serbia 1903, https://sr.wikisource.org/sr-el/Ustav_Kraljevine_Srbije_(1903)#Deo_I._Oblik_vladavine,_državna_vera_i_državna_oblast, 20 Sep. 2019.
54. Constitution of the Kingdom of Serbia 1903, Art. 3, https://sr.wikisource.org/sr-el/Ustav_Kraljevine_Srbije_(1903)#Deo_I._Oblik_vladavine,_državna_vera_i_državna_oblast, 20 Sep. 2019.
55. Constitution of the Kingdom of Serbia 1903, Art. 189, https://sr.wikisource.org/sr-el/Ustav_Kraljevine_Srbije_(1903)#Deo_I._Oblik_vladavine,_državna_vera_i_državna_oblast, 20 Sep. 2019.
56. Constitution of the Kingdom of Serbia 1903, Art. 190, https://sr.wikisource.org/sr-el/Ustav_Kraljevine_Srbije_(1903)#Deo_I._Oblik_vladavine,_državna_vera_i_državna_oblast, 20 Sep. 2019.
57. Constitution of the Kingdom of Serbia 1903, Art. 191, https://sr.wikisource.org/sr-el/Ustav_Kraljevine_Srbije_(1903)#Deo_I._Oblik_vladavine,_državna_vera_i_državna_oblast, 20 Sep. 2019.

Constitution of 1903 contained organizational provisions and guidelines concerning the material position of priests and teachers of religion in the Kingdom of Serbia.

*26. The* Constitution *of the Kingdom of SCS from 1921*,[58] following modern tendencies in the then international – legal and constitutional practice, affirmed the principles of *freedom of religion, religious equality* (*legal equality*) and *public confession of religion*, guaranteeing them to members of 'all religious communities that have already received legal recognition' in the kingdom. It treated the Serbian Orthodox (SOC) and Roman Catholic Church (RCC) as *privileged churches* and left space and the possibility for 'other religions' to *acquire legal personality* based on special laws. It gave everyone the right to independently regulate their internal structure and religious affairs, as well as to manage their property (and finances) in accordance with the regulations in force at the time. Unlike the one from 1903, this Constitution guaranteed the individual the right and opportunity *not to publicly profess his religion*, in the sense that it was his *private matter*, as well as not to participate in religious services if he did not want to. It opened the possibility for an individual to *deinstitutionalize* a religious orientation. It gave 'adopted and recognized religions' the right to 'maintain ties, in accordance with the law, with their supreme religious leaders outside the borders of the state, if their spiritual regulations require it'. This provision aimed to affirm and establish the legal position of the RCC in the country, whose structure and organization have a universal character. This also applied to certain Protestant churches whose 'federal' headquarters were located in Northern and Western Europe.[59] The 1921 Constitution also stipulated that 'expenditures for religious purposes provided for in the state budget shall be divided between adopted and recognized religions, in proportion to the number of their faithful and the actual proven necessity'.[60] It forbade religious representatives to abuse 'spiritual authority for political purposes', especially during the performance of religious service and duties.[61] In today's sense, this was the first constitutional provision that concerned the prohibition of the *abuse of religion for political purposes*. Finally, it guaranteed parents or guardians the right to enrol their children in religious instruction 'at will', 'separated by religion', in accordance with the principles of the church to which they belong.[62] From this historical distance, it can be said that the Constitution of 1921, in the religious field, strived primarily for the creation of 'parity', equality and balance in the relations between the SOC and the RCC on the *Balkan historical border* in the context of strengthening the influence of the Ecumenical Movement in the Protestant part of Europe. The immediate

58. Constitution of Kingdom of Serbs, Croats and Slovenes 1921 https://www.uzzpro.gov.rs/doc/biblioteka/digitalna-biblioteka/Ustav%20Kraljevine%20Srba,%20Hrvata%20i%20Slovenaca.pdf, 5 Mar. 2024.

59. At the beginning of the 1920s, various thematic departments of the Ecumenical Movement were created – for 'Faith and Order', 'Life and Work', etc.

60. The same principles of distribution of material resources to religious subjects are also present in the valid thematic regulations in the Republic of Serbia.

61. Constitution of Kingdom of Serbs, Croats and Slovenes 1921, Art. 12, https://www.uzzpro.gov.rs/doc/biblioteka/digitalna-biblioteka/Ustav%20Kraljevine%20Srba,%20Hrvata%20i%20Slovenaca.pdf.

62. Constitution of Kingdom of Serbs, Croats and Slovenes 1921, Art. 16, para. 3, https://www.uzzpro.gov.rs/doc/biblioteka/digitalna-biblioteka/Ustav%20Kraljevine%20Srba,%20Hrvata%20i%20Slovenaca.pdf.

future showed that it created the preconditions for the later acquisition of the legal personality of the Reformed and Evangelical Christian Church, as well as the Jewish Community (JC) and the Islamic Community in Yugoslavia, based on special laws adopted during 1929–1931.

27. *The* Constitution *of the Kingdom of Yugoslavia from 1931* completely took over the principles of the previous Constitution concerning *freedom of religion, religious equality*, and *public confession of religion*, expanding them with the term 'freedom of thought'. Following the example of tendencies in international practice at the time, in that manner, the 'religious nature and potentials' of different philosophical beliefs and directions were formally equated with historical and traditional religions in Yugoslavia. This Constitution also prohibited the presence of political content during religious ceremonies, including the practice of political (party) agitation.[63] It tried and to a large extent succeeded in 'uniting' the presence of the principles of *supra-nationality* and *religious pluralism*, 'rationalizing' the content of the latter. This 'symbiosis' opened the door to the induction of the principles of *secularity* and later ideological *secularism,* as well as *militant atheism and antitheism,* as the ruling 'religious value system and framework' in Southeast Europe throughout the twentieth and early twenty-first centuries.

28. *The* Constitution *of the Federal People's Republic of Yugoslavia (FPRY) from 1946*, as the first Constitution of communist (atheist) Yugoslavia, was characterized by *ideological colouration.* It considered religion as an 'opium for the masses and a brake' to social progress and development. Formally – legally, like all previous constitutions, it also contained provisions on the principles of freedom of religion and equality of citizens before the law, regardless of religious affiliation.[64] A qualitative deviation from the pre-war period was the newly adopted principle of strict separation of church and state.[65] Its application in practice was reflected in expressed hostility and repressive policy towards religious subjects in the country.[66] This Constitution also contained provisions on the *prohibition of the abuse of the church for political purposes* and the *prohibition of the existence of political organizations on religious grounds*. However, it also provided for the *possibility of allocating material state assistance* to religious entities.[67] Otherwise, it *deprived them of the right to keep records of registers* (births, deaths, and marriages), which caused numerous problems that have not been completely resolved to this day. This Constitution defined *religious hatred* as a *criminal offence.* Since it established the federal system of Yugoslavia and gave federal units the right and opportunity to have their own constitutions,[68] this 'federal' act transferred the legal right to regulate the

63. Constitution of the Kingdom of Yugoslavia 1931, Art. 11, https://royalfamily.org/wp-content/uploads/2014/01/constitution.pdf, 5 Mar. 2024.
64. Constitution of the Federal People's Republic of Yugoslavia from 1946, https://www.arhivyu.rs/en/leksikon-jugoslavije/konstitutivni_akti_jugoslavije, 5 Mar. 2024.
65. Constitution of the Federal People's Republic of Yugoslavia from 1946, *supra* n. 64, Art. 25.
66. Information of the Federal Commission for Religious Affairs, confidential, number 452/3, 31 Oct. 1964, Archives of Yugoslavia, fund 144, folder 76, 1964.
67. Constitution of the Federal People's Republic of Yugoslavia from 1946, *supra* n. 64, Art. 25.
68. Constitution of the Federal People's Republic of Yugoslavia from 1946, *supra* n. 64, Art. 11.

position of churches and religious communities to the jurisdiction of six Yugoslav republics, today independent states – Slovenia, Croatia, BiH, Serbia, Montenegro and Macedonia (today the Northern Republic of Macedonia) after the end of the Second World War.[69] The Constitution of 1946 defined that the education system was separated from the church,[70] which created a precondition for the process of secularization of education in the state.[71]

*29.* The Constitution *of the SFRY* from April 1963 proclaimed the Autonomous region of KiM to be the Autonomous Province of KiM.[72] In the 'development' of Yugoslav federalism, the autonomous units that were part of SR Serbia essentially had the same position, but among them, there are certain differences (name, different number of representatives in the Council of Peoples, AP Vojvodina had a Supreme Court). In terms of religious issues, it took over the principles of the previous constitution.

*30. The 1974 Constitution of the SFRY* retained almost identical provisions and solutions concerning the position of churches and religious communities as the previous one.[73] Formally, it guaranteed citizens *free confession of religion*, emphasizing 'religious communities were separate from the state and free to perform their religious ceremonies' and that 'they can establish religious schools only for the preparation of priests'.[74] Obviously, the intent was to limit the influence of religious teaching and education only to the 'internal' space of religious communities, 'removing' them from society as a whole. Compared to the previous ones, this Constitution was more restrictive in the formal sense on the issue of 'abuse of religion and religious activity for political purposes', defining them as 'unconstitutional'. In practice, the real target of this provision was the segment of the clergy and religious officials who displayed a public anti-communist orientation. The repressive attitude of the state towards the position of churches and religious communities was also confirmed by the constitutional provisions according to which they 'may, *within the limits determined by law*, have the right to ownership of property'.[75] The provision of this Constitution according to which 'the social community can materially help religious communities', at least from this perspective, seems paradoxical. In

69. For comparison, one can see a great deal of 'structural' similarity of the mentioned 'religious – legal concept' with the one that exists today in the EU, which at the community level left it to the Member States to regulate the religious area with their legislation.
70. Constitution of the Federal People's Republic of Yugoslavia from 1946, *supra* n. 64, Art. 38.
71. Because of the application of this constitutional principle elaborated by later thematic laws, higher education institutions of churches and religious communities were expelled from Yugoslav universities in 1952.
72. Constitution of the Socialist Federal Republic of Yugoslavia 1963, https://www.arhivyu.rs/en/leksikon-jugoslavije/konstitutivni_akti_jugoslavije, 5 Mar. 2024.
73. Constitution of the SFRY in 1974, https://sr.wikisource.org/sr-el/Ustav_Socijalističke_Federativne_Republike_Jugoslavije_(1974)#Glava_-{III}-._SLOBODE,_PRAVA_I_DUŽNOSTI_ČOVEKA_I_GRAĐANINA; 20 Sep. 2019.
74. Constitution of the SFRY in 1974, *supra* n. 73, Art. 174.
75. Their elaboration was represented by provisions of the law on nationalization which confiscated large land holdings from religious subjects and deprived them of their property rights, which, according to the authorities, exceeded the 'permissible and prescribed measure'.

essence, the 'religious policy' of the communist state in this period aimed to completely marginalize and reduce the influence of religious subjects in social life.

*31.* The 1992 *Constitution of the FRY,* a federation made up of the Republic of Serbia and Montenegro with historically identical religious and national identities, guaranteed the principles of *freedom of religion, equal treatment and position of religious communities* and *separation of church and state.*[76] Within its second section which dealt with human rights and civil liberties, there were provisions concerning the *legal equality of religious subjects,*[77] *freedom of belief, conscience, thought and public expression of opinion,*[78] *prohibition of inciting* national, racial and *religious hatred,*[79] freedom of religion and performing religious ceremonies, as well as the right of every citizen *not to declare one's religious belief.*[80] The *Constitution of the Republic of Serbia from 1990,* then a federal unit of the FRY, also in continuity with the previous one and without any innovations, resolved the issue of the legal position of religious entities in Serbia. He prescribed that the freedoms and rights of citizens can be limited only in the conditions determined by the constitution and emphasized that citizens and religious communities are guaranteed *freedom of religion, confession and religious services,* that *religious subjects are separated from the state* and *free to perform religious duties and ceremonies,* in addition to which they can *establish religious schools and charitable organizations.*[81] It also envisaged the possibility that the state could help religious subjects materially.

*32. The* Constitutional *Charter of the State Union of SCG from 2002,*[82] a product with confederate outlines, which was a 'transitional solution' in gaining independence of Montenegro from Serbia (2006), guaranteed in principle the application of universal civil liberties and human and minority rights on its territory. This also indirectly referred to *religious rights and freedoms,* which were not directly stated.

*33.* From this historical distance, it can be said that the constitutions of 1946, 1974, 1990 and 1992 continuously and formally – legally inherited and guaranteed the application of the principles of *freedom of religion* and *equality of religious subjects,* striving for their affirmation, advancement and elaboration in accordance with the international standards of the time. In practice, the ideological signs and real intentions of the Yugoslav authorities prevailed, which were not in favour of religious communities.

---

76. Constitution of the FRY 1992, http://www.podaci.net/_z1/2117756/U-srjugo02v9201-0029.html, 20 Sep. 2019.
77. Constitution of the FRY 1992, *supra* n. 76, Art. 20.
78. Constitution of the FRY 1992, *supra* n. 76, Art. 35.
79. Constitution of the FRY 1992, *supra* n. 76, Art. 42.
80. Constitution of the FRY 1992, *supra* n. 76, Art. 43.
81. Constitution of Serbia from 1990, Art. 41, https://www.arhiva.srbija.gov.rs/cms/view.php?id=1014, 5 Mar. 2024.
82. Constitutional Charter of the State Union of Serbia and Montenegro from 2003, https://en.wikisource.org/wiki/Constitutional_Charter_of_Serbia_and_Montenegro, 5 Mar. 2024.

## The Constitution of the Republic of Serbia from 2006

*34.* Compared to the previous ones, the current Constitution of the Republic of Serbia is most strongly dedicated to issues of *human rights and freedoms*, which are elaborated in a catalogue-like manner.[83] The introductory part confirms the principle of secularity of the state, which is elaborated by the provision that *no religion is and can be established as state or mandatory*.[84] Such a solution fully guarantees the secular character of the state. This Constitution emphasizes that *generally accepted principles and rules of international law and ratified international treaties shall be an integral part of the legal system of the Republic of Serbia and as such applied directly*.[85] A qualitative amendment to previous constitutions is a stronger *principle of non-discrimination* (direct or indirect), which *includes discrimination on religious grounds*.[86] Provisions directly related to the *rights and freedoms of religious entities (churches and religious communities)* are contained in Articles 43, 44 and 49. The Constitution guarantees *freedom of thought, conscience, beliefs, and religion*, as well as the right of each individual to retain their beliefs or religion or to change them according to their own discretion and choice.[87] No person is obliged to declare their religious and other beliefs, and they have the freedom to publicly manifest them in worship, observance, or teaching. *Legal restrictions on freedom of religion or belief* are possible only in conditions that require the *protection of life*, and *security and public safety* in a democratic society, including the need to *prevent incitement or persuasion to religious*, national or racial *hatred*.[88] On the topic of *education*, the Constitution guarantees parents and legal guardians the right to ensure 'religious and moral education' for their children in conformity with their own convictions. It points out that churches and religious communities in Serbia are *equal and separated from the state*, with a guaranteed right to organize *independently their internal structure and religious matters*, *perform religious services in public* and *establish and manage religious schools and social and charitable institutions*.[89] Only the Constitutional Court of the Republic of Serbia may *prohibit the activities of a religious community* if its activities infringe the right to life, the right to mental and physical health, the rights of child, the right to personal and family integrity, the right to property, public safety and order, or if it *incites religious*, national or racial *intolerance*.[90] It is emphasized that in Serbia any incitement to racial, national, and *religious hatred, intolerance and inequality is prohibited and punishable*.[91] This confirms the fact that the current Constitution of Serbia contains and guarantees the highest international legal standards concerning *religious rights and freedoms*.

83. Constitution of the Republic of Serbia from 2006, *supra* n. 4.
84. Constitution of the Republic of Serbia from 2006, *supra* n. 4, Art. 11.
85. Constitution of the Republic of Serbia from 2006, *supra* n. 4, Art. 16.
86. Constitution of the Republic of Serbia from 2006, *supra* n. 4, Art. 21.
87. Constitution of the Republic of Serbia from 2006, *supra* n. 4, Art. 43.
88. *Ibid.*
89. Constitution of the Republic of Serbia from 2006, *supra* n. 4, Art. 44.
90. *Ibid.*
91. Constitution of the Republic of Serbia from 2006, *supra* n. 4, Art. 49.

## Chapter 2. Other Legislation with Regard to Religion

*35.* Based on the Constitutional Principles from 2006, several legal acts have been adopted in the Republic of Serbia that regulate or concern the issue of the position, rights, and obligations of religious entities in the country. The most important are certainly the *Law on Churches and Religious Communities,*[92] *Law on Restitution of Property to Churches and Religious Communities,*[93] *Law on Prohibition of Discrimination,*[94] *Criminal Code of the Republic of Serbia,*[95] *Law on Ministries,*[96] *Labour Law,*[97] *Law on Associations,*[98] *Law on Elementary Education,*[99] *Law on Secondary Education,*[100] *Law on Higher Education,*[101] *Budget Law,*[102] *Law on Value Added Tax (VAT),*[103] *Law on Companies,*[104] *Law on the Registration Procedure with the Serbian Business Registers Agency,*[105] *Law on Public Procurement,*[106] *Family Law,*[107] *Law on Cultural Heritage,*[108] *Law on the Serbian Army,*[109] *Law on Police,*[110] *Law on State and Other Holidays,*[111] etc.

*36.* This part of the encyclopaedia will analyse the provisions of the laws that mostly concern the legal status of churches and religious communities in the Republic of Serbia – Law on Churches and Religious Communities, Law on Restitution of Property to Churches and Religious Communities, Law on Ministries, Law on Prohibition of Discrimination and the Criminal Code. The provisions of other laws that are most closely related to the general topic of this section will be included as well. The provisions of other laws concerning special thematic units (financing of religious communities, education, labour law, culture, family law, etc.) will be presented in the relevant parts of the encyclopaedia.

92. Law on Churches and Religious Communities, Official Gazette of RS, no. 36/2006.
93. Law on Restitution of Property to Churches and Religious Communities, Official Gazette of RS, no. 46/2006.
94. Law on Prohibition of Discrimination, Official Gazette of RS, no. 22/2009.
95. Criminal Code of the Republic of Serbia, Official Gazette of RS, no. 35/2019.
96. Law on Ministries, Official Gazette of RS, nos 44/2014, 96/2015 and 62/2017.
97. Labour Law, Official Gazette of RS, no. 95/2018.
98. Law on Associations, Official Gazette of RS, no. 44/2018.
99. Law on Elementary Education, Official Gazette of RS, nos 55/2013, 101/2017, 27/2018 and 10/2019.
100. Law on Secondary Education, Official Gazette of RS, no. 55/2013.
101. Law on Higher Education, Official Gazette of RS, no. 73/2018.
102. Budget Law, Official Gazette of RS, nos 113/2017, 95/2018, 84/2019.
103. Law on Value Added Tax (VAT), Official Gazette of RS, nos 84/2004 to 83/2015.
104. Law on Companies, Official Gazette of RS, no. 95/2018.
105. Law on Registration Procedure in the Serbian Business Registers Agency, Official Gazette of RS, nos 99/2011 and 31/2019.
106. Law on Public Procurement, Official Gazette of RS, no. 91/2019.
107. Family Law 2015, Official Gazette of RS, nos 18/2005, 72/2011 and 6/2015.
108. Law on Cultural Heritage, Official Gazette of RS, nos 71/1994 and 99/2011.
109. Law on the Serbian Army, Official Gazette of RS, nos 116/2007, 88/2009 and 36/2018.
110. Law on Police, Official Gazette of RS, no. 87/2018.
111. Law on State and Other Holidays, Official Gazette of RS, no. 4/2001.

## Law on Churches and Religious Communities

*37.* The Law on Churches and Religious Communities from 2006 regulates the legal status and activities of religious entities in the Republic of Serbia. It is structured into *four parts – General Provisions, Legal Status of Churches and Religious Communities, Activities of Churches and Religious Communities*, and *Transitional and Final Provisions.*

*38.* The first part of the Law covers and elaborates on the Constitutional Principles of *Freedom of* Religion, *Prohibition of Religious Discrimination and Restrictions on Religious Freedom.* In this regard, the Law guarantees all citizens *the right to freedom of conscience and religion,*[112] implying the freedom to 'have or to have not, to hold or to change religion or belief', to 'profess faith in God', as well as that the mentioned manifestation of belief can be 'individual, public (in community with others) or private'. It is achieved by participating in religious services and ceremonies. In that context, everyone has the right to 'religious instruction and teaching', 'cherishing and developing religious tradition', as well as the freedom to 'develop and advance religious education and culture'.[113] Already in the introductory part, the Law guaranteed *individual* and *collective religious freedoms and rights* to the citizens of Serbia. In order to further protect them, it was emphasized that 'no one shall be subjected to coercion' which could impair the said rights, nor be 'harassed, discriminated against or privileged' because of their religious convictions.[114] The law provided for the possibility of restricting them only in cases of endangering the 'right to life and health, the right of the child, the right to personal and family integrity, and right to property', as well as due to possible 'instigation to religious, national or racial intolerance'.[115] Citing the Constitution, other laws and ratified international treaties, the Law underlines that restrictions on the exercise of religious freedoms may be undertaken solely with the aim of 'protecting democratic order in society, public safety and order, morals, and protecting the freedom and rights of others'.[116] In conclusion of the first part, it prescribes that there is *no state religion in the Republic of Serbia.*[117]

*39.* The second part of the Law regulates three important issues concerning the *legal status of religious entities – autonomy, registration and property and financing.* As entities of religious freedom, it defines: 'traditional churches and religious communities, confessional communities and other religious organizations'.[118] At the very beginning of the analysis, it is crucial to emphasize that this distinction has *an exclusively terminological – and not qualitative – status character.* This was confirmed by the *Constitutional Court of the Republic of Serbia in 2013* – at the request

112. Law on Churches and Religious Communities, *supra* n. 92, Art. 1.
113. Law on Churches and Religious Communities, *supra* n. 92, Art. 1, para. 2.
114. Law on Churches and Religious Communities, *supra* n. 92, Art. 2.
115. Law on Churches and Religious Communities, *supra* n. 92, Art. 2, para. 2.
116. Law on Churches and Religious Communities, *supra* n. 92, Art. 3.
117. Law on Churches and Religious Communities, *supra* n. 92, Art. 2, para. 3.
118. Law on Churches and Religious Communities, *supra* n. 92, Art. 4.

of the National Assembly – after *four proposals for determining the unconstitutionality and two initiatives for initiating proceedings to assess the constitutionality of several provisions* of the Law on Churches and Religious Communities.[119] The Law on Churches and Religious Communities elaborates on the constitutional principle of *freedom of association and assembly* and precisely defines the issue of the *autonomy of churches and religious communities*, as well as their autonomous regulations. It guarantees all citizens the right *to freedom of association and public assembly for the purpose of manifesting religious convictions*,[120] and churches and religious communities *independence, freedom,* equality before the law, and *autonomy* in determining their religious identity, internal order and organization, as well as independently conduct their internal and public affairs.[121] The state has no right to 'obstruct the application of autonomous regulations' of religious entities, but at their request, it can 'provide assistance' in the enforcement of internal final decisions and judgments.[122] Therefore, the state figures as *a guarantor of the autonomy of religious entities* and the direct application of their internal regulations. *Priests and religious officials* are elected by the churches and religious communities themselves 'in compliance with their autonomous regulations', which, among other things, regulate the performance of religious services and duties.[123] The clergy are *free and independent* in performing their religious services. The state cannot hold them accountable for religious activities if they are conducted in accordance with the autonomous legislation of churches and religious communities.[124] They enjoy all other public (civil and political) rights except those that are prohibited by their autonomous legislation.[125] The Law guarantees priests and religious officials *confidentiality of communications entrusted to them during confession*, in the sense that they may not be summoned to testify to state authorities.[126] In case of deprivation of freedom, the relevant state body is obliged to immediately inform the religious community to which the respective religious servant belongs.[127] Finally, the state 'protects their official uniform, symbols of rank and dignity', fully respecting the autonomous legislation of religious communities.[128]

---

119. At the session held on 16 Jan. 2013, the Constitutional Court of the Republic of Serbia brought a decision (No. IUz-455/2011) on: (1) Rejection of the proposal to establish unconstitutionality and rejected the initiative to initiate proceedings to review the constitutionality and compliance with the ratified international treaty of Art. 4, Art. 7 para. 2, Arts 10–16, Art. 18, Art. 26 para. 2, Art. 29 para. 2, Art. 31 paras 2 to 4 and Art. 40 of the Law on Churches and Religious Communities; (2) unconstitutionality and initiative to initiate proceedings to review the constitutionality of the provisions of Art. 8 paras 3–5 and para. 9, Arts 9, 24 and 27, Art. 32 paras 3–5 and Art. 43 of the Law from item 1; (3) for determining the unconstitutionality of the Law from item 1 in its entirety.
120. Law on Churches and Religious Communities, *supra* n. 92, Art. 5.
121. Law on Churches and Religious Communities, *supra* n. 92, Art. 6.
122. Law on Churches and Religious Communities, *supra* n. 92, Art. 7.
123. Law on Churches and Religious Communities, *supra* n. 92, Art. 8, paras 1 and 2.
124. Law on Churches and Religious Communities, *supra* n. 92, Art. 8, paras 3 and 4.
125. Law on Churches and Religious Communities, *supra* n. 92, Art. 8, paras 5 and 6.
126. Law on Churches and Religious Communities, *supra* n. 92, Art. 8, para. 7.
127. Law on Churches and Religious Communities, *supra* n. 92, Art. 8, para. 8.
128. Law on Churches and Religious Communities, *supra* n. 92, Art. 8, para. 9.

*40.* Religious entities in the Republic of Serbia registered *pursuant to this Law* have the *status of a legal entity*[129] which can also be acquired by their organizational units and institutions in accordance with autonomous regulations and the decision of the relevant authority. Both can be terminated and erased from the register by the same procedure.[130]

*41.* The law also defines the *typology of churches and religious communities.* 'Traditional churches' are those that *have centuries-long historic continuity* in the Republic of Serbia and *whose legal personality* is acquired pursuant to separate legislation – SOC, RCC, Slovak Evangelical Church a.v. (SECAV), Reformed Christian Church and Evangelical Christian Church a.v.[131] 'Traditional religious communities' in the Republic of Serbia also have *centuries-long historic continuity*, with *legal personality* pursuant to special legislation – the Islamic Religious Community and Jewish Religious Community.[132] The law recognized the SOC as 'exceptional historical, state-building, and civilizational role in forming, preserving and developing the identity of the Serbian people', as well as *continuity with the legal personality* acquired pursuant to the Document on Spiritual Authority ('Načetanija') adopted by the National Assembly of the Principality of Serbia from 1836.[133] The Law recognized the RCC continuity with the legal personality acquired pursuant to the Law on the Concordat between the Kingdom of Serbia and the Holy See from 1914[134] as well as the SECAV, Evangelical Christian Church and the Reformed Christian Church on the basis of the same Laws of the Kingdom of Yugoslavia from 1930.[135] The JC was recognized continuity with legal personality based on the Act on Religious Community of Jews from 1929[136] and the Islamic Community pursuant to the Act on Islamic Religious Community from 1930.[137] 'Confessional communities' in Serbia are all religious entities that have acquired *legal personality* pursuant to an application in accordance with the Acts on Legal Position of Religious Communities in Socialist Yugoslavia from 1953 to 1977.[138]

*42.* In the part related to the *registration of religious entities*, the Law stipulates that 'the ministry responsible for religious affairs keeps the Register of Churches and religious communities'.[139] The *registration procedure*, which is conducted with the aim of registering in the said Register of the Ministry of Justice, and *for the purpose of acquiring legal personality*, for 'traditional churches and religious communities', it means submitting an *application* containing the name, address, name and surname of the authorized person who represents it. 'Other religious organizations'

---

129. Law on Churches and Religious Communities, *supra* n. 92, Art. 9, para. 1, and Art. 20, para. 6.
130. Law on Churches and Religious Communities, *supra* n. 92, Art. 9, paras 2 and 3.
131. Law on Churches and Religious Communities, *supra* n. 92, Art. 10, para. 1.
132. Law on Churches and Religious Communities, *supra* n. 92, Art. 10, para. 2.
133. Law on Churches and Religious Communities, *supra* n. 92, Art. 11, paras 1 and 2.
134. Law on Churches and Religious Communities, *supra* n. 92, Art. 12.
135. Law on Churches and Religious Communities, *supra* n. 92, Art. 13.
136. Law on Churches and Religious Communities, *supra* n. 92, Art. 14.
137. Law on Churches and Religious Communities, *supra* n. 92, Art. 15.
138. Law on Churches and Religious Communities, *supra* n. 92, Art. 16.
139. Law on Churches and Religious Communities, *supra* n. 92, Art. 17.

are required to enclose the *decision on founding* with the names, surnames, a number of identification documents and signatures of the founders[140] which must be at least 0.001% of the total number of adult citizens with residence in the Republic of Serbia. Religious entities wishing to register for the first time must submit to the Ministry *a statute or another document* containing a description of their organizational structure (rights and obligations of members, list of organizational units of legal entities), a description of religious teachings, ceremonies, goals and basic activities, as well as data on permanent sources of income.[141] The law prevents a religious organization entry into the Register whose name contains a name or part of the name reflecting the identity of registered religious organizations, or one whose application for registration is already in procedure.[142] The Ministry is obliged to process the application within sixty days from the day of receipt of the complete documentation, whereby this deadline may be extended for an additional thirty days if it is necessary to supplement the documentation. After ninety days, the request of the religious community with incomplete documentation is refuted, and if the Ministry does not make a decision on registration within the prescribed period, it will be deemed that the registration of a religious entity in the Register has been approved.[143] From the adoption of the Law in 2006 until today, there have been no problematic cases regarding the submission of requests for registration of religious organizations in the Republic of Serbia. This is confirmed by the fact that by the middle of 2019, twenty-six *new ones* were entered in the mentioned register. The Ministry of Justice may *pass a decision refuting the request* for registration of a religious entity whose teaching, aims, ceremonies and activities are contrary to the Constitution and public order of the Republic of Serbia or if they endanger the right to life, health, freedom, human and family rights.[144] The Law also emphasized that when passing any decision on the application for entry to the Register, it will 'take into consideration the decisions of the European Court for Human Rights', as well as 'administrative and court decisions of several EU countries'.[145] This testifies to the commitment of the Republic of Serbia to the values inherited by the European Union (EU) in the field of religion. The *content of the Register* consists of data related to the name, seat and address, organizational units and territorial organization of a religious entity; name and surname of his authorized person; number and date of registration decision; data on religious schools, cultural and charitable institutions and associations; as well as data on business activity.[146] The religious entity is obliged to inform the Ministry of any change of the stated data within thirty days. The content and method of keeping the Register are prescribed by the *Rulebook of the Ministry of Justice* issued by the Minister.[147] By decision of the Ministry, a religious organization may be deleted from the Register, pursuant to the *final court ruling if it is ascertained* that it pursues goals other than those stated when

140. Law on Churches and Religious Communities, *supra* n. 92, Art. 18.
141. *Ibid.*
142. Law on Churches and Religious Communities, *supra* n. 92, Art. 19.
143. Law on Churches and Religious Communities, *supra* n. 92, Art. 20, paras 1, 2 and 7.
144. Law on Churches and Religious Communities, *supra* n. 92, Art. 20, para. 4.
145. Law on Churches and Religious Communities, *supra* n. 92, Art. 20, para. 5.
146. Law on Churches and Religious Communities, *supra* n. 92, Art. 21.
147. *Ibid.*

registered.[148] A religious organization may initiate an *administrative dispute* against such a decision.[149] In case of deletion from the Register, the provisions of state regulations on associations shall apply to the property of a religious entity, and the competent body for religious affairs shall supervise its application.[150]

*43.* The third part of the Law elaborates on issues related to the activities of religious organizations – worship, education, construction, social – charity (charitable) and cultural. Premises for performing religious services (temples, buildings, and other premises) are defined as a 'protected and inviolable' place where religious subjects perform liturgies, services, and other religious activities. They can also be held in public, that is, open spaces and places of historical significance, at the request of the relevant institutions and in agreement with religious communities and organizations. This refers to hospitals, army and police facilities, prisons, schools, and various social institutions.[151] In accordance with their needs and other thematic laws, religious entities can independently undertake construction activities, i.e., erecting temples and other accompanying facilities (rectories, monastery lodgings, administrative-management buildings, schools, boarding schools, hospitals, residential buildings, production facilities, etc.).[152] When drafting urban planning acts, local self-administration authorities are 'obliged to consider' the needs of religious entities. The procedure of construction or reconstruction of religious facilities may be conducted on the basis of a decision of the Church or religious community, upon obtaining necessary licences and permits in accordance with pertinent law and regulation, and the consent of the competent Ministry of Construction, Transport and Infrastructure. Local self-governments may also be a financial partner in the construction of religious buildings if they allocate funds for that in a timely manner. The Law on Churches and Religious Communities also stipulates that burials may be carried out in religious buildings and on their land pursuant to a decision of the competent body of a religious entity.[153] Finally, in compliance with the law, within the framework of their social and charity activities, they can establish separate institutions and organizations, which are independent of their religious services. Such activity must be clearly indicated, by posting the full name of the religious organization.[154]

### Rulebook on the Content and Method of Keeping the Register of Churches and Religious Communities

*44.* The Rulebook on the Contents and Method of Keeping the Register of Churches and Religious Communities[155] was adopted by the Minister of Justice,

148. Law on Churches and Religious Communities, *supra* n. 92, Art. 22.
149. Law on Churches and Religious Communities, *supra* n. 92, Art. 23.
150. Law on Churches and Religious Communities, *supra* n. 92, Arts 24 and 25.
151. Law on Churches and Religious Communities, *supra* n. 92, Art. 31, paras 1–5.
152. Law on Churches and Religious Communities, *supra* n. 92, Art. 32.
153. *Ibid.*
154. Law on Churches and Religious Communities, *supra* n. 92, Art. 33.
155. Rulebook on the Contents and Method of Keeping the Register of Churches and Religious Communities, Official Gazette of RS, no. 64/2006; (further in footnotes referred to as: Rulebook on Keeping the Register of Churches and Religious Communities).

pursuant to the Law on Churches and Religious Communities.[156] It regulates and defines the *procedure for the registration* of religious entities and the *content* and *method* of its management.

*45.* From the Orthodox Churches, the *Patriarchate of the SOC and all its Eparchies in Serbia* and the world are entered in the register, as well as the *organizational unit of the Romanian Orthodox Church Eparchy 'Dacia Felix'* with headquarters in Deti (Romania) and administrative headquarters in Vršac (Banat, Serbia).[157]

*46.* The 'Catholic Church in Serbia' (Roman Catholic and Greek Catholic) is entered in the Register pursuant to the application of its Bishops' Conference and includes all Dioceses of the RCC in Serbia and the then Apostolic Exarchate for Greek Catholics.[158]

*47.* Under the name 'Islamic Community in Serbia' (ICinS), its meshihats, muftis and organizational units were entered in the Register, which this community reported based on its internal regulations.[159]

*48.* The Association of Jewish Communities of Serbia with registered organizational units is registered under the name 'Jewish Community in Serbia'.[160]

*49.* 'Confessional communities and other religious organizations' are entered in the Register under their registered names.[161] When other 'religious organizations' establish associations and unions such as 'spiritual and evangelical churches of Serbia and other associations', their organizational units are entered in the Register as independent religious entities.[162] This Regulation stipulates that – *a religious*

156. Law on Churches and Religious Communities, *supra* n. 92, Art. 21, para. 4.
157. Rulebook on Keeping the Register of Churches and Religious Communities, *supra* n. 155, Art. 2; Note: Since the Canon Law of the Ecumenical (Universal) Orthodox Church prohibits the existence of parallel jurisdictions of several local (autocephalous) Orthodox Churches in the same territory, the SOC and ROC signed an Agreement in 2009 which gives the Eparchy of ROC the right to exist and carry out its mission exclusively in Banat (part of AP Vojvodina of the Republic of Serbia) for the needs of Romanian believers, and the SOC Eparchy of Timisoara and its surroundings in the Republic of Romania for the needs of local SOC believers. Only once this Agreement was signed could ROC 'Dacia Felix' be entered in the Register of Churches and Religious Communities in the Republic of Serbia.
158. Rulebook on Keeping the Register of Churches and Religious Communities, *supra* n. 155, Art. 3; Note: By Decision of the Vatican in 2019, the Greek Catholic Exarchate in Serbia turned into the Diocese of the Greek Catholic Church (GCC), whose Bishop sits in Ruski Krstur in AP Vojvodina.
159. Rulebook on Keeping the Register of Churches and Religious Communities, *supra* n. 155, Art. 5.
160. Rulebook on Keeping the Register of Churches and Religious Communities, *supra* n. 155, Art. 6.
161. Rulebook on Keeping the Register of Churches and Religious Communities, *supra* n. 155, Art. 7.
162. Rulebook on Keeping the Register of Churches and Religious Communities, *supra* n. 155, Art. 7, para. 2.

*organization may be established by a minimum of one hundred adult citizens residing in the Republic of Serbia* or *one hundred foreign citizens with permanent residence* on its territory.[163]

*50.* As a preventive measure against *attempted abuse*, the Rulebook also exhaustively states the obligation of founders (of social and humanitarian organizations, educational, cultural and publishing institutions, information and missionary media, economic entities, as well as cultural and social associations or non-governmental organizations) to harmonize the name and activity of the organization with the Law prior to registration.[164] It stipulates that the date of the first application of a religious organization must be entered in the Register and Decision on Registration according to previously valid laws and regulations. In this way, a religious organization can carry out its activities based on a previously legalized application *without the obligation to be entered in the Register*, 'provided that its activities are not limited by law'.[165] In this context, it is important to emphasize that a *religious organization that does not have an application and does not want to be entered in the Register enjoys religious freedoms like all other entities in the Republic of Serbia* unless its activities are in conflict with Article 3 of the Law on Churches and Religious Communities.[166] Specifically, it can exist unhindered and perform its mission and rituals. Since it does not have the status of a legal entity, it cannot apply for financial assistance from the state. This Rulebook prescribes the form and content of the Register book, which consists of columns in which the data provided for in Article 21 of the Law on Churches and Religious Communities are entered.[167] The entry of a religious organization in the Register is made pursuant to the mentioned Decision, while changes can be made exclusively based on a *written decision* or a *decision* of the Minister of Justice.[168] Deletion from the Register shall be done by 'crossing out the register sheet and entering the date of the decision on deletion in the appropriate column'.[169] Data from the Register is public.[170]

---

163. Rulebook on Keeping the Register of Churches and Religious Communities, *supra* n. 155, Art. 7, para. 3.
164. There were cases of attempts to register 'religious organizations' that had solely material – financial motives. Eventual acquisition of legal personality would allow them exemption from various taxes, cheaper acquisition, and rental of real estate, etc. Also, some already registered 'religious organizations' hold religious ceremonies very rarely or not at all, which leads to the conclusion that they do not believers or followers at all.
165. Rulebook on Keeping the Register of Churches and Religious Communities, *supra* n. 155, Art. 7, para. 6.
166. Rulebook on Keeping the Register of Churches and Religious Communities, *supra* n. 155, Art. 7, para. 7.
167. Rulebook on Keeping the Register of Churches and Religious Communities, *supra* n. 155, Arts 8–10.
168. Rulebook on Keeping the Register of Churches and Religious Communities, *supra* n. 155, Arts 12–14.
169. Rulebook on Keeping the Register of Churches and Religious Communities, *supra* n. 155, Art. 15.
170. Rulebook on Keeping the Register of Churches and Religious Communities, *supra* n. 155, Art. 18.

## Register of Churches and Religious Communities

*51.* Pursuant to the Law on Churches and Religious Communities and the Rulebook on the Content and Method of Keeping the Register of Churches and Religious Communities, the SOC, RCC, SECAV, Reformed Christian Church, Evangelical Christian Church, the JC, the Islamic Community and the Eparchy of the Romanian Orthodox Church (ROC) 'Dacia Felix' with its headquarters in Deti (Republic of Romania) and administrative headquarters in Vršac (Banat, AP Vojvodina) are entered in their Register in Serbia as legal entities. Protestant churches and communities are also entered in the Register on the basis of the adopted decisions – Seventh-day Adventist Church, Evangelical Methodist Church, Church of Jesus Christ of Latter-day Saints, Evangelical Church in Serbia, Church of Christ's Love, Spiritual Church of Christ, Union of Christian Baptist Churches in Serbia, Nazarene Christian Religious Community, Church of God in Serbia, Protestant Christian Community in Serbia, Church of Christ Brethren in Serbia, Free Belgrade Church, Jehovah's Witnesses, Zion Sacrament Church, Union of Seventh-day Adventist Reform Movement, Protestant Evangelical Church Spiritual Centre, Evangelical Church of Christ, Union of Baptist Churches in Serbia, Charismatic Community of Faith in Serbia, Buddhist Religious Community Nichiren Daishonin, Golgotha Church in Serbia, Theravada Buddhist Community in Serbia, Biblical Centre – 'Good News', First Roma Christian Church Leskovac, Vaishnava Religious Community – ISKCON.[171]

## Ministries Organization Act

*52.* With the adoption of the Law on Ministries in 2014,[172] the former Office for Relations with Churches and Religious Communities of the Government of the Republic of Serbia ceased to exist, and its successor became the *Administration for Cooperation with Churches and Religious Communities*[173] as a *special body within the Ministry of Justice*.[174] The Law prescribes that it 'perform duties of state administration and specialized tasks concerning the *affirmation and development of freedom of religion*; *cooperation of the state with churches and religious communities and improvement of their position in society*; *affirmation of religious principles and contents of Serbian national identity; assistance in the protection of religious components in the cultural and ethnic identity of national minorities; missions, pilgrimages and other forms of religious tourism; state cooperation with SOC eparchies abroad; development and affirmation of the values of religious culture; support for the development of religious education and assistance in the process of its inclusion in the state education system; providing support and assistance in sacral construction and in the protection of church cultural heritage; providing assistance in protecting the legal and social position of churches and religious communities, exercising their statutory rights, regulating and improving the social and material*

171. List of Churches and Religious Communities, Ministry of Justice of the Republic of Serbia, https://www.mpravde.gov.rs/registar/1138/spisak-crkava-i-verskih-zajednica-.php, 03 Sep. 2020.
172. Law on Ministries, *supra* n. 96.
173. The term Administration for Religions has become familiar in everyday use, and will be used further in the text.
174. Law on Ministries, *supra* n. 96, Art. 9.

*position of churches and religious communities* (clergy, religious officials, pupils and students of religious schools), as well as other tasks determined by law'.[175] The Administration for Religions pays special attention to the application of the *principle of positive discrimination* of the so-called minority religious communities. Based on the results of the analysis of the Ministry of Justice entitled: 'Comparative – legal analysis of the position of religious communities in the surrounding EU member states – Slovenia, Croatia, Hungary, Romania, Bulgaria and Greece', it can be concluded that the current status of the Administration for Religions in Serbia largely coincides with the status and position of related bodies in the mentioned countries, which as a rule form integral parts in the ministries of culture, human and minority rights or justice.[176]

### Law on Restitution of Property to Churches and Religious Communities

*53.* Starting with the goal of eliminating the *historical injustice* inflicted on religious communities in socialist Yugoslavia on the basis of the application of its regulations on agrarian reform, nationalization and sequestration in the period after the Second World War, the *Law on Restitution of Property to Churches and Religious Communities*[177] was adopted simultaneously with the Law on Churches and Religious Communities in Serbia. It stipulates the conditions, method, and procedure of returning confiscated property without market compensation. This also applies to religious endowments and societies throughout the country.[178] The law emphasizes that the return of confiscated property is based on the principles of *equal legal treatment of all religious entities, autonomy of their will in initiating proceedings, protection of legal security of current conscientious owners and third parties*, as well as *urgent action.*[179] As a goal, the law proclaimed the return of property to religious entities *in kind* or *in the form of other appropriate property.*[180] Issues that are not regulated by this Law are regulated by provisions of other regulations concerning property rights, obligations, housing, and other property issues.[181]

*54.* 'Churches and religious communities' and 'their legal successors' are 'entities with the right to restitution' in accordance with internal regulations.[182] As 'entities of obligations' to return property or financially compensate, the Law designated 'the Republic of Serbia, companies and other legal entities' who at the time of its entry into force were the owners of the confiscated property.[183] If another legal person proves that the property was 'acquired by a legal transaction at market price at the time of transfer of ownership or other rights that contain the right of disposal',

175. Law on Ministries, *supra* n. 96, Art. 9, para. 2.
176. *Source*: Ministry of Justice of the Republic of Serbia and its Administration for Religions, http://www.vere.gov.rs/cir/Siteview.asp?ID=4, 21 Sep. 2019.
177. Law on Restitution of Property to Churches and Religious Communities, *supra* n. 93.
178. Law on Restitution of Property to Churches and Religious Communities, *supra* n. 93, Art. 1.
179. Law on Restitution of Property to Churches and Religious Communities, *supra* n. 93, Arts 2 and 3.
180. Law on Restitution of Property to Churches and Religious Communities, *supra* n. 93, Art. 4.
181. Law on Restitution of Property to Churches and Religious Communities, *supra* n. 93, Art. 5.
182. Law on Restitution of Property to Churches and Religious Communities, *supra* n. 93, Art. 6.
183. Law on Restitution of Property to Churches and Religious Communities, *supra* n. 93, Art. 7.

it remains the owner of the property, and the Republic of Serbia is obliged to pay monetary compensation to the previous owner. If this is not the case, it is obliged to return the property to the religious entity.[184] Natural persons, who 'in the meantime by lawful (encumbrance or non-encumbrance) legal transaction' acquired the right of ownership over property confiscated from religious subjects, are not bound to return it nor pay monetary compensation for it.[185] Finally, if a legal or natural person in the process of transferring property from state to private in an illegal manner (by fictitious legal acts and transactions, which is determined in court proceedings) alienates (appropriates or unreasonably enriches himself) property of a religious subject, they are obliged to return it or to pay market value compensation to the religious subject at the moment of entry into force of this Law. If such a person does not exist, the Republic of Serbia is obliged to pay monetary compensation.[186]

*55.* The subject of return is property that at the time of seizure was owned by religious entities – agricultural land, forests and forest land, construction land, residential and commercial buildings, apartments and business premises, as well as movables of cultural, historical or artistic significance.[187] The law stipulates that the person obliged to return to a religious entity is obliged to return the right of ownership and statehood to the confiscated property if it is in 'approximately the same form and condition' in which it was at the time of confiscation. If this is not the case, the property can be partially returned with the payment of an additional difference in market value.[188] Real property is not returned in cases where the right of ownership cannot be acquired (if it is outside of legal transactions), if restitution would 'significantly impede the work and functioning of state bodies' (health, cultural, educational, etc.), as well as if it would cause 'disproportionate damage' or 'disrupt the economic and technological sustainability and functionality of the business entity' (cause great losses, dismissal of a large number of employees, prevent the performance of activities, etc.).[189] In the above cases, the property will be returned to the religious entity even if it represents illegal property of the taxpayer or if it has been leased.[190] Unless otherwise agreed with the religious subject, the lessee has the right to use the property for his activity 'under the conditions stipulated in the contract', but 'no longer than two years from the day the decision on the return of property becomes final'.[191] Religious entities to which property is returned are released from mortgage obligations arising from the moment of their confiscation until the day the law enters into force, which is guaranteed by the Republic of Serbia.[192] Easements deleted by nationalization are re-established if it does not breach the rights of third parties.[193] The law stipulates that 'movables of cultural, historical or

184. *Ibid.*
185. Law on Restitution of Property to Churches and Religious Communities, *supra* n. 93, Art. 8.
186. *Ibid.*
187. Law on Restitution of Property to Churches and Religious Communities, *supra* n. 93, Art. 9.
188. Law on Restitution of Property to Churches and Religious Communities, *supra* n. 93, Art. 10.
189. Law on Restitution of Property to Churches and Religious Communities, *supra* n. 93, Art. 11.
190. *Ibid.*
191. Law on Restitution of Property to Churches and Religious Communities, *supra* n. 93, Art. 12.
192. Law on Restitution of Property to Churches and Religious Communities, *supra* n. 93, Art. 13.
193. Law on Restitution of Property to Churches and Religious Communities, *supra* n. 93, Art. 14.

artistic significance' are also returned to religious entities. If they are an integral part of the collections of public museums, galleries and other related institutions, the conditions and details of their use shall be regulated by a contract between the religious entity and their holder.[194]

*56.* In case the property cannot be returned, the religious entity is entitled to *monetary compensation*. If the bondager is the state, it is paid in *government bonds* issued for that purpose. If the taxpayer is a legal or natural person, *in cash*.[195] An additional possibility for both parties is compensation in property. The *amount of compensation for confiscated property* according to the established methodology is determined by the *Directorate for Restitution*, starting with the condition of the property at the time of confiscation and its value at the time of the first instance decision.[196] The Law has determined that in the process of restitution of property, religious entities will be credited with the already paid compensation, according to previously valid regulations. Religious entities 'cannot claim compensation on the basis of lost profits due to the impossibility of using the property from the time when it was confiscated', as well as on the basis of 'its maintenance in the period from the day of confiscation until its return'.[197] A certain satisfaction is provided by the right to *financial recourse* from the Republic of Serbia, or rather the fact that it belongs to religious entities in the case of return of confiscated property based on an encumbered legal transaction.[198]

*57.* The Law on Restitution precisely defines the *competence* and *role of the Directorate for Restitution of the Republic of Serbia*, as a special organization that conducts the procedure and decides on requests for the return of property to religious entities, and the payment of financial compensation. It provides expert assistance to claimants and restitution obligors, keeps prescribed records, and reports to the Government on a quarterly basis on the work performed.[199] Religious entities were required *to initiate proceedings* for property restitution, compensation or indemnity by 30 September 2008,[200] enclosing with it information related to the type, size and location of the property, as well as the act, manner and time of its confiscation.[201] They were required to provide proof of the capacity of the applicant (immediate previous owner or his legal successor), excerpt from the register in case of property, data from the land cadastre, as well as other supporting documents.[202] In case of unavailability of evidence, the Administration officially provided them from the obligor or third parties, who were obliged to present them under the threat

194. Law on Restitution of Property to Churches and Religious Communities, *supra* n. 93, Art. 15.
195. Law on Restitution of Property to Churches and Religious Communities, *supra* n. 93, Art. 16.
196. Law on Restitution of Property to Churches and Religious Communities, *supra* n. 93, Art. 17.
197. Law on Restitution of Property to Churches and Religious Communities, *supra* n. 93, Art. 19.
198. Law on Restitution of Property to Churches and Religious Communities, *supra* n. 93, Art. 20.
199. Law on Restitution of Property to Churches and Religious Communities, *supra* n. 93, Arts 21 and 22.
200. Law on Restitution of Property to Churches and Religious Communities, *supra* n. 93, Arts 23 and 25.
201. Law on Restitution of Property to Churches and Religious Communities, *supra* n. 93, Art. 26.
202. *Ibid.*

of a fine.[203] The parties in the proceedings (religious entity and restitution obligor) could also propose *an amicable solution* or *settlement* (which has the validity of an executive document), with the mediation assistance of the Administration, which ensured that it be executed. Such settlement is entered in the decision on all individual requests and issues.[204] The *decision of the Directorate on compensation* orders the obligor to perform his obligation within no longer than three months under the threat of forced execution. The decision shall be submitted to the parties in the proceedings no later than six months from the day of submission of the duly drafted request.[205] No appeal may be filed against the decision, but an *administrative dispute* may be initiated.[206] The Decision on the return of property, financial compensation or remuneration is *brought by the courts* (in case of real property or return of movable property of cultural, historical or artistic significance) or the *Ministry of Finance* if compensation is given in bonds or a monetary amount is paid.[207] Finally, the Law on Restitution stipulates that as of 1 May 2006, 'no possession of property is permitted' which, according to its provisions, is 'subject to restitution', or has 'a mortgage, pledge or lease' on such property.[208]

*58. The Law on Restitution of Confiscated Property and Compensation from 2015*[209] stipulates that the newly appointed *Agency for Restitution* performs activities that relate to the implementation of this Law and the law governing the restitution of property to churches and religious communities, in the sense that *it conducts proceedings and decides on requests for restitution of property (compensation), provides professional assistance to applicants and restitution obligors, keeps records prescribed by law, reports to the Government once a year through the Ministry of Finance on performed tasks within its competence*, as well as other tasks prescribed by law.[210]

### Law on Associations

*59.* The Law on Associations in the Republic of Serbia from 2018[211] prescribed that the association is a 'voluntary and non-governmental non-profit organization based on the freedom of association of several natural and legal persons, established for the purpose of achieving and promoting a certain common general goal or interest, which is not prohibited by the Constitution or the Law'.[212] Its provisions also apply to matters not regulated by special law, which includes *churches and religious communities*. This Law stipulates that the goals and activities of the association 'may not be aimed ... at inciting and encouraging inequality, hatred and

203. Law on Restitution of Property to Churches and Religious Communities, *supra* n. 93, Art. 27.
204. Law on Restitution of Property to Churches and Religious Communities, *supra* n. 93, Arts 28 and 29.
205. Law on Restitution of Property to Churches and Religious Communities, *supra* n. 93, Art. 31.
206. Law on Restitution of Property to Churches and Religious Communities, *supra* n. 93, Art. 32.
207. Law on Restitution of Property to Churches and Religious Communities, *supra* n. 93, Art. 33.
208. Law on Restitution of Property to Churches and Religious Communities, *supra* n. 93, Art. 36.
209. Law on Restitution of Confiscated Property and Compensation, Official Gazette of RS, nos 72/2011, 108/2013, 142/2014 and 88/2015 – US.
210. Law on Restitution of Confiscated Property and Compensation, *supra* n. 209, Art. 55.
211. Law on Associations, *supra* n. 98.
212. Law on Associations, *supra* n. 98, Art. 2.

intolerance based on racial, national, *religious* or other affiliation or orientation'.[213] Interpretation according to which religious subjects also belong to 'associations' has caused numerous controversies. The essence of the critics' attitudes could be reduced to pointing out the fact that religious entities, in comparison with other associations, essentially differ in their 'vertical' (transcendent, 'otherworldly') determinants and functions. They critically perceive the dogmatic interpretation of the provisions of this Law as 'horizontalization' and 'banalization' of faith, religion, and religious entities, which are forcibly deprived of the essential aspect of religious identity *(vertical).*

**Law on Prohibition of Discrimination**

*60.* The constitutional principles of non-discrimination in Serbia were elaborated by the Law on Prohibition of Discrimination from 2009.[214] It stipulates that discrimination and discriminatory treatment means 'any unwarranted discrimination, unequal treatment or omission (exclusion, limitation or preferential treatment) in relation to individuals or groups, as well as to members of their families or persons close to them, in an open or covert manner, based on actual or presumed personal characteristics'.[215] The mentioned characteristics include *religious beliefs*.[216] Therefore, 'association for the purpose of discrimination is prohibited', or more exactly 'activities of organizations or groups aimed at violating the Constitution, rules of international law and freedoms and rights guaranteed by law', which would result in 'incitement to national, racial, *religious* and other hatred, division or enmity'.[217] The Law has defined 'causing and inciting inequality, hatred and enmity, on the grounds of nationality, *race or religion,* language, gender, political or sexual orientation and disability' as a severe form of discrimination.[218] Article 18 explicitly *prohibits religious discrimination*, which includes conduct contrary to the principle of free expression of faith or belief, that is, 'denying an individual or group of persons the right to acquire, maintain, express and change faith or belief', as well as 'the right to express oneself in private or public or act in accordance with one's beliefs'. The law does not consider discrimination as 'conduct of priests, that is to say, religious officials which is in keeping with religious doctrine, beliefs or objectives of churches and religious communities entered in the Register', and in accordance with the Law on Churches and Religious Communities.[219] This Law also prohibits discrimination against 'national minorities and their members on the basis of nationality, ethnic origin, *religious beliefs* and language'.[220]

---

213. Law on Associations, *supra* n. 98, Art. 3.
214. Law on Prohibition of Discrimination, *supra* n. 94.
215. Law on Prohibition of Discrimination, *supra* n. 94, Art. 2.
216. Law on Prohibition of Discrimination, *supra* n. 94, Art. 2, para. 1, item 1.
217. Law on Prohibition of Discrimination, *supra* n. 94, Art. 10.
218. Law on Prohibition of Discrimination, *supra* n. 94, Art. 13.
219. *Ibid.*
220. Law on Prohibition of Discrimination, *supra* n. 94, Art. 24.

*61.* The provisions of the Labour Law from 2018[221] which regulates the rights, obligations and responsibilities arising from employment, are also thematically connected to this Law in one part. It too 'forbade direct and indirect discrimination of persons seeking employment' and employees, *inter alia*, based on *religion.*[222] Also, 'it is not considered a justified reason' to terminate an employment contract due to the *religion of the employee, who cannot be terminated due to their religion.*[223] This Law additionally strengthened the prohibition of religious discrimination in employment and work in the Republic of Serbia.

### Criminal Code of the Republic of Serbia

*62.* The current Criminal Code (CC) in the Republic of Serbia was adopted in 2019.[224] It defines and prescribes *criminal offences for violations of freedom of religion and discrimination based on religion.* The first is a violation of the freedom to *profess one's religion or practising a religion*, for which the perpetrator will be 'punished with a fine or imprisonment up to one year'.[225] The same punishment will be given to an individual for *coercing* another to express his religious conviction. If such an offence is committed by an official, 'he shall be punished by imprisonment of up to three years'.[226] Whoever publicly exposes an individual or group *to ridicule* in connection with their affiliation to a certain race, *religion*, nationality or other personal characteristics shall be punished with a fine or a term of imprisonment of up to one year.[227] It is also a criminal offence to incite national, racial, and *religious hatred and intolerance* among peoples and ethnic communities, for which a sentence of 'imprisonment from six months to five years' is applicable.[228] If the offence is committed in conditions of 'coercion, maltreatment, compromising security, exposure to derision or desecration of monuments of graves and religious symbols', the offender will receive a sentence of one to eight years in prison. If it is an official (who abuses his position or authority) whose offences result in violence or other serious consequences for the coexistence of peoples, national minorities or ethnic groups, he will be sentenced to one to ten years in prison.[229] As a fourth criminal offence, the CC also recognized 'failure to report the criminal offense and the offender'. The perpetrator, if he is not a 'religious confessor of the offender', shall be punished by imprisonment for a term between six months and eight years.[230] For 'inciting ... religious hatred and intolerance by conduct at a sports event or public assembly' which results in violence or physical confrontation, a prison sentence of one to five years is envisaged, with an accompanying fine. If this

221. Labour Law from 2018, *supra* n. 97, Art. 18, para. 1.
222. Law on Prohibition of Discrimination, *supra* n. 94, Art. 18.
223. Law on Prohibition of Discrimination, *supra* n. 94, Art. 183.
224. Criminal Code of the Republic of Serbia, *supra* n. 95.
225. Criminal Code of the Republic of Serbia, *supra* n. 95, Art. 131.
226. *Ibid.*
227. Criminal Code of the Republic of Serbia, *supra* n. 95, Art. 174.
228. Criminal Code of the Republic of Serbia, *supra* n. 95, Art. 317.
229. *Ibid.*
230. Criminal Code of the Republic of Serbia, *supra* n. 95, Art. 332.

offence is committed by a group, the leader receives from three to twelve, and the other perpetrators from two to eight years in prison.[231]

*63.* The CC also prescribes *serious crimes* against religious subjects and their followers. The crime of genocide includes 'the intent of the perpetrator to destroy, in whole or in part, a national, ethnic, racial or religious group', 'ordering the killing or causing serious physical or mental harm', 'inflicting on the group conditions of life that lead to its complete or partial physical destruction', or 'the application of measures intended to prevent births within the group or their forcible relocation to another group'.[232] The *criminal offence of Crimes against Humanity* refers to a perpetrator who, in violation of the rules of international law, as part of a wider and systematic attack directed against the civilian population, 'orders ... persecution or expulsion on political, religious, racial, national, ethnic, cultural, sexual or any other grounds', and for which a sentence of imprisonment of at least five years to life imprisonment is provided.[233] *War Crimes against Civilian Population* also is a serious crime, and if the perpetrator in violation of the rules of international law during war, armed conflict or occupation 'orders...deportation or forced conversion to another religion', he shall be punished by imprisonment for a term not less than five years.[234] For the criminal offence of *War Crimes against the Wounded and Sick*, the perpetrator who during the armed conflict 'orders that...*religious staff* be subjected to bodily injuries, torture and inhuman treatment', shall be punished by imprisonment of a minimum of five years.[235]

*64.* The current CC in Serbia prescribes several other criminal acts that refer to religious subjects and their believers. For the destruction of cultural heritage during war or armed conflict, among them *religious facilities and institutions*, a sentence of three to fifteen years in prison is applicable.[236] *Racial and other discrimination* represents a 'violation of fundamental human rights and freedoms guaranteed by universally accepted rules of international law and international treaties ratified by Serbia', and 'on the grounds of differences in race, colour or *religion*' is punishable by imprisonment from six months to five years.[237] Also, a perpetrator who 'disseminates or propagates texts, images and any other representation of ideas or theories that advocate or incite hatred' against any person or a group based on their *religious affiliation* shall be punished with imprisonment from three months to three years.[238] A person who 'publicly approves, denies the existence, significantly reduces the gravity of genocide, crimes against humanity and war crimes committed against a group of persons or a group member...based on race, skin colour, *religion*, state, national or ethnic affiliation in a manner that may lead to violence or incitement to hatred', shall be punished with imprisonment for a term between six

231. Criminal Code of the Republic of Serbia, *supra* n. 95, Art. 344a.
232. Criminal Code of the Republic of Serbia, *supra* n. 95, Art. 370.
233. Criminal Code of the Republic of Serbia, *supra* n. 95, Art. 371.
234. Criminal Code of the Republic of Serbia, *supra* n. 95, Art. 372.
235. Criminal Code of the Republic of Serbia, *supra* n. 95, Art. 373.
236. Criminal Code of the Republic of Serbia, *supra* n. 95, Art. 383.
237. Criminal Code of the Republic of Serbia, *supra* n. 95, Art. 387.
238. Criminal Code of the Republic of Serbia, *supra* n. 95, Art. 387, para. 4.

months and five years.[239] Finally, the CC prescribes that whoever 'publicly threatens to commit a criminal offense against a person or group of persons...because of their religious affiliation' shall be punished by imprisonment for a term between three months and three years.[240]

### Statistical data

*65.* According to the data of the Ministry of Internal Affairs (MIA) of the Republic of Serbia,[241] during 2010–2019, four different criminal offences related to freedom of religion were committed in the country in accordance with the provisions of the CC – 'Violation of freedom of religion and belief' (Article 131), 'Violation of reputation due to racial, religious, national or other affiliation' (Article 174), 'Incitement to national, racial and religious hatred and intolerance' (Article 317) and 'Racial and other discrimination' (Article 387). When it comes to 'Violation of the freedom to profess one's religion and perform religious rites', one criminal offence was committed in 2011, 2016 and 2018. In the case of 'Reputation breach due to racial, religious, national or other affiliation', three acts were committed in 2011, and one in 2012, 2013, 2017 and 2018. In this period, most crimes were related to 'Incitement to national, racial and religious hatred and intolerance' (Article 317 of the CC) – namely: thirty-two (2010), fifty-seven (2011), forty-three (2012), thirty (2013), forty-nine (2014), forty-eight (2015), nineteen (2016), fifteen (2017) and twelve (2018). The mentioned criminal offences were mostly not motivated by religious hatred but appeared as a result of verbal conflicts, anonymous threats or writing graffiti and slogans to the detriment of different nationalities (Croatian, Serbian, Roma, Hungarian, Bulgarian, etc.). Finally, when it comes to acts related to 'Racial and other discrimination', there were one in 2010, 2011, 2017 and 2018, and two in 2014, 2015, 2016 and 2019.[242] As can be seen from the presented, the number of crimes related to freedom of religion in the Republic of Serbia is continuously declining in the second decade of the twenty-first century, especially in the period from 2016 to 2019.[243]

---

239. Criminal Code of the Republic of Serbia, *supra* n. 95, Art. 387, para. 5.
240. Criminal Code of the Republic of Serbia, *supra* n. 95, Art. 387, para. 6.
241. The number of criminal offences, criminal charges and perpetrators for criminal offences of Arts 131, 174, 317 and 387 of the CC registered on the territory of the Republic of Serbia from 2010–2019, MIA, 2021.
242. *Ibid.*
243. *Source*: Ministry of the Interior of the Republic of Serbia.

## Chapter 3. Typology of the System

*66.* An attempt to determine and possibly define the nature of the system of religious law in the Republic of Serbia implies the existence of certain criteria, as well as its comparison with the same criteria in other countries. Since the Republic of Serbia is a candidate country for EU membership, it is expedient to compare the most important criteria of its system with those of EU Member States from the region of Southeast Europe.

*67.* Probably the most important criterion is the *procedure for registration* of religious entities. In comparison to Slovenia, Croatia, Hungary, Romania, Bulgaria and Greece, registration in Serbia implies a very simple procedure, after which religious entities acquire legal personality with the competent authority. The procedure is *uniform*, which results in the fact that all registered religious entities have *identical legal status*. In Hungary, Romania and partly in Greece, this procedure is two-tiered, with the result that the lower category (first phase of registration) of religious entities is a type of *religious association*, while the higher category (with a completed two-stage procedure) consists of *registered churches*. The conditions for changing the status of a religious association into a recognized church are *much stricter* than the conditions for founding the association itself. 'Registered churches', 'recognized religions' and 'church legal entities' *in practice enjoy a wider range of rights and privileges* than 'religious organizations', 'religious associations' and 'religious legal entities'. The former is recognized as a public law entity and religious associations as a private law entity.[244] Both in the Republic of Serbia and in the mentioned countries, 'traditional churches and religious communities', 'registered churches', 'recognized religions' and 'church legal entities' have *preferential treatment in the registration procedure*. Those recognized under previous legislation have acquired legal personality under an *abbreviated* and/or *facilitated procedure*. The decision in the Republic of Serbia that respects the existence of special laws which recognize the legal personality of certain religious entities in the past is *a good choice*. It *avoids discretionary decision-making* when entering into the register.

*68.* Another important criterion is the *conditions for registration*, which can be temporal, *quantitative* and *qualitative*. Temporal ones do not exist in Serbia, unlike in Croatia, Hungary, and Romania. The absence of this condition facilitates registration and acquisition of legal personality. The quantitative condition refers to the *number of signatories (believers) required for the registration* of a religious entity. In Serbia, this number is one hundred – the second mildest condition in comparison with the mentioned countries. *Qualitative conditions for registration* (name of the church or religious community; its address; name, surname and title of the person authorized to represent church or religious community; the decision to establish a religious organization with names, surnames, numbers of identification documents

244. More in: *Comparative-Legal Analysis of the Position of Religious Communities in the Surrounding Countries of the EU Member States – Slovenia, Croatia, Hungary, Romania, Bulgaria and Greece*, Ministry of Justice of the Republic of Serbia, 2016, p. 98.

and signatures of founders of at least 0.001% of adult citizens of the Republic of Serbia residing in the Republic of Serbia or foreign citizens with permanent residence in the territory of the Republic of Serbia; statute of a religious entity with a description of the organizational structure, method of management, rights and obligations of members, method of establishment and termination of the organizational unit, list of organizational units with the status of a legal entity and other data of importance for a religious organization; presentation of the basics of religious learning, religious rites, religious goals and basic activities of a religious organization; and data on permanent sources of income) are almost identical in all countries. The difference is the fact that the verification of conditions is performed by different institutions – parliament, government or the competent ministry.[245]

*69.* If issues of procedure and conditions for registration of religious entities are considered the most important criteria for determining the typology of the system, based on the above, it can be concluded that the current Serbian system has a very *mild, liberal and simple character*. Its criteria are easily achievable in practice for any newly established religious organization.

245. *Ibid.*, 99.

# Part II. Religious Freedom in General

*70.* All aspects of religious freedom in the Republic of Serbia are regulated primarily by the provisions of the Constitution and the Law on Churches and Religious Communities. They are further elaborated by other thematic laws and bylaws.

*71.* Social rights of priests and religious officials are regulated by the Law on Health Insurance,[246] Law on Health Care,[247] Law on Pension and Disability Insurance (PIO),[248] Law on Contributions for Compulsory Social Insurance,[249] as well as the Decree on the Payment of Contributions for Pension, Disability and Health Insurance for Priests and Religious Officials.[250]

*72.* Property rights and tax reliefs for churches and religious communities are regulated by the Law on VAT,[251] Law on Republic Administrative Fees,[252] Law on Accounting and Auditing,[253] and the Law on Restitution of Property to Churches and Religious Communities.[254]

*73.* Religious instruction in public schools is regulated primarily by the Laws on Elementary Education[255] and Secondary Education.[256]

*74.* It has already been mentioned that the Constitution of the Republic of Serbia guarantees every citizen the right to *freedom of thought, conscience, beliefs and*

246. Law on Health Insurance from 2016, Official Gazette of RS, nos 109/2005, 110/2012, 119/2012, 123/2014, 126/2014, 106/2015 and 10/2016.
247. Law on Health Care, Official Gazette of RS, nos 107/2005, 2/2009, 99/2010, 57/2011, 119/2012, 45/2013, 93/2014 and 106/2015.
248. Law on Pension and Disability Insurance (PIO), Official Gazette of RS, nos 34/2003, 84/2004, 101/2005, 63/2006, 107/2009, 101/2010, 93/2012, 108/2013 and 142/2014.
249. Law on Contributions for Compulsory Social Insurance, Official Gazette of RS, nos 84/2004, 61/2005, 62/2006, 5/2009, 101/2011, 7/2012, 108/2013, 68/2014, 112/2015 and 5/2016.
250. Decree on payment of contributions for pension and disability and health insurance for priests and religious officials from 2012, Official Gazette of RS, no. 46/2012.
251. Law on Value Added Tax (VAT), Official Gazette of RS, nos 86/2004 – corrigendum, 61/2005, 61/2007, 93/2012 and 83/2015.
252. Law on Republic Administrative Fees, Official Gazette of RS, nos 51/2003, 101/2005, 54/2009, 70/2011, 93/2012, 65/2013, 57/2014, and 112/2015.
253. Law on Accounting and Auditing, Official Gazette of RS, no. 62/2013.
254. Law on Restitution of Property to Churches and Religious Communities, *supra* n. 93.
255. Law on Elementary Education, *supra* n. 99.
256. Law on Secondary Education, *supra* n. 100.

*religion, to express religious beliefs,* as well as the *right of parents and legal guardians to provide their children with religious education* in accordance with their beliefs. Also, religious entities (churches and religious communities) are *equal* and *separated from the state, freely and autonomously perform their activities and mission,* and can be banned only if 'their activities infringe the right to life, right to mental and physical health, the rights of child, right to personal and family integrity, right to property, public safety and order', or if it 'incites and encourages religious, national or racial intolerance'.[257] All the stated principles, freedoms and rights *are taken from international conventions* governing fundamental human rights and religious freedoms.

257. Constitution of the Republic of Serbia from 2006, *supra* n. 4, Art. 44.

## Chapter 1. Individual Religious Freedom

75. The Constitution of the Republic of Serbia guarantees every *citizen freedom of thought, conscience, beliefs, and religion*, and prohibits the 'imposition' of religious beliefs, determinations[258] and *any form of religious discrimination* (direct and indirect). Every individual enjoys *a guaranteed right to equal legal protection*;[259] an adult individual has legal capacity and freedom of independent decision-making,[260] which includes the choice or change of religious beliefs and affiliations.[261] Each person is guaranteed the right to *conscientious objection*, i.e., the possibility of choosing to fulfil military duty in accordance with the principles of his faith without the obligation to carry and/or use weapons.[262]

76. In a broader sense, which also touches on the issue of freedom of religion, the Constitution guarantees to each individual the *freedom of opinion and expression* (speech, writing, art, etc.), which may be restricted by law solely to protect the values of a democratic society (rights and reputation of others, to uphold the authority and objectivity of the court, to protect public health and morals of a democratic society, and national security).[263] An individual is guaranteed the *freedom to express his or her national affiliation*,[264] as well as the *right to take part in the management of public affairs under equal conditions*.[265] Every citizen enjoys the right to *freedom of assembly* indoors and outdoors,[266] to *property* acquired by the law,[267] as well as the right *to work* in terms of freedom to choose an occupation freely under *equal* conditions.[268] An individual, as an *equal* spouse, has the right *to freely enter and dissolve a marriage*, regardless of whether he or she is in a marital or extramarital union.[269] The Constitution also guarantees the *right to education* (elementary education is mandatory and free, whereas secondary education is free), while all citizens have access to higher education under *equal* conditions.[270]

77. The Law on Churches and Religious Communities also guarantees every citizen the right to freedom of conscience and religion[271] as well as cherishing and developing their religious tradition (worship), education and culture.[272] It has prohibited any form of religious discrimination[273] and provided for the possibility of

258. Constitution of the Republic of Serbia from 2006, *supra* n. 4, Art. 11.
259. Constitution of the Republic of Serbia from 2006, *supra* n. 4, Art. 21.
260. Constitution of the Republic of Serbia from 2006, *supra* n. 4, Art. 37.
261. Constitution of the Republic of Serbia from 2006, *supra* n. 4, Art. 43.
262. Constitution of the Republic of Serbia from 2006, *supra* n. 4, Art. 45.
263. Constitution of the Republic of Serbia from 2006, *supra* n. 4, Art. 46.
264. Constitution of the Republic of Serbia from 2006, *supra* n. 4, Art. 47.
265. Constitution of the Republic of Serbia from 2006, *supra* n. 4, Art. 53.
266. Constitution of the Republic of Serbia from 2006, *supra* n. 4, Art. 54.
267. Constitution of the Republic of Serbia from 2006, *supra* n. 4, Art. 58.
268. Constitution of the Republic of Serbia from 2006, *supra* n. 4, Art. 60.
269. Constitution of the Republic of Serbia from 2006, *supra* n. 4, Art. 62.
270. Constitution of the Republic of Serbia from 2006, *supra* n. 4, Art. 71.
271. Law on Churches and Religious Communities, *supra* n. 92, Art. 1.
272. Law on Churches and Religious Communities, *supra* n. 92, Art. 1, para. 2.
273. Law on Churches and Religious Communities, *supra* n. 92, Art. 2.

restricting the freedom of religion of an individual only as prescribed by the Constitution and laws, and in accordance with ratified international treaties.[274]

**Religious Freedoms and Rights of Members of the Serbian Army**

*78.* *The Law on the Serbian Army*[275] provided for organizing of religious service in the army, stipulating that it was forbidden to 'favour or deprive' its members in his/her 'rights and duties', including their religious affiliation.[276] The goal of organizing religious service in the armed forces is *to guarantee freedom of religion* to its members[277] and shall be regulated by the Government. It is then implemented based on a special agreement between the Ministry of Defence and churches in Serbia.[278] The law also stipulates that a *disciplinary offence* is any 'act that insults the dignity of subordinates, especially with regard to gender, *religious beliefs* or nationality … '.[279] This provision especially protects military personnel who are members of *religious and national minorities* in the Republic of Serbia.

*79.* Pursuant to the *Law on the Serbian Army*[280] and the *Law on Government*,[281] the *Decree on Religious Service in the Serbian Army* was adopted in Serbia in 2012.[282] It defined religious service in the army as 'an organized type of activity of traditional churches and religious communities in the military environment', which includes 'worship, religious services, and other religious activities' in for that purpose, specially equipped places of worship (temples, buildings, chapels, etc.). It is performed by an 'authorized dignitary and a high-ranking member of a traditional church or religious community, canonically competent to priests and religious officials who perform religious service'.[283] The Decree also emphasizes that religious service in the Army is organized to *ensure the freedom of religion*, or rather 'to strengthen the spiritual and moral values' of its members, 'nurturing military virtues and patriotism', as well as 'shaping civic responsibility'.[284] The goal is the 'establishment, development, maintenance and increase of operational capabilities' of the Army. The decree prohibits 'missionary work of churches and religious communities in the military environment'. Commanders, heads of units and directors of institutions of the Ministry of Defence and the Serbian Army bear the responsibility for religious service in the Army.[285] Military persons participate in religious service 'exclusively of their own free will and conviction', without any 'coercion that could endanger freedom of religion' and with mandatory respect for all military rules and obligations.[286] They 'may not be harassed, discriminated against or privileged'

274. Law on Churches and Religious Communities, *supra* n. 92, Art. 2, para. 2 and Art. 3.
275. Law on the Serbian Army, *supra* n. 109.
276. Law on the Serbian Army, *supra* n. 109, Art. 25.
277. Law on the Serbian Army, *supra* n. 109, Art. 13.
278. Law on the Serbian Army, *supra* n. 109, Arts 26 and 27.
279. Law on the Serbian Army, *supra* n. 109, Art. 149, para. 1, item 5.
280. Law on the Serbian Army, *supra* n. 109, Art. 26.
281. Law on Government, Official Gazette of RS, no. 16/2011; Art. 42, para. 1.
282. Decree on Religious Service in the Serbian Army, Official Gazette of the RS, no. 22/2012.
283. Decree on Religious Service in the Serbian Army, *supra* n. 282, Art. 2.
284. Decree on Religious Service in the Serbian Army, *supra* n. 282, Art. 3.
285. Decree on Religious Service in the Serbian Army, *supra* n. 282, Art. 4.
286. Decree on Religious Service in the Serbian Army, *supra* n. 282, Art. 5.

because of their religious beliefs, belonging or non-belonging to the respective religious community, or due to participation or non-participation in religious life.[287] Members of the Army have an *obligation to mutually accept and respect* religious feelings and rights, especially in cases where they 'represent something sacred' for individuals.[288] Therefore, they are not allowed activities aimed at the acceptance of the religion of the other (*prohibition of proselytism*).[289] The last two provisions bear special significance to the preservation of religious identity of *minorities* in the Serbian Army.

*80.* Worship and other religious activities in the Army are performed by *priests and religious officials*, who are appointed by religious communities in accordance with internal and autonomous regulations. At the same time, they have the status of *professional military personnel*. Depending on their affiliation with a particular church or religious community, these persons may be *military priests* (SOC), *military chaplains* (RCC), *military imams* (ICS) and *military rabbis* (JC). Their assistants do not have the right to perform worship independently, although they have the rank of *non-commissioned officer*.[290] Both enjoy numerous social and labour rights – health care, PIO, the right to salary, compensation and other benefits, as well as other rights based on their status, in accordance with the law.[291] *Evaluation of the work* of military priests is performed by *superior officers* in the organizational unit of the General Staff of the Serbian Army, based on the opinion of an authorized religious dignitary and of religious officers and assistants directly by their *superior military priests*.

*81.* The Decree stipulated that if it is established that in the total number of members of the Army there are *100–500 believers* of a certain traditional church or religious community, *one military priest (religious officer)* will be assigned to perform religious service. If there are *500–1,000 of them*, they will receive *two military priests* (religious officials). For every *subsequent one thousand believers, an additional priest* will be provided.[292] If the number of members of a certain *confessional community* or *other religious organization* in the Army reaches the specified numbers, the Ministry of Defence will conclude an *agreement with it on the exercise of religious service* and accept into employment its priest (religious official). The *assistant priest* with the rank of non-commissioned officer accepts the position at the suggestion of his priest (religious officer).[293] Like a priest, he is accepted into professional military service with the consent of an authorized religious dignitary (bishop, mufti, rabbi, etc.) for which they are additionally trained to work according to the programme of the General Staff of the Serbian Army.[294] Their professional military service ceases when their religious community denies them the

287. Decree on Religious Service in the Serbian Army, *supra* n. 282, Art. 6.
288. Decree on Religious Service in the Serbian Army, *supra* n. 282, Art. 7.
289. Decree on Religious Service in the Serbian Army, *supra* n. 282, Art. 8.
290. Decree on Religious Service in the Serbian Army, *supra* n. 282, Art. 9.
291. Decree on Religious Service in the Serbian Army, *supra* n. 282, Art. 10.
292. Decree on Religious Service in the Serbian Army, *supra* n. 282, Art. 11.
293. Decree on Religious Service in the Serbian Army, *supra* n. 282, Art. 12.
294. Decree on Religious Service in the Serbian Army, *supra* n. 282, Art. 13.

right to perform religious activities based on autonomous regulations, about which the authorized religious dignitary informs the General Staff in writing.[295] When performing religious service in the Army, military priests (religious officers) *do not carry or use weapons*, command only their assistants and advise the unit commander on *religious and moral issues*. They are also guaranteed *the secrecy of information during confession*, in accordance with religious regulations. Pursuant to the *Rule of Service of the Serbian Army*, priests and religious officials may wear a beard, have the designation of their speciality on their uniforms and be addressed according to the rank they have in their religious community. Orthodox priests in uniforms have a cross with a trefoil on each arm on their military plaques, military rabbis have a Star of David, chaplains have a flat cross, imams have a crescent moon, and Protestant church officials have a cross within a rose. In case of their deprivation of liberty by the military police, the commander of the unit shall immediately inform the authorized religious dignitary.[296]

*82*. The primary activity of priests and religious officials in the Serbian Army refers to planning and performing worship, religious ceremonies and other religious activities, holding lectures on spiritual and moral topics, equipping worship facilities with the necessary items, supervising the work of subordinate military priests (religious officials), taking preventive measures against inappropriate behaviour and negative phenomena (suicide, substance abuse, sectarian activities, theft, etc.), cooperation with moral authorities and psychologists of the command and unit on various issues, pastoral and advisory work, church choir, participation in multinational operations, etc. In the formal-legal sense, they carry out their activities on the basis of the approval of the Ministry of Defence[297] and in accordance with the autonomous regulations of their religious community and planning documents of the General Staff and unit commands.[298] The inviolable place of worship can be changed at the proposal of a religious dignitary or priest and determined by the commander of the barracks, also based on their proposal.[299] Worship services may be performed outside the place of worship in the barracks, with the approval of the commander and the consent of the military priest.[300]

*83*. A *special agreement on exercise of religious service in the Serbian Army* between the Ministry of Defence and traditional churches and religious communities regulates the principles and competencies of its organization and performance, as well as the status, position, rights, formation positions and activities of military priests (religious officers). It also contains provisions concerning the specifics of planning and performing the activities of military priests, information on their authorized dignitary, the required number of military priests in the Army, the manner of their admission to military service, performance appraisal, participation in

295. Decree on Religious Service in the Serbian Army, *supra* n. 282, Art. 14.
296. Decree on Religious Service in the Serbian Army, *supra* n. 282, Art. 15.
297. Decree on Religious Service in the Serbian Army, *supra* n. 282, Art. 23.
298. Decree on Religious Service in the Serbian Army, *supra* n. 282, Art. 24.
299. Decree on Religious Service in the Serbian Army, *supra* n. 282, Art. 25.
300. Decree on Religious Service in the Serbian Army, *supra* n. 282, Art. 26.

international activities, termination of service, *rights of believers in the Army, application of the principle of positive discrimination, etc.*[301] Military priests and their assistants shall be deployed at the Military Academy, the Military Medical Academy, other military health institutions, and their subordinate units.[302]

*84.* The *organization of religious service* in the Army is under the *authority of the General Staff*. The chain of command implies that military priests at the operational and tactical levels in the units are under the command of their military officers. The Decree also guarantees them the *existence of a parallel autonomous religious hierarchy*, according to which assistants are subordinated to their military priests (religious officials),[303] while priests are responsible to their dignitaries for the religious activity according to the provisions of canonical and autonomous law.[304] In case the unit does not have a military priest for the religion to which the soldier of one of the traditional churches or religious communities belongs, he can fulfil his religious needs with a military priest from another unit (command). A soldier can be provided with the *right to specific food* in the unit, as well as the right to leave during religious holidays established by law. The military priest serving in a unit is obliged to assist the military believer of one of the *confessional communities* or *other religious organizations* in exercising *his right to specific food*, as well as in terms of *leave and absence from the barracks during religious holidays* established by law. Based on the application of the principle of *positive discrimination* in the Army, it is envisaged that if the number of members of a certain traditional church or religious community decreases over time below the numbers defined in Article 11 of the Decree, they are guaranteed the number of military priests they had before that reduction.[305] Finally, members of the Serbian Army and members of their families abroad (in defence delegations of the Republic of Serbia, for education, during participation in multinational operations, etc.) also *exercise their freedom of religion* through an *authorized military priest* of their religious community, based on with the consent of the competent religious dignitary.[306]

### Other Regulations Related to Individual Religious Freedoms

*85.* In the legal system of the Republic of Serbia, there are several other laws that address the issue of individual freedom of religion.

*86.* The Law on Police from 2018[307] stipulates that a police officer 'has the right to salary compensation' in case of absence from work on the day of a state and *religious holiday* which is a non-working day.[308]

---

301. Decree on Religious Service in the Serbian Army, *supra* n. 282, Art. 16.
302. Decree on Religious Service in the Serbian Army, *supra* n. 282, Art. 17.
303. Decree on Religious Service in the Serbian Army, *supra* n. 282, Art. 19.
304. Decree on Religious Service in the Serbian Army, *supra* n. 282, Art. 20.
305. Decree on Religious Service in the Serbian Army, *supra* n. 282, Arts 21 and 22.
306. Decree on Religious Service in the Serbian Army, *supra* n. 282, Art. 28.
307. Law on Police, *supra* n. 110.
308. Law on Police, *supra* n. 110, Art. 194.

*87.* The Law on Execution of Criminal Sanctions from 2011[309] stipulates that a convict has the right to a religious service, to hold and read religious literature, as well as the right to a visit from a religious official. If there is a sufficient number of convicts of the same religion in the institution (prison), the warden must, at their request, allow the authorized priest to visit them regularly, or to organize regular religious services and/or teaching. A convict cannot be coerced to attend a religious service or visit a religious official.[310] This Law regulates that a religious service is to be held in penitentiaries in a 'separate and specially designated space of the institution', while the duration and manner are more closely regulated by the act on its house rules. Today, spaces for worship exist in all the largest such institutions in the Republic of Serbia – Niš, Požarevac and Sremska Mitrovica.

*88.* The *Law on Patients' Rights from 2013*[311] guarantees the right of all patients to receive visitors in accordance with the house rules during their stay in the health institution, including *priests and religious officials*.[312] In all the largest clinical and hospital centres in the Republic of Serbia, there are *hospital chapels* in which regular worship services are performed by permanent or authorized priests of all religious communities. Retired priests with identical competencies and tasks are most often hired in smaller hospitals.

*89.* Finally, the *Law on Granting of Identity Card from 2011*[313] stipulates that a person who 'according to nationality, *religion* or folk customs' wears a hat or scarf as an integral part of the costume or clothing 'may be photographed' with said them, in accordance with the regulations on taking biometric data.[314] This provision refers to the practice of rights of members of 'minority religious communities' in the Republic of Serbia and has as its goal to affirm the principle of positive discrimination in this area as well.

*90.* Individual freedom of religion is guaranteed to all citizens of the Republic of Serbia, and they enjoy and exercise it to the fullest. 'Religious services' are also available to those who, due to difficult and special living conditions (patients and prisoners) and work (members of the security organs), need them the most. It is also enjoyed and exercised by members of 'minority religious communities' in almost all areas of life and work.

309. Law on Execution of Criminal Sanctions, Official Gazette of RS, nos 85/2005, 72/2009 and 31/2011.
310. Law on Execution of Criminal Sanctions, *supra* n. 309, Art. 113.
311. Law on Patients' Rights, Official Gazette of RS, 45/2013.
312. Law on Patients' Rights, *supra* n. 311, Art. 13, item 7.
313. Law on Granting of Identity Card, Official Gazette of RS, nos 62/2006 and 36/2011.
314. Law on Granting of Identity Card, *supra* n. 313, Art. 10, para. 8.

## Chapter 2. Collective Religious Freedom

*91.* The Constitution of the Republic of Serbia contains several provisions that also concern collective (in theory called 'corporate') religious freedoms and rights in the immediate and broader sense. Like other legal entities in the country, religious entities (churches and religious communities) may establish *media* (television, radio stations, newspapers, etc.) without censorship and work bans, except in cases where they disseminate information that poses a threat to state security, directly call for violence, war, or *religious hatred, discrimination and intolerance.*[315] Collective religious freedoms and rights are based on the constitutional principle of *freedom of association*, which citizens exercise through the establishment and operation of associations. These can be banned by the Constitutional Court only if they *incite religious hatred.*[316] The Constitutional Provision calling on all citizens to 'develop the spirit of tolerance, understanding and cooperation' is of great importance for the affirmation of the principles of *religious pluralism and tolerance* in the Republic of Serbia, especially in the fields of *education, culture, and information*, regardless of ethnic, cultural, linguistic, or *religious identity*.[317] In this context, every citizen and especially state, provincial and local self-government bodies are obliged to 'protect cultural and historical heritage, as well as goods of public interest'.[318] The provision relating to the right to preservation of specificity of national minorities is closely related to the exercise of the right to collective freedom of religion.[319]

*92.* The Law on Churches and Religious Communities guarantees all citizens of the Republic of Serbia the possibility and the *right to collective expression of religion* or *religious belief.*[320] *Collective religious entities* (churches and religious communities)[321] base their legal personality on the legal provision of the *freedom of association and assembly of citizens*, who create and constitute religious entities *as collective entities*. Their goal is the realization of religious freedom and the expression of religious beliefs of their members.[322] Only *collective religious entities* registered in accordance with the law may have the *status of a legal entity*[323] in Serbia and the consequent opportunity to perform *various types of activities* in society (worship, education, construction, social and charitable (humanitarian), cultural, etc.).[324] Only they can enjoy *independence, autonomy,* and *equality* before the state[325] as well as its *financial assistance.*[326] Thus, the collective aspect of freedom

315. Constitution of the Republic of Serbia from 2006, *supra* n. 4, Art. 50.
316. Constitution of the Republic of Serbia from 2006, *supra* n. 4, Art. 55.
317. Constitution of the Republic of Serbia from 2006, *supra* n. 4, Art. 81.
318. Constitution of the Republic of Serbia from 2006, *supra* n. 4, Art. 89.
319. Constitution of the Republic of Serbia from 2006, *supra* n. 4, Art. 79.
320. Law on Churches and Religious Communities, *supra* n. 92, Art. 1, para. 2.
321. Law on Churches and Religious Communities, *supra* n. 92, Art. 4.
322. Law on Churches and Religious Communities, *supra* n. 92, Art. 5.
323. Law on Churches and Religious Communities, *supra* n. 92, Art. 9, para. 1 and Art. 20, para. 6.
324. Law on Churches and Religious Communities, *supra* n. 92, Arts 31–50.
325. Law on Churches and Religious Communities, *supra* n. 92, Arts 6–8.
326. Law on Churches and Religious Communities, *supra* n. 92, Art. 28.

of religion in the Republic of Serbia, in many areas, is a prerequisite for the existence of all other types of religious freedoms and rights. In Serbia today, there are thirty-four registered collective religious entities, i.e., churches and religious communities.[327] Many of them contain numerous organizational units and thematic institutions with the status of a legal entity, which also testifies to the full realization of the right to collective freedom of religion in the Republic of Serbia.

**Religious Aspect of the Rights of National Minorities**

*93.* Members of national minorities are guaranteed 'special protection (of the state) for the purpose of exercising full equality and preserving their identity' by the Constitution of the Republic of Serbia.[328] They are guaranteed the right to 'express, preserve, nurture, develop and publicly express their national, ethnic, cultural and *religious characteristics*; to the use of their symbols in public places; to use their language and script in state, provincial and local authorities, especially in the areas where they are most represented; to education in their own language in state institutions and institutions of the autonomous provinces; the establishment of private educational institutions; the use of names and surnames in their mother tongue as well as the names of streets, settlements, etc.; to full, timely and impartial information in their own language, including the right to express, receive, send and exchange information and ideas'; and finally the right to 'establishment of its own media in accordance with the law'.[329] Based on the law, provincial regulations may establish and develop additional rights of persons belonging to national minorities.

*94.* The Law on Prohibition of Discrimination, among other things, prohibits discrimination against national minorities based on 'religious affiliation and religious beliefs'.[330] The Law on Protection of Rights and Freedoms of National Minorities prohibits 'any form of discrimination on national, ethnic, racial, linguistic, religious or any other ground against national minorities and members of national minorities'.[331] Finally, the Law on Employees in Public Administration provides for affirmative action measures for the employment of persons belonging to national minorities in order to achieve their adequate representation in state and provincial bodies, as well as bodies of local self-government units.[332]

*95.* Many other legal acts contain provisions against discrimination of national minorities, with the possibility of taking affirmative action measures to improve their position. Members of national minorities in Serbia fully exercise their religious freedoms and rights (to worship, religious education, religious culture, etc.) within the RCC, ICS, Protestant churches, JC, and other religious entities.

327. *Source*: Ministry of Justice of the Republic of Serbia.
328. Constitution of the Republic of Serbia from 2006, *supra* n. 4, Art. 14.
329. *Source*: Office for Human and Minority Rights of the Government of the Republic of Serbia.
330. Law on Prohibition of Discrimination, *supra* n. 94, Art. 24.
331. Law on Protection of Rights and Freedoms of National Minorities, Official Gazette of the FRY, no. 11/2002, Art. 3; Official Gazette of Serbia and Montenegro no. 1/2003 – Constitutional Charter and Official Gazette of the RS, nos 72/2009, 97/2013 and 47/2018.
332. Law on Employees in Public Administration, Official Gazette of RS, nos 113/2017, 95/2018 and 86/2019; Art. 15.

## Other Collective Religious Rights

*96. The Law on State and Other Holidays from 2011*[333] stipulates that *religious holidays – Christmas and Easter –* are also celebrated as state holidays in the Republic of Serbia.[334] In this regard, employees of different religions are entitled to non-working days during the following religious holidays: *Orthodox* on the first day of their Patron Saint's Day, Good Friday and the first day of Easter; *Roman Catholics and members of other Christian religious communities* on Good Friday concluding with the second day of Easter according to their calendar; *Muslims* on the first day of Eid al-Fitr and Eid al-Adha; and *Jews* on the first day of Yom Kippur.[335] In addition to the mentioned non-working religious holidays, Orthodox believers in Serbia celebrate some of them as working days: Saint Sava as the *Day of Spirituality* (27 January), the *Remembrance Day for victims of the Holocaust, genocide and other victims of fascism in the Second World War* (22 April), *St. Vitus Day (Vidovdan)* as a memorial to the Battle of Kosovo (28 June) and *Remembrance Day of Serbian Victims in the Second World War* (21 October).[336]

333. Law on State and Other Holidays, Official Gazette of RS, nos 4/2001, 101/2007, 92/2011.
334. Law on State and Other Holidays, *supra* n. 333, Art. 2.
335. Law on State and Other Holidays, *supra* n. 333, Art. 4.
336. Law on State and Other Holidays, *supra* n. 333, Art. 5.

## Chapter 3. Organizational Religious Freedom

*97.* The Constitution guarantees every citizen of the Republic of Serbia freedom of religion, including *the choice of the form of its expression* (at religious ceremonies, attending religious services or classes, individually or in community with others, and manifesting religious beliefs in private or public), in a way that does not *jeopardize the morals of democratic society, freedoms,* and the *rights of others.*[337] Churches and religious communities are equal and separated from the state and have the right *to independently regulate their internal structure* and *religious matters* (performing religious services, establishing and managing religious schools, social and charitable institutions, etc.).[338]

*98.* The Law on Churches and Religious Communities guarantees religious communities' autonomy and independence in *determining internal order and organization,* as well as *conducting internal and public affairs.*[339] In addition, if they deem it appropriate, they may request and enjoy assistance from the state in the protection and application of their autonomous regulations,[340] in accordance with which they themselves elect priests and religious officials and regulate the manner of worship.[341] Churches and religious communities in the Republic of Serbia may establish *organizational units and institutions* with the *status of a legal entity* and subsequently request their deletion from the Register.[342] Also, at the request of the competent authorities, they may perform religious services and ceremonies in hospitals, military and police facilities, institutions for the execution of criminal sanctions, schools and institutions of social and child care, in public places, open spaces and places of cultural and historical significance. In accordance with separate law (obtaining building permits) and in cooperation with local authorities, they can independently build temples and other buildings for purposes of service and worship (rectories, lodgings, administrative buildings, schools, boarding schools, hospitals, residential buildings, production facilities, etc.). The law stipulates that burials may take place in temples and other religious facilities owned by Churches and religious communities, based on their decision.[343] Finally, religious communities may *establish various social and charitable institutions* with clearly indicated activities which are separate from religious service.[344]

*99.* The mentioned non-working and working celebrations of religious holidays envisaged by the Law on State and Other Holidays, during which citizens directly exercise their religious rights (they go to worship services and religious ceremonies), can also be included under the organizational freedom of religion. In this context, it should be noted that labour legislation does not provide for the possibility of

337. Constitution of the Republic of Serbia from 2006, *supra* n. 4, Art. 43, para. 3.
338. Constitution of the Republic of Serbia from 2006, *supra* n. 4, Art. 44.
339. Law on Churches and Religious Communities, *supra* n. 92, Art. 6.
340. Law on Churches and Religious Communities, *supra* n. 92, Art. 7.
341. Law on Churches and Religious Communities, *supra* n. 92, Art. 8, paras 1 and 2.
342. Law on Churches and Religious Communities, *supra* n. 92, Art. 9, paras 2 and 3.
343. Law on Churches and Religious Communities, *supra* n. 92, Art. 32.
344. Law on Churches and Religious Communities, *supra* n. 92, Art. 33.

performing religious services during working hours. In the Republic of Serbia, there is a widespread *religious custom and practice* that companies and various institutions as collectives celebrate *their Patron Saint Day*.[345] Pursuant to the Law on the Serbian Armed Forces and the Decree on Religious Service, the issue of organizing religious service and determining the worship space for the exercise of religious rights of soldiers is regulated. Examples of organizational units and institutions of religious entities in Serbia are the Museum of the SOC, the Religious Charitable Guardianship of the Archbishopric of Belgrade and Karlovac, the Institute of RCC for Culture, History and Spirituality 'Ivan Antunović', the Humanitarian Organization of the SOC 'Čovekoljublje' and 'Caritas' of the RCC, Ecumenical Humanitarian Organization of Protestant Churches, Traditional Association ICS 'Gajret', Jewish Historical Museum and Amateur Theatre 'King David', etc.[346]

*100.* The Republic of Serbia is committed to the affirmation and development of all aspects of freedom of thought, conscience, and religion, in conditions of the existence of 'cooperative separation' in relation to its religious subjects. This represents an integral part of the programme commitment of the Government of the Republic of Serbia in the context of the European integration process. The 'religious' spirit and the provisions of the European Convention on Human Rights play a major role in society in the Republic of Serbia. This is best evidenced by the fact that their essence is an 'organic' part of the Constitution of the Republic of Serbia, as well as all subsequent regulations governing issues of religious rights and freedoms, modelled on the highest world standards.

345. Throughout the history of the SOC, the Patron Saint Day is an authentic traditional religious custom practised by Serbs in all parts of the world. This religious holiday represents the celebration of a Christian saint as a heavenly protector of the family. An essential spiritual and symbolic event during the celebration of the Patron Saint Day is the cutting of the Feast cake. The cutting of the cake in honour of a certain Saint is performed by a priest in the Church, usually after the Liturgy, in the presence of family members, after which a serving or 'Table of Love' is held in the host's house for family and guests.

346. *Source*: Ministry of Justice.

# Part III. Legal Status of Religious Communities

## Chapter 1. Formal Status of Religious Communities

*101.* The Constitution of the Republic of Serbia stipulates that it is *a secular state* from which its *churches and religious communities are separated.*[347] Religious entities in the country have an *autonomous status* in relation to the state.[348]

*102.* The Law on Churches and Religious Communities gives *registered religious entities* the status of a *legal person,*[349] which can be acquired and subsequently lost by their organizational units and institutions, in accordance with autonomous regulation.[350] In the Republic of Serbia, there are *traditional churches and religious communities* (with centuries-old historical continuity and legal personality acquired on the basis of previously valid laws: SOC, RCC, Slovak Evangelical Church, Reformed Christian Church, Evangelical Christian Church, Islamic Community,[351] JC) and since 2009 the Diocese of the Romanian Church 'Dacia Felix' with its seat in Deti (Romania) and administration in Vršac,[352] whereby the SOC is recognized as having a special *historical and civilizational role* in forming and preserving the *spiritual and national identity* of the majority Serbian nation.[353] *Confessional communities* (numerous Protestant churches registered based on the law in former Yugoslavia in 1977), as well as *other religious organizations,*[354] have a legal personality. This is a *terminological distinction*, with all registered religious entities, thirty-four of them, *enjoying the same legal treatment and scope of religious rights and freedoms.*[355] It is essential to note that the *act of registration is not*

347. Constitution of the Republic of Serbia from 2006, *supra* n. 4, Arts 11 and 44.
348. Constitution of the Republic of Serbia from 2006, *supra* n. 4, Art. 44.
349. Law on Churches and Religious Communities, *supra* n. 92, Art. 9, para. 1 and Art. 20, para. 6.
350. Law on Churches and Religious Communities, *supra* n. 92, Art. 9, paras 2 and 3.
351. In real life in the Republic of Serbia, there is an organizational division of the Islamic Community, which is reflected in the activities of ISC and IZS. Without interfering in the internal affairs of this religious community, the state continuously helps the life and work of both its divisions, striving to achieve harmonious relations and social consonance.
352. Law on Churches and Religious Communities, *supra* n. 92, Art. 10, paras 1 and 2.
353. Law on Churches and Religious Communities, *supra* n. 92, Art. 11, paras 1 and 2.
354. Registered after the adoption of the Law in 2006. To date, there are a total of twenty-six of them in Serbia.
355. *Source*: Ministry of Justice of the Republic of Serbia.

*a precondition for the existence* of the respective religious entity in Serbia but represents *only a framework and an assumption for the full enjoyment of their religious rights and freedoms.*

*103*. The Ministry of Justice of the Republic of Serbia is responsible for the status and legal issues of religious entities in Serbia. The Ministry keeps the mentioned *Register of Churches and Religious Communities* in the country, based on Article 17 of the Rulebook on the Content and Method of Keeping the Register. *Legal personality* allows religious subjects to fully enjoy religious freedoms, rights, and obligations, including *financial assistance* and *state support.*[356] The procedure for registration of religious entities (submission of applications, conditions and deadlines for registration, decision-making, international legal context, as well as the possibility of a potential administrative dispute) is regulated by Articles 18 to 23 of the Law on Churches and Religious Communities, as well as the Rulebook on the Content and Method of Keeping the Register. The detailed content of their provisions is presented in the appropriate part of the encyclopaedia.

*104*. The religious policy of the Republic of Serbia and the accompanying regulations give it a *liberal character*. This is best evidenced by the fact that since the adoption of the Law on Churches and Religious Communities (2006) until mid-2019, twenty-six newly established religious communities have been registered in the country.

356. Based on Art. 28 of the Law on Churches and Religious Communities.

## Chapter 2. Autonomy of Religious Communities

*105.* The Constitution of the Republic of Serbia stipulates that its churches and religious communities *have an autonomous status in relation to the state.*[357]

*106.* The Law on Churches and Religious Communities has elaborated on this constitutional provision, guaranteeing religious subjects' *autonomy* and *independence* in determining and manifesting religious identity, defining internal order and organization, as well as conducting public affairs.[358] The state figures as a *guarantor* of *autonomous religious regulations*, whereby at the request of the religious entities themselves, it can aid in its enforcement and application.[359] The autonomous status of the religious entities extends to their individual context and level in the sense that priests and religious officials are elected in accordance with the mentioned autonomous regulations.[360] They are 'independent' in the performance of their *religious services*, for which the state cannot hold them accountable if it takes place in accordance with autonomous religious regulations.[361] Priests are also guaranteed the *secrecy of facts and circumstances learned during confession*, the content of which they are not obliged to testify before state bodies.[362] Finally, the state 'protects their official uniform, as well as the designations of the rank and dignity of priests and religious officials', respecting the application of autonomous religious regulations.[363]

357. Constitution of the Republic of Serbia from 2006, *supra* n. 4, Art. 44.
358. Law on Churches and Religious Communities, *supra* n. 92, Art. 6.
359. Law on Churches and Religious Communities, *supra* n. 92, Art. 7.
360. Law on Churches and Religious Communities, *supra* n. 92, Art. 8, paras 1 and 2.
361. Law on Churches and Religious Communities, *supra* n. 92, Art. 8, paras 3 and 4.
362. Law on Churches and Religious Communities, *supra* n. 92, Art. 8, para. 7.
363. Law on Churches and Religious Communities, *supra* n. 92, Art. 8, para. 9.

## Chapter 3. Fundamental Rights and Religious Communities

*107.* In accordance with the proclaimed principles of human rights and freedoms, the Constitution of Serbia, accepting and applying generally accepted rules of international law and ratified international treaties,[364] explicitly prohibits all forms of discrimination, including that based on religion.[365] Restriction of religious freedoms and prohibition of activities of religious entities are possible only in the conditions provided by the Constitution and the law.[366] In Serbia, any incitement to racial, national, and religious hatred, intolerance and inequality is prohibited and punishable.[367]

*108.* The basic rights and freedoms directly or indirectly enjoyed by religious entities and their members (priests, representatives and believers) are the *protection of national minorities,*[368] *gender equality,*[369] the *right to dignity and free development of his personality,*[370] *right to life,*[371] *prohibition of slavery and right to liberty,*[372] *right to a fair trial,*[373] *right to freedom of movement,*[374] to *inviolability of home and the right to property,*[375] the *right to protection of personal data,*[376] *freedom of thought and expression,*[377] the *right of encouragement and respect for diversity,*[378] the *right to freedom of the media,*[379] *electoral right,*[380] *the right to participate in the management of public affairs,*[381] *freedom of assembly and freedom of association,*[382] the *right to inheritance*[383] and the *right to work,*[384] *the right to marry and equality of spouses,*[385] *the right to legal aid,*[386] *the right to social protection, pension insurance and education,*[387] as well as the *right to preserve one's specificity and associate with one's compatriots.*[388] It is especially important to point

364. Constitution of the Republic of Serbia from 2006, *supra* n. 4, Art. 16.
365. Constitution of the Republic of Serbia from 2006, *supra* n. 4, Art. 21.
366. Constitution of the Republic of Serbia from 2006, *supra* n. 4, Arts 43 and 44.
367. Constitution of the Republic of Serbia from 2006, *supra* n. 4, Art. 49.
368. Constitution of the Republic of Serbia from 2006, *supra* n. 4, Art. 14.
369. Constitution of the Republic of Serbia from 2006, *supra* n. 4, Art. 15.
370. Constitution of the Republic of Serbia from 2006, *supra* n. 4, Art. 23.
371. Constitution of the Republic of Serbia from 2006, *supra* n. 4, Art. 24.
372. Constitution of the Republic of Serbia from 2006, *supra* n. 4, Arts 26 and 27.
373. Constitution of the Republic of Serbia from 2006, *supra* n. 4, Art. 32.
374. Constitution of the Republic of Serbia from 2006, *supra* n. 4, Art. 39.
375. Constitution of the Republic of Serbia from 2006, *supra* n. 4, Arts 40 and 58.
376. Constitution of the Republic of Serbia from 2006, *supra* n. 4, Art. 42.
377. Constitution of the Republic of Serbia from 2006, *supra* n. 4, Art. 46.
378. Constitution of the Republic of Serbia from 2006, *supra* n. 4, Art. 48.
379. Constitution of the Republic of Serbia from 2006, *supra* n. 4, Art. 50.
380. Constitution of the Republic of Serbia from 2006, *supra* n. 4, Art. 52.
381. Constitution of the Republic of Serbia from 2006, *supra* n. 4, Art. 53.
382. Constitution of the Republic of Serbia from 2006, *supra* n. 4, Arts 54 and 55.
383. Constitution of the Republic of Serbia from 2006, *supra* n. 4, Art. 59.
384. Constitution of the Republic of Serbia from 2006, *supra* n. 4, Art. 60.
385. Constitution of the Republic of Serbia from 2006, *supra* n. 4, Art. 62.
386. Constitution of the Republic of Serbia from 2006, *supra* n. 4, Art. 67.
387. Constitution of the Republic of Serbia from 2006, *supra* n. 4, Arts 69–71.
388. Constitution of the Republic of Serbia from 2006, *supra* n. 4, Arts 79 and 80.

out the Constitutional Provision that indicates the need to *develop a spirit of tolerance* for all citizens.[389] The Constitution also guarantees numerous *economic rights* to religious entities and their members.[390] All the above-mentioned basic rights provided by the Constitution are elaborated and specified by distinct laws.

389. Constitution of the Republic of Serbia from 2006, *supra* n. 4, Art. 81.
390. Constitution of the Republic of Serbia from 2006, *supra* n. 4, Arts 82–96.

## Chapter 4. Contractual Religious Freedom

*109.* An example of a bylaw that directly concerns contractual religious freedoms in the Republic of Serbia is the Government Regulation on Funds for encouraging programmes or the missing portion of funds for financing programmes of public interest implemented by associations from 2018.[391] It determines the conditions, criteria, scope, manner and procedure of allocation and return of funds by which the state encourages programmes of public interest implemented by associations 'to achieve common or general goals and interests' that are not contrary to the Constitution and law.[392] Although churches and religious communities are considered 'associations' in the professional community, it is essential to point out that this Regulation stipulates that it 'does not apply to the financing and co-financing of programmes that are regulated by separate law'.[393] Most of its provisions concerning the conditions and procedures for the allocation of funds are also applied by the Administration for Religions of the Ministry of Justice when providing financial assistance to religious entities in the Republic of Serbia so that they are fully legal, fair, efficient and transparent, and under complete supervision and control. The significance of this Regulation is reflected primarily in the fact that it precisely defines the entities and procedures for the implementation of all public competitions in which religious entities in the Republic of Serbia also participate. Their finalization implies the signing and implementation of agreements between religious entities and the competent state body (the Republic of Serbia, autonomous province, or local self-government). The mentioned agreements represent the necessary legal precondition, framework, and basic instrument for the transfer of state budget funds for support and assistance to churches and religious communities, to their accounts which were specially designated and opened for those purposes.

*110.* The Regulation specifies the annual plans and calendar of public tenders, criteria for selection of programmes to be financed, application procedures for the competition, composition of commissions for its implementation and control, decision-making procedure, participation of professional public in it, use of funds, monitoring of programme implementation, reporting, evaluation, etc.[394] Within the consideration of the *programme financing*, details concerning the area and territory of its implementation, time and duration, goal, type and scope of activities, as well as the total number of persons required for its implementation are given.

*111.* In accordance with the Regulation, the *annual plan for announcing various types of public tenders* with all relevant data (on the donor, field, name and period

391. Government Regulation on Funds for encouraging programmes or the missing portion of funds for financing programmes of public interest implemented by associations from 2018, Official Gazette of RS, no. 16/2018 (further referenced as Government Regulation on Funds).
392. Government Regulation on Funds, *supra* n. 391, Arts 1 and 2.
393. Government Regulation on Funds, *supra* n. 391, Art. 2.
394. Government Regulation on Funds, *supra* n. 391, Art. 3.

of announcing) is published by the competent authority on its website by 31 January of the current year.[395] *Criteria for the selection of programmes* to be financed are the field, duration, number of beneficiaries and sustainability; the degree to which its objectives are linked to the public interest; possible co-financing by other entities (from own revenues, budget, EU, donations, legacies, etc.); legality and efficiency of use of budget funds; as well as degree of *fulfilment of contractual obligations*.[396] *The open competition* for the allocation of funds is announced by the competent state body, and it usually contains information on fields of public interest, possible participants in the competition, the amount of funds allocated, the necessary tender documentation to be submitted with the completed programme form, duration of competition and programme, etc. The key general criteria for associations to obtain state financial support are *legality* and *restricted spending of funds*. Namely, they can be used *exclusively for the implementation of a certain programme* and *in accordance with the contract* between the competent authority and the association.[397]

*112.* For participation in the competition, associations *apply* to the competent authority within the prescribed period,[398] and the authority then forms a *commission for its implementation* according to an internal act. Members of the commission are obliged to sign a statement that there will be *no conflict of interest* during the decision-making process, and if it is determined that it exists, they must withdraw from the commission.[399] The commission determines the list of *evaluations and rankings of programmes that applied* to which the applicants have the right to object. The decision on the selection of the programme is made by the competent body within thirty days from the expiration of the deadline for submitting complaints.[400] Depending on the case and necessity, and in accordance with the internal act of the body, the commission for evaluating the competition may include *representatives of the professional public*.[401] From the above, it is evident that the procedure of conducting and realizing public open competitions in the Republic of Serbia has a completely *transparent character* and is subject to *criticism and judgment of the professional and general public*.

*113.* The *transfer of funds allocated in the competition* is performed by the competent authority in accordance with the regulations governing the issue of opening accounts for users of public funds. The *agreement* between the two parties defines mutual rights, obligations and responsibilities (subject and deadline for programme implementation, amount of funds, security instruments in case of their unintended spending or non-fulfilment of the obligation which results in the obligation to return, etc.).

395. Government Regulation on Funds, *supra* n. 391, Art. 4.
396. Government Regulation on Funds, *supra* n. 391, Art. 5.
397. Government Regulation on Funds, *supra* n. 391, Art. 11.
398. Government Regulation on Funds, *supra* n. 391, Art. 5.
399. Government Regulation on Funds, *supra* n. 391, Art. 8.
400. Government Regulation on Funds, *supra* n. 391, Art. 9.
401. Government Regulation on Funds, *supra* n. 391, Art. 10.

*114.* Before concluding the contract, *the user of funds* (association) is obliged to submit to the competent authority a statement certifying that all data stated in the tender documentation *are correct*, that he has not already secured funds from other sources for the same purpose, and that he implements an *anti-corruption policy* internally.[402]

*115.* The *competent authority* monitors the implementation of the programme for which it approved the funds through *notification* and *control* of *periodic, narrative, and financial reports* of the beneficiaries.[403] It undertakes both *announced* and *unannounced monitoring visits* of its representatives who review the beneficiary's documentation. Control may be performed t*hrough cooperation and agreement with an auditor.*[404] The competent authority shall notify the beneficiary about the performed assessment and content of the mentioned reports, which include recommendations for elimination of deficiencies, who have eight days for supplementing and amending the report.[405] The beneficiary is also *obliged* to take all necessary measures in order to *avoid* or *eliminate the existence of conflicts of interest* when using earmarked funds and inform the competent authority about all types of *conditions and risks* that could occur.[406] The beneficiary may also request from the competent body the *redistribution of earmarked funds*, which could be approved only after obtaining *written consent* or *signing an annex to the contract.*[407]

*116.* If it is determined that the allocated funds were *misused*, the competent authority is obliged to initiate the procedure for *termination of contract* with the beneficiary and request the return of funds with interest.[408] It makes a *report* on the implemented financial support from the budget of the Republic of Serbia to associations in the previous calendar year. In order to improve efficiency at the internal level, the competent authority may conduct an *evaluation* of the degree and quality to which the *objectives of the programme* for which it awarded funds in the competition *have been achieved.*[409] Concrete statistical data on the type and scope of financing for religious entities in the Republic of Serbia will be presented in the appropriate part of the encyclopaedia.

402. Government Regulation on Funds, *supra* n. 391, Art. 11.
403. Government Regulation on Funds, *supra* n. 391, Art. 13.
404. Government Regulation on Funds, *supra* n. 391, Art. 12.
405. Government Regulation on Funds, *supra* n. 391, Arts 14 and 16.
406. Government Regulation on Funds, *supra* n. 391, Art. 17.
407. Government Regulation on Funds, *supra* n. 391, Art. 18.
408. Government Regulation on Funds, *supra* n. 391, Arts 19 and 20.
409. Government Regulation on Funds, *supra* n. 391, Art. 21.

# Part IV. International, Transnational and Regional Effects on Religious Communities

## Chapter 1. International Law Effects on Religious Communities

*117.* The Kingdom of Yugoslavia after the First World War and the SFRY after the Second World War were founders of the League of Nations and the UN. After the break-up of SFRY in 1991, pursuant to *Resolution no. 55/12 of the UN General Assembly*, the FRY was forced to rejoin the UN on 1 November 2000.[410] In this way, the Republic of Serbia, legal successor of the former Yugoslavia, at the beginning of the twenty-first century, strengthened its affiliation and confirmed its obligation to apply the legal acts of this World Organization.

*118.* This is confirmed by the provisions of the current Constitution, which emphasizes that generally accepted rules of international law and ratified international treaties are '*an integral part of the legal system of the Republic of Serbia, and applied directly*' on its territory.[411] This ensures full harmonization of the constitutional order of the state with international standards of the *rule of law* and *protection of human rights and freedoms*, while within the judiciary, part of the national sovereignty has been transferred *to international courts*. This represents the highest level of respect for the principles of the rule of law and the protection of fundamental human rights and freedoms, *including religious rights and freedoms*.

*119.* As emphasized in Article 194, paragraph 4 of the Constitution of the Republic of Serbia, *ratified international treaties may not be in noncompliance with the Constitution*. However, the fifth paragraph of the same article pointed out that laws and other general acts enacted in Serbia *may not be in noncompliance with ratified international treaties*. In accordance with the stated provisions, *the Constitutional Court* of the Republic of Serbia has the authority *to decide on the compliance of laws and other general acts with ratified international treaties, as well as on the compliance of ratified international treaties with the Constitution*, according to Article 167 of the Constitution. The presented constitutional provisions signify that the *international agreements* are above the laws and other general acts of the

410. *Source*: Ministry of Foreign Affairs, Republic of Serbia, and the United Nations (UN), http://www.mfa.gov.rs /sr/ index.php/spoljna-politika/multilaterala/un?lang=cyr, 21 Jan. 2019.
411. Constitution of the Republic of Serbia from 2006, *supra* n. 4, Art. 16, para. 2.

Republic of Serbia on the hierarchical ladder of the legal order, but *below the Constitution*. However, not all international treaties have weaker legal force than the Constitution. Article 18, paragraph 2 of the Constitution of Serbia stipulates that it guarantees and as such *directly implements human and minority rights* guaranteed by ratified international treaties. This provision means that the provisions of international treaties guaranteeing human and minority rights are of the *same legal force as the provisions of its Constitution* in the legal order of the Republic of Serbia.

*120.* After the Second World War, Yugoslavia adopted the *UN Universal Declaration of Human Rights* in 1948.[412] Article 18 underlines that everyone has the right to '*freedom of thought, conscience and religion*' (including the *freedom to change one's religion*), as well as 'the right to, alone or in community with others and in public or private, manifest his religion or belief in teaching, practice, worship and observance'. The Declaration affirms the principles of *freedom of peaceful assembly and association*[413] as well as non-discrimination, sameness and equality before the law and on religious grounds.[414] The spirit of these still pertinent provisions is contained in all subsequent relevant international and national acts and regulations concerning the issue of freedom of religion and the legal status of religious entities. It represents an organic part and '*backbone*' of the valid legal regulations in the Republic of Serbia.

*121.* The *International Covenant on Civil and Political Rights of the UN from 1966*[415] was also ratified by the SFRY. It also states that 'everyone shall have the right to freedom of thought, conscience and religion', that is the freedom to profess, accept, change, preach and practice religion or belief at one's own discretion, 'individually or in community with others'.[416] The Covenant affirmed *the right to freedom of association* and the need to protect the *social dimension of religious life* in a democratic society,[417] as well as the *principle of non-discrimination based on religion or belief*.[418] It underlined that no one shall be subjected to any form of coercion due to his or her religious affiliation, expression or non-expression,[419] and religious freedoms *may be subject to restrictions* only as prescribed by law.[420] *The States Parties* to the Covenant *undertook* half a century ago that parents or legal guardians would provide their children with 'religious and moral education' in accordance with their own convictions and beliefs[421] and that they will 'take steps

---

412. Universal Declaration of Human Rights UN 1948, www.ohchr.org, 20 Feb. 2020.
413. Universal Declaration of Human Rights UN 1948, *supra* n. 412, Art. 20.
414. Universal Declaration of Human Rights UN 1948, *supra* n. 412, Arts 2 and 7.
415. UN International Covenant on Civil and Political Rights in 1966, Official Gazette of the SFRY, no. 7/1971.
416. UN International Covenant on Civil and Political Rights in 1966, *supra* n. 415, Art. 18, para. 1.
417. UN International Covenant on Civil and Political Rights in 1966, *supra* n. 415, Art. 22.
418. UN International Covenant on Civil and Political Rights in 1966, *supra* n. 415, Art. 2, para. 1.
419. UN International Covenant on Civil and Political Rights in 1966, *supra* n. 415, Art. 18, para. 2.
420. UN International Covenant on Civil and Political Rights in 1966, *supra* n. 415, Art. 18, para. 3.
421. UN International Covenant on Civil and Political Rights in 1966, *supra* n. 415, Art. 18, para. 4.

towards the adoption of legal measures' that will enable all citizens, including members of '...religious minorities',[422] *to exercise the rights provided for in the Covenant*. They include *equal legal and judicial protection for all*.[423] Thus, in the mid-1960s, a more intensive process of *harmonization of national legislation with proclaimed international standards began*.

*122*. The *Declaration on the Elimination of All Forms of Intolerance and Discrimination Based on Religion or Belief* was adopted and proclaimed Resolution no. 36/55 of the UN General Assembly on 25 November 1981.[424] This declaration also emphasizes that 'everyone shall have the right to freedom of thought, conscience, and religion of their choice, individually or in community with others and in public or private', as well as manifest his religion or belief in 'worship, observance, practice or teaching'.[425] In addition, 'no one shall be subject to coercion which would impair his freedom to have a religion or belief of his choice',[426] and legal restrictions on religious freedom may be imposed only with the aim of defending democratic values and order in society.[427] The Declaration also states that '*no one shall be subjected to discrimination* by any State, institution, group of persons, or person on the *grounds of religion or belief*'[428] (Article 2, paragraph 1), whereby the *expression intolerance and discrimination based on religion or belief* means 'any distinction, exclusion, restriction or preference based on religion or belief and having as its purpose or as its effect nullification or impairment of the recognition, enjoyment or exercise of human rights and fundamental freedoms on an equal basis'.[429] This discrimination would be contrary to the *principles of human dignity* and the *UN Charter*.[430] The Declaration thus stipulates that 'all States shall take effective measures to *prevent and eliminate discrimination on the grounds of religion or belief* in the recognition, exercise and enjoyment of human rights and fundamental freedoms in all fields of civil, economic, political, social and cultural life', making all efforts 'to enact or rescind legislation where necessary to prohibit any such discrimination,

422. UN International Covenant on Civil and Political Rights in 1966, *supra* n. 415, Art. 27.
423. UN International Covenant on Civil and Political Rights in 1966, *supra* n. 415, Art. 2, paras 2 and 4, and Art. 26.
424. UN Declaration on the Elimination of All Forms of Intolerance and of Discrimination Based on Religion or Belief, https://www.ohchr.org/EN/ProfessionalInterest/Pages/ReligionOrBelief.aspx, 21 Feb. 2019.
425. UN Declaration on the Elimination of All Forms of Intolerance and of Discrimination Based on Religion or Belief, *supra* n. 424, Art. 1, para. 1.
426. UN Declaration on the Elimination of All Forms of Intolerance and of Discrimination Based on Religion or Belief, *supra* n. 424, Art. 1, para. 2.
427. UN Declaration on the Elimination of All Forms of Intolerance and of Discrimination Based on Religion or Belief, *supra* n. 424, Art. 1, para. 3.
428. UN Declaration on the Elimination of All Forms of Intolerance and of Discrimination Based on Religion or Belief, *supra* n. 424, Art. 2, para. 1.
429. UN Declaration on the Elimination of All Forms of Intolerance and of Discrimination Based on Religion or Belief, *supra* n. 424, Art. 2, para. 2.
430. UN Declaration on the Elimination of All Forms of Intolerance and of Discrimination Based on Religion or Belief, *supra* n. 424, Art. 3.

and to take all appropriate measures to combat intolerance on the grounds of religion or belief'.[431] It also stipulated the right of parents or legal guardians to organize, in accordance with their religion or beliefs, moral education in the best interests of the child, starting with the 'spirit of understanding, tolerance, friendship among peoples, peace and universal brotherhood'. In this process, neither parents nor children may be subjected to pressure or any form of discrimination.[432] The Declaration exhaustively states that freedom of thought, conscience and religion implies and includes the freedom to *assemble in connection with religion and establish places on religious grounds, establish charitable and humanitarian institutions, use necessary articles to perform religious services, disseminate relevant publications, teach a religion or belief in suitable places, receive voluntary financial support and contributions from individuals and institutions, train and appoint religious leaders and officials, celebrate religious holidays,* as well as *establish interfaith dialogue at the national and international levels.*[433] All signatories have agreed to *incorporate these religious rights and freedoms into national legislation* 'in such a manner that everyone shall be able to avail himself of such rights and freedoms in practice'.[434] The essence of all the mentioned provisions of international legal acts concerning the freedom of religion is contained in both the Constitution and the laws that guarantee their application in the Republic of Serbia.

**Examples of Cooperation of the Republic of Serbia with Specialized UN Agencies**

*123.* Today, the Republic of Serbia cooperates with specialized agencies and UN representatives through *various mechanisms of consultations and periodic answers to posed questions.*

*124.* Based on Article 27 of the International Covenant on Civil and Political Rights, other applicable international and regional acts, as well as national legislation, the UN General Assembly adopted the *Declaration on the Rights of Persons Belonging to National or Ethnic, Religious and Linguistic Minorities (Resolution 47/135)* on 18 December 1992. The Member States agreed to 'protect the existence and national, ethnic, *religious* or linguistic *identity of minorities* and to support the conditions for its promotion' and to 'adopt appropriate legislative and other measures to achieve this goal'.[435] The UN General Assembly then adopted Resolution 72/184 on 19 December 2017, entitled *Effective Promotion of the Declaration on the Rights of Persons Belonging to National or Ethnic, Religious and Linguistic Minorities*, affirming the aforementioned positions.[436]

---

431. UN Declaration on the Elimination of All Forms of Intolerance and of Discrimination Based on Religion or Belief, *supra* n. 424, Art. 4.
432. UN Declaration on the Elimination of All Forms of Intolerance and of Discrimination Based on Religion or Belief, *supra* n. 424, Art. 5, paras 1–5.
433. UN Declaration on the Elimination of All Forms of Intolerance and of Discrimination Based on Religion or Belief, *supra* n. 424, Art. 6.
434. UN Declaration on the Elimination of All Forms of Intolerance and of Discrimination Based on Religion or Belief, *supra* n. 424, Art. 7.
435. *Source*: Office for Human and Minority Rights of the Republic of Serbia.
436. *Ibid.*

*125.* In its commentary on the UN Secretary General's Report on Human Rights and Cultural Diversity and the measures taken to promote and protect minority rights, the Republic of Serbia informed the UN High Representative at the end of 2018 that it remains committed to further affirmation and development of freedom of thought, conscience and religion, that it provides regular assistance to its churches and religious communities for the protection of legal and social status, autonomy and equal treatment, as well as the exercise of other rights established by the Constitution and laws. This especially refers to 'minority' religious communities in relation to which the competent state bodies actively and continuously apply the principle of 'positive discrimination'. The Republic of Serbia explained its actions with the position that 'the mission of churches and religious communities represents a significant factor in democratization and progress of society', which is why the state strives for constant improvement of mutual relations with its religious subjects, which are 'good and stable', and is accompanied by 'constant strengthening of interchurch and interreligious dialogue'.[437] The mentioned principles of the religious policy of the Republic of Serbia are based on the strategic and programme commitments of its Government related to the strengthening and acceleration of the process of European integration.

*126.* When it comes to *measures taken to protect and promote minority religious rights*, the Republic of Serbia informed the UN High Representative that it takes into full account the examples of positive practice in the field of protection of religious freedom and its implementation in the national legislation of neighbouring EU countries (Slovenia, Croatia, Hungary, Romania, Bulgaria and Greece). In response to one of the most frequently asked questions, it was pointed out that in several Eparchies of the SOC (Vranje, Timok, Braničevo, Banat), Dioceses of the RCC and Protestant Churches, Islamic and Jewish Communities, *religious services are regularly held in national minority languages*, depending on the local needs and requirements of the believers. In the SOC Eparchy of Vranje, religious service for Orthodox believers is performed in Bulgarian (in Bosilegrad, Donja and Gornja Ljubata, Rajičinovac, Bresnica, Bistra, Bistri izvor, etc.); in the Eparchy of the RPC 'Dacia Felix' in Banat in thirty-nine parishes (Vršac, Pančevo, Mramorak, Veliki and Mali Torak, Bela Crkva, Jankov Most, Uzdina, Straža, Orešac, Kovin, Nikolince, Omoljica, Jabuka, Glogonja, Deliblat, Središte, Markovac – Romanian Greek Catholic Parish, Grebenca, Vlajkovica, Margita, etc.) by twenty-seven Romanian priests (three are Romanian citizens) in Romanian; as well as in the SOC Eparchy of Timok in the Vlach language by nine Vlach priests. Worship services in Hungarian, Croatian, Slovenian, English, and Serbian are performed in the dioceses of the RCC for its believers and in German and Hungarian within the Reformed Christian and Slovak Evangelical Churches. The Islamic Community uses Bosnian, Arabic, Roma, Albanian and Serbian in worship, and the JC uses Hebrew and Serbian.[438] The UN representative was also informed about the important fact that in 2017, *an initiative was launched to establish interfaith dialogue at the international*

437. *Source*: Ministry of Justice.
438. *Ibid.*

*(multilateral and bilateral), regional (multilateral and bilateral) and internal levels*, with the aim of creating social preconditions for reconciliation, development and integration in the economic and political fields, primarily in the region of Southeast Europe.[439]

*127.* In the *Third UN Periodic Report on the Implementation of the International Covenant on Civil and Political Rights* in September 2016, the Republic of Serbia informed the UN that the current Law on Churches and Religious Communities (2006) provides for a *liberal and simple procedure* for registering new religious entities, that it does not prohibit but stimulates the *acquisition of their legal personality*, as well as that the registration itself is not a condition for the existence and operation of religious entities but a precondition for the full enjoyment of all their rights. In this context, the valid *terminological distinction* of religious entities into traditional, confessional and newly established churches and religious communities should be observed, which in *practice enjoy all the rights and freedoms guaranteed by the Constitution and the law in the same manner and to the same extent.*[440]

*128.* In the period 2017–2019, the Republic of Serbia also regularly reported to the *Human Rights Council of the UN General Assembly* on the implementation of its measures (Decision A/HRC/RES/37/38) in the fight *against intolerance, negative stereotypes, stigmatization, discrimination, incitement to violence and violence based on religion or belief.* Special accent was placed on emphasizing full respect for freedom of religion and the prohibition of religious discrimination in the country, especially members of religious 'minorities'. She pointed out the need for further improvement of the existing interreligious dialogue at the regional and internal levels. In May 2017, she informed the *UN Special Representative on Cultural Rights* that through various programmes of higher and secondary theological education at faculties, seminaries and madrasas, Serbia is helping to improve the process of religious education, whose direct bearers and beneficiaries in many cases are women. Many of the mentioned religious educational institutions in Serbia are accredited by the competent Ministry of Science, Education and Technological Development, which means that they are *equal in status and rights* with other educational institutions in the country. An example of the measures taken to respect and ensure the rights of women in the religious field is the long-term successful cooperation and assistance of state bodies to churches of the Reformation (Slovak Evangelical Church and Reformed Christian Church), within which *female priests with episcopal and priestly dignity are active.* The Republic of Serbia fully accepts and guarantees the application of the autonomous regulations of the mentioned Protestant churches related to the religious status, rights and duties of women. In accordance with their competencies, the state authorities have, on several occasions, at the request of the communities themselves, financially supported the appearance of certain pastors at international conferences dealing with the topic of women's rights.

439. *Source*: Administration for Religions of the Ministry of Justice.
440. *Ibid.*

# Chapter 2. Transnational Law Effects on Religious Communities in Serbia

*129.* Within the *Organization for Security and Co-operation in Europe (OSCE)* as a transnational and regional arrangement based on the principles of *Chapter 8 of the UN Charter*, the Member States are gathered around the pursuit of a secure and peaceful world. Aware that it cannot exist without respect for human rights and fundamental freedoms, they agreed that they must respect the values and principles of democracy and the rule of law, including *religious rights and freedoms*. Yugoslavia, a founder of OSCE and a signatory to the Helsinki Final Act in 1975, and its successor – the Republic of Serbia, has been a member of this organization since 10 November 2000. By signing the fundamental documents of the OSCE (the *Helsinki Final Act*, the *Paris Charter* and the *Istanbul Document*) at the Ministerial Meeting in Vienna on 27 November 2000, the Republic of Serbia accepted all norms, standards and obligations arising from membership in this organization.[441]

*130.* Chapter 7 of the *Declaration of the Helsinki Final Act*[442] states that respect for basic human rights implies respect for the right of all citizens to 'opinion, conscience and religion', regardless of race, gender, language or any other determinant. States Parties committed themselves to respecting the *freedom of the individual to profess and practice his or her religion or belief individually or in association with others, in accordance with his or her own choice*. This is especially applicable to members of *national minorities,* where respect for and application of religious rights and freedoms will be an important aspect of *good interstate relations* in the context of their ongoing cooperation with the UN. In Chapter 10 of the Helsinki Final Act, the OSCE States Parties undertook to fulfil in 'good faith' all their obligations under international law in accordance with the signed agreement, including those concerning international standards for the adoption of internal laws and regulations. They accepted the *supremacy of UN acts in relation to all other international treaties or agreements* in accordance with Article 103 of the UN Charter.

*131.* The Paris Charter of 21 November 1990[443] reaffirmed the principle that every individual has the right to freedom of thought, conscience, and religion, as well as the right to confess and practice them individually or in a community with others, in equal conditions for all before the law. The Member States strengthened their commitment to combat all forms of discrimination, hatred, and xenophobia, including those based on religion.

*132.* The *1999 OSCE Istanbul Document*,[444] which focused primarily on security issues in Europe at the end of the twentieth century, the determination of the

441. https://www.mfa.gov.rs/spoljna-politika/srbija-u-medjunarodnim-organizacijama/oebs, 5 Mar. 2024.
442. Declaration of the Helsinki Final Act, https://fer.org.rs/wp-content/uploads/2018/11/helsinski_zavrsni_akt.pdf, 15 Jan. 2019.
443. Paris Charter of 21 Nov. 1990, https://www.osce.org/mc/39516?download=true, 15 Jan. 2019.
444. Istanbul Document, https://www.osce.org/mc/39569?download=true, 15 Jan. 2019.

members to respect and apply all *religious rights and freedoms* as an indispensable aspect and foundation of peacekeeping in Europe, especially in its Southeast, in the former Yugoslavia, was repeated.

## Chapter 3. Regional Law Effects on Religious Communities

*133.* In the international framework, there are also *regional legal frameworks and instruments* related to religious issues. These regional instruments contain essentially the same provisions as those listed at the wider international level. Bearing in mind the geographical position and strategic political orientation of the Republic of Serbia, of all regional organizations, the EU and the Council of Europe (CoE) are of the greatest importance for it.

**European Union**

*134.* With the entry into force of the *Stabilisation and Association Agreement (SAA) with the EU*[445] on 1 September 2013,[446] the Republic of Serbia received the status of an *EU accession candidate state*. The two most important obligations it undertook in this act were the *establishment of a free trade zone* and the *harmonization of national legislation with its law*. Negotiations on the SAA between the EU and Serbia began in November 2005. This Agreement, as well as the accompanying Interim Agreement on Trade and Trade-Related Matters (TTAs), were signed in April 2008. On 14 June 2010, the Council of Foreign Ministers of EU Member States brought a decision on the beginning of the ratification of the Stabilization and Association Agreement with Serbia. It was ratified by the European Parliament on 19 January 2011, and the ratification process in the EU Member States was completed on 18 June 2013 with ratification by Lithuania.[447]

*135.* At the Summit of the European Council on 28 June 2013, the decision was made to open negotiations on Serbia's membership in the EU. In the period from January 2014 to December 2019, *eleven intergovernmental conferences between Serbia and the EU* were held in Brussels, at which a *total of eighteen negotiating chapters were opened.*[448] Chapter 23 'Judiciary and Fundamental Rights' (opened at the Third Conference in July 2016) is of particular importance for the topic of this encyclopaedia, as well as the one concerning 'Financial and Budgetary Provisions' (Chapter 33 opened in June 2018). On 26 June 2017, the National Assembly of the Republic of Serbia adopted the Law on Amendments to the Law on Ministries, pursuant to which the *Ministry of European Integration* was established. Thus, the Office for European Integration of the Government of Serbia ceased to exist.

445. Which has the status of an international agreement.

446. The Stabilisation and Association Agreement between the EU, its Member States and the Republic of Serbia, no. 103/2007, can also be found on the Internet address: https://www.mei.gov.rs/upload/documents/sporazumi_sa_eu/ssp_prevod_sa_anexima.pdf.

447. Ministry of European Integration of the Republic of Serbia, https://www.mei.gov.rs/srl/srbija-i-eu/sporazum-o-stabilizaciji-i-pridruzivanju/, 5 Mar. 2024.

448. In the following order: Chapter 32 on *Financial Control* and Chapter 35 on *Normalization of Relations Between Belgrade and Pristina* 2015; Chapter 23 *Judiciary and Fundamental Rights*, Chapter 24 *Justice, Freedom and Security*, Chapter 5 *Public Procurement* and Chapter 25 *Science and Research* 2016; Chapter 20 *Enterprise and Industrial Policy*, Chapter 26 *Education and Culture*, Chapter 7 *Intellectual Property Law*, Chapter 29 *Customs Union*, Chapter 6 *Company Law* and Chapter 30 *External Relations* 2017; Chapter 13 *Fisheries*, Chapter 33 *Financial and Budgetary Provisions*, Chapter 17 *Economic and Monetary Policy* and Chapter 18 *Statistics* 2018, as well as Chapter 9 *Financial Services* and Chapter 4 *Free Movement of Capital* in 2019.

This data additionally testifies to the fact that Serbia attaches primary strategic weight and special importance to its process of European integration and EU membership, as one of the most important foreign policy priorities.

*136.* If the issue of European integration is viewed today from a historical, cultural-civilizational and religious point of view, it can be stated that the most important historical-civilizational constituents of European identity are Hellenic-Roman and Judeo-Christian, with subsequent admixtures of Islam and the attainments of the Enlightenment. The 'religious' stronghold of the EU Development Strategy is the principle of *('valuable') neutrality*, which is based on the foundations and methodology *of economic and political integration* of Member States. The EU, as well as the whole world at the beginning of the twenty-first century, is experiencing a *process of pronounced secularization*, followed by the *consequent relativization of the influence of Christian values and principles* in the social and public life of its members. It is accompanied by significant *scientific and technological development*. For the emerging 'universal value system' of which the EU is an 'organic' part, and on which the 'new world architecture' should rest, the greatest significance and use value of religions are reflected in their *ethical (moral) potential*, which needs to be reshaped, synthesized and universally applied.

### Community Ecclesiastical Law and Legislation

*137.* At the beginning of the twenty-first century, due to the *economic crisis* and *the crisis of identity*, interest in the issue of the *relationship between religion and politics*, that is, the *state* and the *church*, began to grow in the EU. The development strategists of the European project concluded that culture (including *religion* and the *Church*) and higher education are essential preconditions and the basis for further development of integration processes. In the religious-methodological sense, the *Western-Christian (Roman Catholic and Protestant) framework and approach* according to which the final 'unity of diversity' can be reached based on economic-political integration were confirmed. Gradually, there was a need for a more precise definition and an attempt to legally shape the 'desirable form' in the relations between the *state and the church* and at the *community level*. This became even more topical with the accession of new *predominantly Orthodox* EU states, which brought to the Union their cultural and civilizational features, experiences, 'potential' and needs.[449] In such circumstances, the EU has paid considerable attention to the *legacy issues of former communist countries* (now candidates or EU members), especially to the issues of *state interference in the religious field*, the *influence and role of religion in the transition process*, as well as *restitution*.[450] It is undisputed

449. EU Member States with a predominant Orthodox population are Greece and Cyprus with about 12 million inhabitants. New members Romania and Bulgaria have a population of 19.4 and 7 million, respectively. Orthodox candidate countries for EU membership are Serbia with nearly 7 million inhabitants, Montenegro with 627.5 thousand, Northern Macedonia with more than 2 million and BiH with 3.32 million inhabitants. Also, in Poland, one of the EU's most populous countries, there are some 8 million Orthodox believers.

450. Robbers Gerhard, *'State and Church in the European Union'*, in: *State and Church in the European Union*, Gerhard Robbers, Bogoljub Sijaković (ed.), Orthodox Theological Faculty, Institute for Theological Research, Belgrade, 2012, 9.

that the legal systems of EU Member States, as well as their neighbours, have common historical and cultural-civilizational, that is, Christian roots.[451]

*138.* According to the number of believers, *more than half* of the religious community in today's EU is represented by *Roman Catholics*, followed by *Protestants* and *Anglicans*. At the beginning of the twenty-first century, in the period of the last momentum of enlargement, there was a general agreement in the EU that in the future, Orthodox, Muslims, Jews and atheists will also have a significant influence in its development.[452]

*Table 4 EU Citizens by Religion in 2012*

| | *(In %)* |
|---|---|
| Roman Catholics | 55.40 |
| Protestant | 13.40 |
| Anglican | 6.70 |
| Orthodox | 3.10 |
| Muslim | 2.90 |
| Jewish | 0.30 |
| Other religions and atheists | 18.25 |

*Source*: 'State and Church in the European Union', in: *State and Church in the European Union, supra* n. 450, 9.
*Note*: The United Kingdom left the EU at the end of January 2020, after forty-seven years of membership. In that way, the religious structure of the EU itself was changed.

*139.* The *different systems of state and church law* that exist today in EU countries are a consequence of 'different outcomes of the Reformation and religious wars' in Europe in the sixteenth and seventeenth centuries. The basic typology, which in practice has numerous transitional forms, implies the existence of a *state church*, a *distinct separation of state and church*, and the so-called *general separation* that implies a more open cooperation of the two entities in solving common social problems. In many countries from the last group, mutual relations are regulated by *agreements between the state and the church*, which define the areas and the existing level of cooperation and leave room for its interdisciplinary improvement. All three of these models actually strive to overcome the 'anti-church and anti-religious mood' in EU countries and aim to give 'more space and freedom' for the church to act in obligation to respect human rights.[453]

451. *Ibid.*
452. Such attitudes, based on the principles of sameness and equality of all EU regions, were legally enshrined in the non-ratified Draft European Constitution from 2004.
453. Robbers, *supra* n. 450, 9–10.

*140.* At the beginning of the twenty-first century, it was envisaged that the EU, at the community level and in the religious field, would be empowered to create assumptions and provide space for the smooth functioning of all its 'religious' entities, in the broadest sense of the word. It was based on the need to respect and preserve the principles of religious freedom, religious neutrality (secularity), existing institutions of state and church law, as well as subsidiarity.[454] This leads to the conclusion on the lack of any intention for a more precise definition of the religious identity of the EU. Article 6 of the Draft Constitution, based on Article 9 of the European Convention for the Protection of Human Rights and Fundamental Freedoms, guarantees the right of religious persons to self-determination. The issue of religion was in fact treated as an important precondition for the existence of a common constitutional tradition of the Member States,[455] with the EU striving for 'equal respect for the position of churches, religious associations and communities, philosophical and non-confessional organizations their status and recognizing their identity and contribution'. That is why she wanted to establish an 'open, transparent and regular dialogue' with all her religious entities.[456]

*141.* Based on the *1997 Treaty of Amsterdam,*[457] the Draft Constitution, in Article I-52, proclaimed and affirmed the principle of *neutrality of the EU* in relation to its religious and philosophical subjects, as well as in relation to the *legal systems of its Member States.* It is important that the EU recognized not only its religious subjects as *subjects of community law*, primarily *Christian churches*, but also other religious and philosophical subjects without *discrimination.*[458]

*142.* Despite the complete relativization of church criteria in terms of 'what and how we may or may not believe', the Draft Constitution did not literally treat religious entities in the EU only as part of civil society (*NGOs*) but recognized their special *identity and contribution* in upgrading community social life.[459] It gave EU citizens the opportunity to take the initiative to *call a referendum* on *church (religious) issues* or the possible conclusion of an agreement between the *Community and religious entities*, as well as the *Community with third countries.*[460] In defining such powers, the Draft Constitution referred to Article 307 of the said *Treaty Establishing the European Community,*[461] which gave it the *right to monitor* and *assess*

454. Draft European Constitution, Arts 5 and 6 paras 2 and 3, http://publications.europa.eu/resource/cellar/7ae3fd7e-8820-413e-8350-b85f9daaab0c.0005.02/DOC_1, 13 May 2019.
455. Draft European Constitution, *supra* n. 454, Art. I-7.
456. Draft European Constitution, *supra* n. 454, Art. I-52, paras 1 and 3.
457. Treaty of Amsterdam, https://eur-lex.europa.eu/legal-content/EN/TXT/PDF/?uri=CELEX:11997D/TXT, 6 Mar. 2024.
458. Draft European Constitution, *supra* n. 454, Art. II-81 prohibited discrimination based on religion and belief, and Art. II-82 emphasized the principle of respect for different cultures, religions and languages within the EU. The principle of equality is confirmed by Arts 282, 300 and 308 of the Treaty Establishing the European Community.
459. Draft European Constitution, *supra* n. 454, Art. I-47, paras 3 and 4.
460. Draft European Constitution, *supra* n. 454, Art. I-52, para. 3. For example, with the Holy See as a subject of international law.
461. Treaty Establishing the European Community, https://eur-lex.europa.eu/legal-content/EN/TXT/?uri=CELEX%3A12002E%2FTXT, 20 Feb. 2019.

*compliance of contracts between members and third countries with a community agreement*, except for agreements that the member signed with a third country before the entry into force of the community agreement.[462] The Union's further powers in the field of religion have been limited by respect for the principle of *subsidiarity* as defined in Article 5 of the Treaty Establishing the European Community.[463]

*143.* Since the EU primarily strives to preserve the existing diversity and specificity, all concrete powers in regulating this issue have remained at the level of Member States.[464] This primarily supervisory-regulatory function of the Union is confirmed by Article 6 of the Draft Constitution, which specifically indicates the obligation of the EU to respect the national identity of its members.[465]

*144.* Secondary sources of religious law in the EU, for example, are *Council Directive establishing a general framework for equal treatment in employment and occupation* in October 1989 and the *Council Directive* on Television Broadcasting Activities in November 2000.[466] Both regulations refer to the principle of *prohibition of insulting religious feelings* through *equal treatment in the employment* of citizens regardless of their religious beliefs, as well as during television advertising.

*145.* The attempt and process of the emergence of state and church law at the EU community level are accompanied by the 'deinstitutionalization of institutionalized churches'.[467] The nature and intention of the emerging legal regulations at the community level primarily imply an *attempt to define a framework* for the integration of widely understood religious entities into the system of strategically projected (economic-political) development of the Union. It includes the aspiration to establish a multilayered interreligious dialogue of numerous religious entities, as well as the EU's dialogue with third countries. In the whole context, the EU intends to leave the essential and concrete powers in the field of church law to its Member States.

*146. EU Charter of Fundamental Rights from 2016*[468] confirmed the principles that *everyone has the right to freedom of thought, conscience and religion*, that is

462. Robbers, *supra* n. 450, 14.
463. 'Arbitrary' involvement of the Union in the field of religion is foreseen only if the common projected objective the Member States cannot achieve in mutual relations.
464. Robbers, *supra* n. 450, 12.
465. Article 151 of the Treaty Establishing the European Community, which primarily deals with education, defines the preservation, protection, and development of the cultural diversity of the members as its competence. The ecclesiastical and legal heritage also belongs to its domain.
466. Directive 89/552/EEC, https://eur-lex.europa.eu/legal-content/EN/TXT/?uri=CELEX%3A31989L0552 and Directive 2000/78/EC, https://eur-lex.europa.eu/legal-content/EN/TXT/?uri=celex% 3A32000L0078, 20 Feb. 2019.
467. Robbers, *supra* n. 450, p. 12.
468. Charter of Fundamental Rights of the European Union (2016/c 202/02), Ministry of European Integration of the Republic of Serbia, https://www.mei.gov.rs/upload/documents/eu_dokumenta/povelja_osnovna_prava_jul_20.pdf, 25 Dec. 2019.

the freedom to change religion or belief and freedom, to manifest it through worship, teaching, practice, and observance, either alone or in private in community with others and in public or in private. It recognized the right to conscientious objection in accordance with the national laws of the Member States governing the exercise of this right.[469] In this context, the EU prohibits all forms of religious discrimination and respects religious diversity.[470]

## Comparison of Serbia and EU Member States from the Region

*147.* In the *Screening Report of the Republic of Serbia for Chapter 23 'Justice and Fundamental Rights' in 2013*,[471] it is pointed out that in the Republic of Serbia, freedom of thought, conscience, belief and religion are fully guaranteed by the Constitution and laws and enjoyed in practice, on an individual and collective level, in accordance with the highest international and European standards.

*148.* In 2016, the Ministry of Justice of the Republic of Serbia drafted the already mentioned document entitled 'Comparative legal analysis of the position of religious communities in the surrounding EU member states – Slovenia, Croatia, Hungary, Romania, Bulgaria and Greece',[472] with the aim of identifying examples of positive practice in the field of protection of the collective aspect of freedom of religion in these countries, for the purpose of their implementation in Serbian legislation in the context of the EU accession process. One of the goals was to determine the harmonization of Serbian regulations with European standards in this area.

*149.* The results of the analysis showed that in all the mentioned countries of Southeast Europe, almost simultaneously after 2000, special laws were adopted which regulated the *legal status of churches and religious communities* and the *procedure of their registration* and that their *content was mostly similar*. The exception is Greece, where the position and status of smaller religious organizations were regulated in 2014. These laws in all mentioned countries contain provisions that protect the *freedom of religion* and prescribe its content, *classify religious entities* (churches and religious communities), regulate the *procedure of their registration*, define the *legal status* and state the *rights and privileges* of registered religious organizations. They paid special attention to the issue of *registration* of religious entities and the manner in which they acquire *legal personality*. Both in the Republic of Serbia and in its EU neighbours, activities of religious entities are regulated in detail by special laws or agreements. In principle, it can be stated that the *legal framework for religious entities is similar in all countries in the region*, with some differences in the *prescribed conditions and procedures for registration*, as well as the *legal status of religious entities after registration*. For example, unlike the Republic of Serbia, in which a religious entity *acquires legal personality by the very act of*

469. Charter of Fundamental Rights of the European Union, *supra* n. 468, Art. 10.
470. Charter of Fundamental Rights of the European Union, *supra* n. 468, Arts 21 and 22.
471. Screening Report for Serbia – Ch. 23 – Justice and Fundamental Rights 2013, Ministry of European Integration of the Republic of Serbia, https://www.mei.gov.rs/upload/documents/skrining/izvestaj_pg_23_16.pdf, 19 Dec. 2019.
472. *Source*: Ministry of Justice of the Republic of Serbia.

*registration*, in Hungary, Romania and to some extent Greece, there is a *two-stage registration procedure* which implies the *keeping and existence of separate registers*. In them, a newly established religious entity first registers in order to acquire a *lower legal status* (*religious association*), and only *after a certain period of time or fulfilment of strict conditions does it obtain the right to submit a request for re-registration acquiring a more beneficial legal position.*[473] *Registration in Serbia* is simpler, faster, and more favourable for smaller and newly established religious entities because it provides them with a more *advantageous legal treatment* (it does not have different categories of legal status). In addition, it is *closer to the proclaimed European and international standards* in the field of protection of freedom of religion.

*150.* As a consequence of the unified registration procedure in Serbia, all registered religious entities have the *same legal status* ('traditional churches and religious communities', 'confessional religious communities' and 'other religious organizations'), while in neighbouring EU countries it differs in the *lower* (religious associations) and *higher* categories (registered churches). In Hungary, it refers to 'religious organizations' and 'registered churches', in Romania to 'religious associations' and 'recognized religions', and in Greece to 'religious legal entities' and 'church legal entities'. It is characteristic of all of them that the higher category *enjoys a wider range of rights and privileges* than the lower one. In addition, registered churches are granted *public law,* and religious associations are mostly granted *private law subjectivity*. The existing typology of religious entities in the Republic of Serbia into 'traditional churches and religious communities', 'confessional religious communities' and 'other religious organizations'[474] *cannot be equated with the division of religious entities into several categories* because they all have *identical legal status*, and *none enjoys special rights or privileges.* Immediately after the unified registration procedure in Serbia, the newly established religious *entity acquires the status of a legal entity and is de jure equated with traditional churches and religious communities.*[475]

*151.* Traditional churches and religious communities in the Republic of Serbia have *preferential treatment in the registration procedure* because they were obliged to submit only an *application* containing the name of the church or religious community, the address of its seat, and the name and capacity of the person authorized to represent it. A similar practice exists in all EU neighbouring countries in the region. In Slovenia and Croatia, churches and religious communities that existed on the day of the entry into force of the current Law on Religious Freedoms *retained the status of a legal entity* and were entered in the Register ex officio. In Hungary and Romania, the law contains a list of religious organizations that were recognized ex officio, while in Bulgaria, religious organizations registered under the law from 1949 *retained the status of a legal entity even after the entry into force of the 2002 law*. Finally, in Greece, in addition to the three traditional religions with previously

473. *Ibid.*
474. Law on Churches and Religious Communities, *supra* n. 92, Art. 4.
475. *Source*: Ministry of Justice of the Republic of Serbia and its Administration for Religions.

acquired legal personality, the Law from 2014 recognized the legal personality of nine new churches and their organizational units. Thus, in these EU countries, several religious organizations that were recognized by previous legislation acquired legal personality by a *shortened or simplified procedure*. However, in both the Republic of Serbia and its neighbours, *there is no single criterion* for selecting religious organizations. This potentially creates room for their discrimination. In that context, the legal framework and approach in Serbia, which respects the objective fact of the existence of special laws that recognize the legal personality of such organizations in the past, *is perhaps the best solution*. It *avoids the discretion of the state* when establishing traditional churches and religious communities.

*152.* When it comes to the *conditions for registration of religious organizations*, they can be divided into *temporal, quantitative and qualitative*. *Temporal conditions* have not been prescribed by Serbian law but exist in Croatia, Hungary, and Romania. The absence of this condition facilitates the registration of newly established religious organizations and provides them with the opportunity to acquire legal personality without a prescribed and unnecessary wait. The most important *quantitative condition* is the number of believers whose signatures the religious entity must submit when entering into the register. In the Republic of Serbia, the Law stipulates that when submitting a request for registration, a religious community must submit a decision on its establishment with the names, surnames, numbers of identification documents and signatures of the founders of at *least 0.001% (one hundred persons* as specified by the Rulebook) adult citizens of the Republic of Serbia with a permanent residence, or foreign citizens with permanent residence on its territory. In Bulgaria, *there is no prescribed condition* for the existence of the necessary number of founders; in Slovenia, ten signatures are enough for the registration of a religious entity, in Croatia 500, in Greece for a religious legal entity 300, in Hungary for a religious association ten and for a registered church around 10,000, and in Romania, the prerequisite is 300 signatures for a religious association and about 19,000 for a registered religion (Figure 2). From the above, it is evident that the quantitative condition in the Republic of Serbia is *one of the most lenient in the region*.

*Figure 2 Number of Believers Necessary to Acquire the Most Favourable Legal Position of Religious Entities in Countries from Southeast Europe*

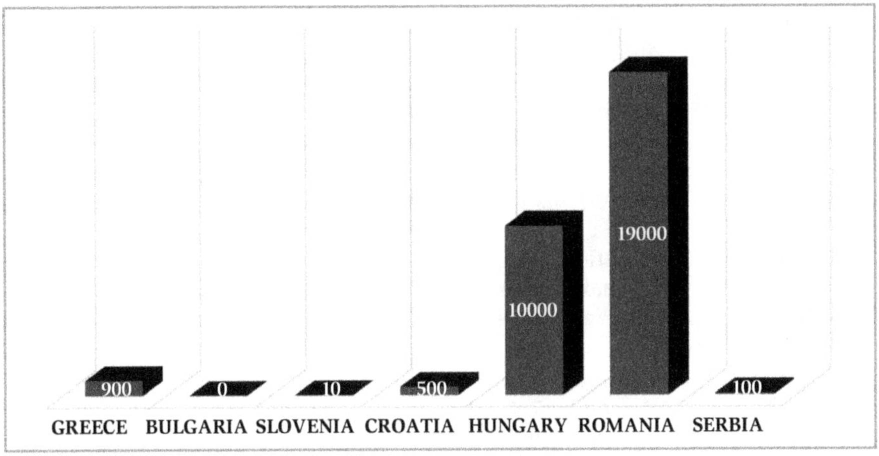


*153.* The problems faced by legislation that does not set a quantitative criterion relate to the tendency towards 'fragmentation' of religious entities, which is accompanied by abuse of their legal position. For example, in Bulgaria, large communities belonging to the same religion are registered as separate religious communities because this allows them to apply independently for state financial assistance. There were also attempts in Serbia to acquire the legal personality of 'religious entities' with financial motives. In this case, too, the Serbian model can be considered a *correct solution* because the prescribed criterion is easily achievable for any newly established religious organization that has enough followers. There are opinions and suggestions that the number of believers founding a new religious entity should be raised in order to avoid attempts to abuse this issue.

*154.* When it comes to *qualitative conditions* for the registration of religious entities, they are almost identical in Serbia and neighbouring EU countries. When applying for registration, all countries request the submission of the *statute* of the religious organization, with a description of the organizational structure, management, rights and obligations of members, establishment and closure of organizational units, presentation of the basic religious teaching, ceremonies, goals and activities of the religious organization, as well as information on its permanent sources of income. The difference being the fact that the verification of submitted documents in Serbia is performed by the Ministry of Justice, in Romania by the Government, and in Hungary by the Parliament.

**Council of Europe**

*155.* The FRY initiated the procedure for joining the CoE on 22 January 2001, after which it received the status of a special guest in its Parliamentary Assembly.[476] The Republic of Serbia became a member of this organization on 3 April 2003. Cooperation with this organization has a special significance for the process of European integration of the Republic of Serbia, having in mind the fact that the activities of the CoE are based on the so-called *Copenhagen Criteria (1993*). They relate to the rule of law, stability of institutions and respect for and protection of national minorities.[477] With the *Law on Ratification of the European Convention for the Protection of Human Rights and Fundamental Freedoms*, adopted in the State Union of SCG in 2003,[478] the state undertook to respect and apply all the provisions of the said Convention. Thus, it accepted the *jurisdiction of the European Court of Human Rights* and *enabled international judicial protection of fundamental rights, including the right to freedom of religion* according to all international and European standards.

*156.* The *European Convention on Human Rights and Fundamental Freedoms of 1950*,[479] like other important international documents in the religious field, affirms the principles and rights of freedom of thought, conscience and religion (religion or belief, its changes, practised alone or in community, in public or private) which may be subject to restrictions only under conditions prescribed by law, and in the function of protecting the values of a democratic society (public order, health, morals, protection of rights and freedoms of others, etc.).[480] The document also proclaims *freedoms of expression, assembly, and association*[481] motivated by *religious reasons*.[482] Article 14 of the Convention prohibits all forms of *discrimination*, including those *based on religious beliefs*. In addition, *Protocol no. 1* to the European Convention for the Protection of Human Rights stated that its signatories will respect the right of parents to provide their children with education and teaching *in accordance with their religious and philosophical beliefs*.

*157.* Yugoslavia (FRY) acceded to another important CoE document in 2001 – the *Framework Convention for the Protection of National Minorities*.[483] The preamble to the document guarantees national minorities the *right to express and*

476. Republic of Serbia in International Organizations, Ministry of Foreign Affairs Republic of Serbia, https://www.mfa.gov.rs/en/foreign-policy/serbia-international-organizations/council-europe, 6 Mar. 2024.
477. https://www.mfa.gov.rs/en/foreign-policy/serbia-international-organizations/council-europe, 6 Mar. 2024.
478. Law on Ratification of the European Convention for the Protection of Human Rights and Fundamental Freedoms of 1950, Official Gazette of SCG – International Agreements, 9/2003, 5/2005 and 7/2005 – corr.
479. European Convention on Human Rights and Fundamental Freedoms, https://www.echr.coe.int/Documents/Convention_SRP.pdf, 15 Jul. 2019.
480. European Convention on Human Rights and Fundamental Freedoms, *supra* n. 479, Art. 9.
481. European Convention on Human Rights and Fundamental Freedoms, *supra* n. 479, Art. 10.
482. European Convention on Human Rights and Fundamental Freedoms, *supra* n. 479, Art. 11.
483. CoE Framework Convention for the Protection of National Minorities, Official Gazette of the FRY, no. 6/1998.

*nurture religious beliefs*, and the Member States committed themselves to tolerance and respect for the cultural, linguistic and *religious* beliefs of persons belonging to national minorities. This includes the right of national minorities to *establish religious institutions, organizations, and associations*.

*158.* In practice, the European Court of Human Rights has had no cases related to the protection of religious rights in the Republic of Serbia thus far.

*159.* As in the case of the UN, the cooperation of the Republic of Serbia with the CoE in the religious field is realized through a *mechanism of periodic consultations and answers to questions*, with the aim of improving harmonization and full implementation of legislation in the Republic of Serbia in accordance with accepted standards of this organization and the EU. In brief, all religious entities in Serbia *enjoy all the rights and freedoms guaranteed by the Constitution and laws in the same manner and to the same extent*. In this regard, the 'traditional churches', *exclusively in terminological terms*, have only verified their centuries-old existence through the Law, while all others acquired *identical legal status after the registration procedure*.[484]

*160.* The FRY acceded to the Framework Convention for the Protection of National Minorities of the Council of Europe, which entered into force in Serbia on 1 September 2001.[485] Based on the foreseen mechanism for cooperation, FRY submitted *its First Periodic Report* on the Implementation of the Convention to the Council of Europe in 2002, which was adopted by the Resolution of the Committee of Ministers on its implementation in Serbia and Montenegro in 2004. The *Second Periodic Report* was submitted to the CoE in 2008 and adopted in 2011. In accordance with Article 25 of the Framework Convention, Serbia submitted to the organization its *Third Periodic Report* for the period 2007–2011, in which it was emphasized that the country as a contracting party, in accordance with its Constitution and laws, guarantees every member of a national minority the *right to express his or her religion or belief*, including the *establishment of religious institutions, organizations and associations*.[486] It is pointed out that members of national minorities in the Republic of Serbia (almost 99% of them) meet their religious needs within the Roman Catholic and Greek Catholic Churches (GCCs) (*Hungarians, Croats, Bunjevaks, Sokci, Czechs, Germans, Slovaks, Bulgarians, Ukrainians, and Ruthenians*), Islamic communities (*Bosniaks, Albanians, Roma, Egyptians, Ashkali, and Gorani*), Slovak Evangelical Churches a.v. (*Slovaks and Germans*), Reformed Christian Churches (*Hungarians*), Jewish Communities (*Jews*), Dioceses of the RPC 'Dacia Felix' (*Romanians*), as well as within the SOC *by their choice (Roma, Vlachs, Bulgarians, Macedonians and Montenegrins*). Religious entities have good

484. *Source*: Administration for Religions of the Ministry of Justice.
485. CoE Framework Convention for the Protection of National Minorities, *supra* n. 483, Art. 29, para. 2.
486. *Source*: Republic of Serbia, Framework Convention for the protection of national minorities – The Third Periodical Report submitted to the Secretary General of the Council of Europe in accordance with Art. 25 of the Framework Convention, 2012, https://www.ljudskaprava.gov.rs/sr/node/133, 20 Dec. 2019.

cooperation with the state body in charge of religious affairs, which is confirmed by the fact that many 'small', mostly Protestant religious communities have been entered in the Register in only a few years – Free Belgrade Church, Jehovah's Witnesses-Christian Religious Community, Zion Sacrament Church, Union of Seventh-day Adventist Reform Movement, Protestant Evangelical Church 'Spiritual Centre' and Evangelical Church of Christ, Eparchy of the ROC 'Dacia Felix', Christian Adventist Church, Evangelical Methodist Church, Church of Jesus Christ of Latter-day Saints, Evangelical Church in Serbia, Church of Christ's Love, Spiritual Church of Christ, Union of Christian Baptist Churches in Serbia, Nazarene Christian Religious Community, Church of God in Serbia, Church of Christ Brethren in Serbia, and the Protestant Christian Community in Serbia. Among their founders were *numerous members of national minorities*, who in this manner also *exercise their right to freedom of religion and the establishment of their religious institutions*. In the *Fourth Periodic Report* to the CoE for 2012–2016, the Republic of Serbia answered questions concerning the exercise of the *right to worship in the languages of national minorities* and the *establishment of religious institutions*. The position was again explained, and precise arguments and data were presented that 'non-traditional' religious entities were not discriminated against in any way in relation to 'traditional' ones, that 'no religious community was granted a special status', and that the state 'adheres to principles of neutrality and impartiality, and even more so' in relation to 'minority' religious communities.[487] All religious entities in the Republic of Serbia have a fair opportunity to submit a request for registration and acquire legal personality, whereby the criteria are applied exclusively in a non-discriminatory manner. This can best be verified directly with the religious leaders in the country, as well as in the Register of Churches and Religious Communities in the Ministry of Justice.

*161.* When it comes to worship in the languages of national minorities, the competent body of the Republic of Serbia, respecting the constitutional principle of separation of state and church, continuously recommends that religious entities perform services and ceremonies in the languages of national minorities as much as possible in accordance with internal religious regulations. In this regard, the data shows that religious entities worship in the languages of national minorities as follows: Islamic Community in Bosnian, Romani, Albanian, Turkish, Arabic and Serbian; SOC, in the Eparchies of Timok and Braničevo in Vlach, in the Eparchy of Vranje in Bulgarian (in Bosilegrad, Donja and Gornja Ljubata, Rajcinovci, Bresnica, Bistra, Bistro Izvor, etc.), and in the Eparchy of Bačka in Romani; RCC and GCC in Hungarian (in the Diocese of Subotica and Zrenjanin), Croatian (Diocese of Srem and Subotica), Serbian and Slovenian (in the Archdiocese of Belgrade and certain parts of the aforementioned dioceses). Within the Exarchate (now the Diocese), the GCC service is performed in Ruthenian, Ukrainian, Church Slavonic and Romanian; JC serves in Hebrew and Serbian; Slovak Evangelical Church in

487. *Source*: Republic of Serbia, Framework Convention for the Protection of National Minorities – The Fourth Periodical Report Submitted to the General Secretary of the Council of Europe in accordance with Art. 25 of the Framework Convention, 2018, https://ljudskaprava.gov.rs/sr/node/22332, 20 Dec. 2019.

Slovak and German; Reformed Christian Church and Evangelical Christian Church in Hungarian; ROC in Romanian in thirty-nine parishes of the Diocese 'Dacia Felix' (in Vršac, Pančevo, Mramorak, Veliki and Mali Torak, Bela Crkva, Jankov Most, Uzdin, Straža, Orešac, Kovin, Nikolinci, Omoljica, Jabuka, Gloganj, Deliblato, Središte, Markovac, Grebenac, Vlajkovac, Margita, etc.), led by twenty-seven Romanian priests (three are Romanian citizens). Article 23 of the Framework Convention stipulates that the rights and freedoms deriving from the principles contained in the Convention, insofar as they are the subject of the European Convention for the Protection of Human Rights and Fundamental Freedoms or in the Protocols thereto, shall be understood in accordance with that Convention. Since freedom of religion is guaranteed by Article 9 of the European Convention, it is clear that the provisions of the Framework Convention must be understood in accordance with the provisions of the European Convention for the Protection of Human Rights and Fundamental Freedoms. In that sense, the Serbian authorities adhere to the understanding of the European Court of Human Rights, which in the case of 'Metropolitan Church of Bessarabia vs. Moldova' took the view in 1999 that 'since religious communities traditionally exist in the form of organized structures, Article 9 must be interpreted in the light of Article 11 of the Convention, which safeguards associative life against unjustified State interference' and that 'autonomous existence of religious communities … is thus an issue at the very heart of the protection which Article 9 affords'.[488] Article 9 of the European Convention for the Protection of Human Rights is interpreted in the court's case as that, in the event of a conflict between the individual and collective aspects of Article 9, it is desirable for collective rather than an individual expression of belief to prevail, because 'the church is an organized religious community based on identical or at least substantially similar views', and is therefore 'protected in its right to exercise faith, to organize and to perform prayers, ritual, religious service and divine worship, and is free to act uniformly and to impose uniformity in all these matters'.[489] Bearing in mind the above understanding of the court, it is clear that the active steps of the state to improve the right of persons belonging to national minorities to worship in their mother tongues can only be reduced to recommendations to churches and religious communities and the encouragement of dialogue between interested parties while refraining from any arbitrary interference in the language issue, which is fully in line with international standards of freedom of religion. All this should be viewed through the prism of the existence of the Law on Official Use of Languages and Scripts,[490] which also applies to religious entities when performing religious worship.

*162.* The CoE was interested in the right of *persons belonging to national minorities to associate based on religious beliefs*. Article 5 of the Law on Churches and Religious Communities was pointed out, which underlined that citizens have

488. European Court of Human Rights, Case of the *Metropolitan Church of Bessarabia and Others v. Moldova*, no. 45701/99, https://hudoc.echr.coe.int/eng#{%22itemid%22:[%22001-59985%22]}, 15 Feb. 2020.
489. *Ibid.*
490. Law on Official Use of Languages and Scripts, Official Gazette of RS, nos 45/1991 to 48/2018.

the freedom of association and public assembly to express their religious beliefs. In practice, there are religious entities in the country that have members of national minorities as their majority members, such as the RCC, Protestant churches, Islamic Community, JC, etc. In accordance with the provisions of the Law that guarantees them autonomous status in relation to state bodies,[491] the mentioned religious entities exercise the right to establish religious institutions, organizations, and associations. Examples of the associations are: 'Maria' and 'Caritas' (RCC), 'Gajret' (IC), 'Ecumenical Humanitarian Organization' (Protestant Churches of the Reformation), 'Chabad Serbia' (JC), etc. The conclusion is that the right of members of national minorities to establish religious institutions, organizations or associations is effectively guaranteed by law, that legal provisions regulating religious communities do not allow discrimination, and that this right is exercised in practice.

*163.* Based on the Fourth Periodic Report on the Implementation of the Framework Convention for the Protection of National Minorities in the Republic of Serbia submitted to the CoE in September 2018, the Advisory Committee of the Framework Convention for the Protection of National Minorities adopted the *Fourth Opinion for Serbia on 26 June 2019.*[492] The authorities of the Republic of Serbia assessed that it was 'based on a constructive analysis of the position of national minorities and dedicated to very important issues'. They pointed out that 'the implementation of the Framework Convention is a continuous process', that their comments on the Fourth Opinion of the Advisory Committee 'are mainly based on the activities undertaken in the country', and that 'all activities are aimed not only at upgrading highly regulated legislation in the field of protection and promotion of the rights of national minorities, but also on the consistent application of the established legislative and institutional framework'.

491. Law on Churches and Religious Communities, *supra* n. 92, Arts 6 and 7.

492. *Source*: Advisory Committee on the Framework Convention for the protection of national minorities, Fourth Opinion on Serbia adopted on 26 Jun. 2019, https://rm.coe.int/4th-op-serbia-en/16809943b6, 15 Jun. 2020.

# Part V. Religion and Politics

## Chapter 1. Religion's Influence in Politics

*164.* The monotheistic concept of religion implies the existence of a spiritual-theoretical 'value' and institutional system, whose key factors are faith in God, the associated set of ceremonies and rituals, as well as religious entities – churches, other religions and believers. All of them are in an interdependent relationship with social circumstances, which is why religion can be defined as 'vertical sociability'.[493] Especially today, religion is largely a value alternative to secularism. The greatest monotheistic religions, especially Christianity, and even more specifically Islam, 'in this world as well' strive to create an immediate community of believers and God, which is why they have primarily an identity, integrative and cohesive nature and potential, with a predominantly 'vertical' determinant.[494]

*165.* In the traditional societies of European countries, there was and still is a *real and unbreakable connection between religion, society and politics.* The spiritual and secular dimension of existence through institutions (church and state) has always permeated at all levels, but also found itself in a certain 'competitive' relationship in the sense of striving to 'better' position oneself in relation to the other and have a greater influence, starting from different strongholds, goals, consequences and origins. In that sense, we can discuss the notions of 'true missionary work', 'cooperation', as well as attempts to instrumentalize the ontological ('otherworldly') for earthly purposes. The mentioned correlation of the two concepts is characteristic of all periods of recent human history. To illustrate, in the Byzantine (Eastern Roman) Empire, the emperor convened church councils but without the right to make decisions in them. In the time of Charlemagne,[495] Frankish King and Emperor (768–814) and protector of the papacy,[496] the Roman Church acquired certain 'political competencies', while this ruler acquired certain 'ecclesiastical ones'.[497]

493. Mantzaridis Georgios M., *Sociology of Christianity*, Christian Cultural Centre, Belgrade, 2004, p. 9.
494. Nikolić Marko, 'Aktuelna međureligijska saradnja na Balkanu', in: *Srbija u Jugoistočnoj Evropi*, Dragan Đukanović, Vladimir Trapara (ed.), *Institut za medjunarodnu politiku i privredu*, Beograd, 2012, pp. 552–568.
495. The first emperor in Western Europe after the collapse of the Western Roman Empire three centuries earlier.
496. Pope John Paul II called him 'Father of Europe' in 2004.
497. Mercier Jacques, *History of the Vatican*, Barbat, Zagreb, 2001, pp. 129–135.

*166.* In Europe today, the question of attempting to find and define the desirable, possible and functional form of the church as a 'vertical' and the state as a 'horizontal' entity, or rather the 'ontological content that lives in this world' (church and religious communities) and 'executive-formal' (state) which should create 'value preconditions' for it. The position and role of religious entities in that sense should be primarily 'value-critical' in the moral sense and the state 'neutral-executive'. Since history testifies that in this correlation the two subjects often 'betrayed' themselves, today it would be desirable, and necessary, for existential reasons, for both to 'remain what they are and should be', and then creatively, in a kind of 'community of complementarity and enrichment', enable each other to perform their various missions and functions. This does not imply the loss of one's own identity, much less the literal application of the principle of separation of church and state, which guarantees the church only the status of a non-governmental organization with individual membership.

## Cultural – Civilization and EU Context

*167.* The *Edict of Milan* in 313 affirmed the principle of freedom, public position, and the 'constitutive' influence of Christian religion in society. Her church was *legalized* during the reign of *Emperor Constantine* (324–337) and *Empress Helena.* These rulers were inspired in their life and work by Christian teaching; they are inscribed in the *Diptychs of the Saints* of the Ecumenical (Universal) Orthodox Church, and are highly respected in the European part of the RCC, on the territory of today's Italian Republic. In the time of Theodosius I (379–395), Christianity became the *state religion* in the empire. After a historical period of 1,600 years, it can be said that the *roots of Europe* are undoubtedly *Christian*, with *Hellenic-Roman, Islamic, Judaic* and *Enlightenment* components and legacy.

*168.* Today's EU is based on the principles of humanism, rationalism, liberal individualism, the rule of law, democracy and human rights, which in the religious sense represent a symbiosis of secularized surrogates of Christian and other religious values and principles. It is not disputed that the 'soul' of human rights, freedom, democracy, and the rule of law, to a greater or lesser extent, can originally be found in the Gospels, the Talmud, and other Holy Books. In the current crisis of European identity, it can be reasonably assumed that the 'fuel for development' of the EU could represent the 'value-critical', integrative, peace-making, social-security, collective and individual-psychological potentials of its religious communities, above all Christian churches which in the EU are the most represented. In that context, both ecumenical and Christian-Islamic dialogue should be affirmed as strategic frameworks and preconditions for the promotion of universal ethical principles on the European continent as well.

*169.* When discussing 'integration' in the modern sense of the word, we should bear in mind the fact that it has numerous denominators with ecclesiastical notions of *universality*[498] and *universalism.*[499] The neologism 'Christian integration' also implies the pursuit of 'unification of all' but based on the values that have been left

498. Which is especially strong in the Eastern (Orthodox) Christian Church.

by the Lord Jesus Christ to the people through the Church.[500] Representatives of the largest religions in today's EU believe that the existing process of primarily 'horizontal' (economic-political) integration on the continent should be *enriched with religious content,* that is to say, with elements of 'vertical' integration and with a predominant aim of further improvement and sustainability of the integrative process. In that context, it is necessary to act preventively on the widespread *practice of abusing Islam for political purposes* in the world in the twenty-first century, which can have very negative consequences on European soil as well. Cells of 'radical Islam', funded by extreme Muslims from the Middle East, exist especially in the Serbian province of KiM and tend to 'spill over' into Western Europe as well. They are also the greatest exponents of organized crime in Southeast Europe and represent a threat to peace and security across the continent.[501]

## Spiritual Roots of Serbian Statehood and Culture

*170.* The SOC has an 'exceptional historical, state-building and civilizational role in forming, preserving, and developing the identity of the Serbian nation'.[502] Through the efforts of *Saint Sava* (1175–1236), prince, monk, educator, writer, diplomat and the first archbishop, the SOC gained *ecclesiastical independence (autocephaly)* from the Ecumenical Patriarchate in 1219, with the status of Archbishopric. Sava then organized the spiritual life of the SOC in eleven eparchies and gave a decisive stamp to the development of *church law* (Hilandar and Studenica Typicon, Namocanon, etc.), Serbian sacral architecture, painting, literature and medicine (he founded hospitals in Hilandar and Studenica monasteries). At the same time, he performed important *state and diplomatic affairs* in the then relations of Serbia with the Bulgarians and Ugrians, maintained complex *church and political relations with Rome (Vatican)*, and established contact with the world of Islam. The most important contribution of Sava to the Serbian people is reflected in the fact that he *Christianized* and *enlightened* them in the period when they lived divided in the areas under the jurisdiction of the then Ohrid Archbishopric, but also in the western parts that were strongly influenced by Latins. Bearing in mind not only the church but also the *national-state interest of the Serbian people,* Sava also prepared the famous *Zakonopravilo or Nomokanon*, a major collection of *church-canonical* and *civil-legal character*, a testament that contains valuable and strategic guidelines for the life of the Serbian people on its historical path. For Serbs, the Namokanon embodies the 'true model of synthesis' of the spiritual and the secular, 'in an authentic Serbian way'. The consequence of direct application of this model was the 'spiritual, identity-shaping and maturing' of the Serbian people and the 'material and political rise' of its state in the Middle Ages. In the historical context,

499. Previously used by the Western (Roman Catholic and Protestant) Christian Church, it has become established in almost all areas of social and scientific life.
500. Serbian Patriarch Pavle, *Presentation at the conference 'Christianity and European Integration'*, Christianity and European Integration, Christian Cultural Centre, Belgrade, 2003, p. 17.
501. Government of the Republic of Serbia, *Albanian Terrorism and Organised Crime in Kosovo and Metohija*, White Book, 2003, https://www.srbija.gov.rs/kosovo-metohija/19991, https://www.media.srbija.gov.rs/medsrp/dokumenti/bela_knjiga1.pdf, 7 Mar. 2023.
502. Law on Churches and Religious Communities, *supra* n. 92, Art. 11, para. 2.

the stated 'synthesis' is terminologically shaped by the notion of the *Saint Sava Testament* in the manner of the 'New Testament of Christ'. In the fourteenth century, the Kosovo Covenant emerged on its foundations as a covenant of boundless sacrificial love for its people, its Church and state, but also for the principles of truth, justice, and freedom. The *practical living* of the mentioned ideals represents *a qualitative guideline of the SOC to its people* in the last eight centuries, thanks to which they survived the temptations of centuries of Ottoman oppression, the massacre of the population in the First and Second World Wars, terror and executions of godless Serbs (Partisans) on their own people in the second half of the twentieth century, as well as the break-up and creation of new nations in the late twentieth and early twenty-first centuries. The *Svetosavlje* as a 'philosophy of life' is 'Orthodoxy of a Serbian style and experience', and 'the path of the God-man Christ who leads to life against all national exclusivity'.[503]

*171.* In medieval Serbia, respected in both the East and the West, two simultaneous processes took place: the *acquisition of autocephaly* by the SOC and *the consolidation and development of the state*. On the foundations of the *Orthodox faith*, Serbia then became a *Christian kingdom*, with the proclaimed goal of creating *stronger institutional frameworks and ties between the SOC and the state*. In their correlation in unchanged proportion, the *value supremacy of the original Christian and Orthodox* in relation to the *national (Serbian) and the state* has remained unchanged throughout history. A Saint of SOC from the twentieth century Nikolaj (Velimirović) explained this 'balanced and common path' of the church (people) and the state with the term 'evangelical nationalism'.[504] In today's circumstances, it could be defined as a *value-corrective critique of the absolutization of the secular.*

*172.* Today, all over the world, in the Balkans, Europe, America and Australia, Serbian citizens exercise their freedom of religion within thirty-nine SOC eparchies and see it as a guarantor of preserving and affirming *Orthodox identity* and *Serbian culture* overall (language, Cyrillic alphabet, science). The SOC continuously teaches them *not to remain locked in narrow national frameworks*, but open to all who have recognized the Saviour in Christ, *regardless of* nationality, skin colour, the language they speak and where they live. In this, one can recognize the universal authenticity, significance, and contribution of the SOC to the preservation of the diversity of European and world spirituality, history, and culture.

### The Period of Disintegration of Yugoslavia and the Beginning of the Twenty-First Century

*173.* The civil war in socialist Yugoslavia at the beginning of the 1990s (1991–1995), to a large extent, although temporarily, marginalized the beneficial

503. Irinej Episkop Bački, *'Kosovo i Metohiju nam ne mogu oteti i nećemo ga dati'*, https://rtv.rs/sk/drustvo/irinej-backi-kosovo-i-metohiju-nam-ne-mogu-oteti-i-necemo-ga-dati_1054440.html, 6 Mar. 2024.

504. In: Address to the Holy Synod of Bishops of the Serbian Orthodox Church – 'Sopoćanska poslanica', Sopoćani Monastery, 21 Feb. 2001, https://svetosavlje.org/sopocanska-deklaracija-2001-godine/, p. 2, 6 Mar. 2024.

social and political influence of religious communities in society. It left very little room for spirituality, peace, tranquillity, and 'internal' and 'external' progress, which are incomparably easier to achieve in *peace*. However, it was the 'hellish experience' and the harsh reality that revived the strength and influence of Christian and other religious ideals in the Republic of Serbia and its surroundings. The role of the SOC and most of its representatives in the war conflict, despite the existence of extremely negative examples, was *crisis-preventive* and *peace-making*. It was symbolized above all by its Patriarch Pavle. It was not exclusively church-missionary but also *critical-corrective* towards all political factors and leaders of parties in the conflict, including the authorities in Serbia. There is documentation available to the public which attests to this.[505] However, the Vatican and representatives of the RCC in Slovenia, Croatia and BiH, as well as the Islamic Community in the war-affected areas, favouring the application of the principle of *self-determination of the people*, undoubtedly advocated the creation of *nation-states within the former Yugoslav republics* and the disintegration of the Yugoslav Federation. Like the representatives of the SOC, they also wrote numerous petitions and appeals to international actors during the war to try to influence the end of the conflict, but in diagnosing its causes, they *mostly attributed the responsibility to the Serbian side*. In this context, the Bishops of the RCC in the Republics of Croatia and BiH[506] repeatedly called for *military intervention* by international forces against Bosnian Serbs, and later the FRY.[507]

*174.* In today's Republic of Serbia, *85% of Orthodox Christians* ('members' of the SOC) cultivate correct relations with the believers of the *RCC, the Islamic and Jewish Communities, as well as the Protestant churches*. From a theoretical point of view, this is logical, since the essence of all monotheistic religions is the aspiration to achieve 'peace in relation to others', where its existence or absence unmistakably testifies to whether individuals and religious groups are only declarative or true believers. Their religiosity has a *predominantly traditional* character, and in a relatively *small percentage, it is piously religious*. However, the constitutional and legal provisions define and clearly delineate secular political and social conditions and space for religious entities, which do not have the illusion that the 'period of symphony' can return in the relations between the state and the church like in Byzantium or medieval Serbia. In the conditions of great challenges in all areas of life, in the *relations between the church and the state*, there is *understanding and cooperation* today, which are based on the common awareness that both entities perform functions aimed at the *well-being of citizens*. In that context, the SOC emphasizes

505. Patriarch Pavle in the Italian Catholic weekly Il Sabato, *'The consumer society is far from Christianity'*, Pravoslavlje, 15 Dec. 1991, no. 594, p. 11; Patriarch Pavle, *'The SOC to its spiritual children about Saint Sava in 1991'*, Glasnik Srpske Patrijaršije, 1991, p. 1; *'Echoes of the stay in Austria – Patriarch Pavle in Vienna and Linz'*, Pravoslavlje, 15 Jan.–1 Feb. 1994, XXVIII year, no. 644–645, p. 2.
506. Letter of the Croatian Bishops to Pope John Paul II dated 18 Dec. 1992, Split magazine 'Slobodna Dalmacija', 30 Dec. 1992, p. 6. This letter states: '...the aggressor cannot be disarmed with papers and international resolutions, but only with the protection of the police and military force, that is, by foreign military intervention'.
507. NATO aggression against the FRY lasted from 24 Mar. to 10 Jun. 1999.

that even today, Saint Sava and Saint King Stefan Prvovenčani – born brothers, who solved all problems with trust and deep faith in God, who gave them strength and wisdom, diplomatic skills, pragmatism and a comprehensive understanding of different interests can be role models for all. That is why they managed to build bridges towards both east and west, preserving the permanent spiritual commitment of their people. And most importantly, their approach and actions resulted in the timely advancement of Serbia, in the religious, cultural and economic sense.

*175.* Today, the Serbian Patriarch emphasizes that the '*principle of cooperative separation and cooperation*' of the state and religious subjects is appropriate for our age, within the framework of when 'everyone should continue to do their job, and help each other when and where necessary'. He denoted the still *largely present atheistic legacy* in Serbia from the time of socialist Yugoslavia as the main obstacle to the realization of the mentioned form of relations. He points out that even today the Church is 'challenged the right to declare itself on the most important issues of today', even in cases when it comes to 'vital issues, the identity of the people and their self-awareness'. Despite everything, the relationship between the church and the state in the Republic of Serbia today is on an 'upward trajectory', with the state 'helping the church in endangered areas, especially in Kosovo and Metohija and Republika Srpska', and 'benefiting the people, the state and the church'.[508]

*176.* When it comes to the current problem related to the situation in the *Autonomous Province of KiM*, the SOC has for several decades called on *all political actors to continue the dialogue without pressure and blackmail* in order to resolve *issues of human rights, freedom of life and functioning of the SOC*, institutional and security protection of its *holy objects*, enabling the *unhindered return of displaced persons*, and *free access to property* for all those from whom it has been unlawfully taken or usurped. She *wholeheartedly supports any responsible dialogue that shall contribute to the rule of law*, as well as *reconciliation between all peoples* living in KiM as the southern province of Serbia. It points out that the province cannot be taken away from Serbia forever without her consent and that the Church '*will not give it because God is slow but sure*'.[509] SOC sees the *solution to the problem* in KiM in the *greatest possible autonomy for Albanians* where they constitute the majority, and likewise for the Serbian population. However, Serbia *cannot recognize a separate state for the Albanians on the territory that is the birthplace of Serbia*, where there are 1,500 churches and monasteries of the SOC, and which testify even today whose territory this was throughout history.

*177.* In the *Republic of Montenegro*, the SOC, until recently for almost three decades, lived and faced 'tragic temptation' and *attempts to seize church property* and *reshape the church and national identity* of the Serbian people living in it.

508. Christmas Epistle of the Serbian Orthodox Church, 'Srpska Pravoslavna Crkva svojoj duhovnoj deci o Božiću 2019. Godine', http://spc.rs.
509. Irinej Episkop Bački, *'Kosovo i Metohiju nam ne mogu oteti i nećemo ga dati'*, https://rtv.rs/sk/drustvo/irinej-backi-kosovo-i-metohiju-nam-ne-mogu-oteti-i-necemo-ga-dati_1054440.html, 6 Mar. 2024.

According to the official census, it has almost 30% Serbs, and the SOC has been present in this country for centuries. In this former Yugoslav republic, today the independent state of Montenegro, *the Law on Freedom of Religion or Belief and Legal Status of Religious Communities* was adopted at the end of 2019, which 'allows for the seizure and desecration of shrines and trampling of endowments of holy founders who dedicated them to God and the Church, and not to any state or authority'.[510] *Article 62* of the mentioned Law, which was adopted in Montenegro at the end of 2019, stipulates that 'religious buildings and land used by religious communities on the territory of Montenegro, which were built or obtained from public revenues of the state or were state-owned until 1 December 1918 and for which there is no evidence of the right of ownership of religious communities, they are *state property* as the cultural heritage of Montenegro'. The state in Montenegro obviously intended to *confiscate* religious buildings for which 'there is no evidence' *from the current owners*. However, she did not foresee her obligation to prove that she was the owner prior to 1 December 2018. Also, *Article 63* foresaw that 'the Property Administration of Montenegro, for facilities and land for which evidence of the right of ownership of religious communities does not exist, will determine *within a year that they are state property ...*'.[511] In that context, the SOC provided exclusively ecclesiastical support to its believers and their peaceful Christian resistance to the injustice inflicted on them, which was *not directed against the statehood of Montenegro*. She appealed to its state bodies to be aware of their responsibility before history and the future and to reconsider its position on the religious rights and freedoms of their citizens and the majority Church in Montenegro. She emphasized that the SOC and its eparchies in Montenegro will '*protect religious rights and freedoms with all available legal means*' in the country while at the same time calling on all relevant actors to *renew a comprehensive dialogue* on this extremely sensitive issue. In its critical attitude towards the actions of the current Montenegrin authorities – its persecutors, the SOC maintained a *good and constructive purpose and role*, emphasizing that the authorities do not understand that they are in the most difficult situation, because according to the Bible, 'not even the gates of hell can overcome the Church'. She told the Montenegrin authorities that they could 'quickly wear themselves out in extinguishing fires by lighting new fires', *contrary to the proclaimed path and goal of Euro-Atlantic integration*, which implies 'respecting at least a hundredth part of the rules of the game in the countries of Atlantic civilization'. The believers of the SOC in Montenegro, as well as everywhere they live, are asking for 'no less and no more than the rights that apply to everyone'.[512] The political climate created after the parliamentary elections at the end of August 2020 suggests that there could be a positive evolution in the attitude towards the SOC in Montenegro.

510. The Communique of the Holy Assembly of Bishops of the Serbian Orthodox Church, http://arhiva.spc.rs/eng/communique_holy_assembly_bishops_2.html, 7 Mar. 2024.
511. After the elections in September 2020, the new authorities in Montenegro, with the decisions of the new parliamentary majority on 20 Jan. 2021, and after the signature of the President of the Republic, began amending the Law on Freedom of Religion in Montenegro.
512. Srpska Patrijaršija, *'Intervju mitropolita Porfirija za Tanjug'*, http://spc.rs/sr/ interview_mitropolita_porfirija_za_tanjug, 05 Jan. 2020.

*178.* The SOC has been residing on the territory of today's *Republic of Northern Macedonia* for centuries. In the context of the *church schism* that has existed since 1957, and which was essentially initiated by ideologized authorities, the SOC made a *principled decision to continue the dialogue* with the 'Macedonian Orthodox Church' (MOC). She is of the opinion that such a dialogue, patient and loving, is necessary with 'lured and seduced children, so that they would return to unify with the Church without which there is no salvation'. The SOC called on the schismatic hierarchy and its believers to accept the centuries-old canonical order of the Orthodox Church, and exclusively on that basis, without extra-clerical motives and anti-clerical influences, make an effort to achieve full church independence *if that was their goal.* Therefore, MOC should condemn the violations of basic human and civil liberties in Macedonia, *especially conscience and religion*, which SOC Archbishop and Metropolitan Jovan of Skopje has been facing for almost a decade. He was imprisoned for years based on a '*politically motivated court decision*'.[513] In addition, the Macedonian authorities have been, through various means of obstruction, *refusing to register the SOC in the register of religious communities* in the country for several decades. After the 'vacuum' and stagnation in interchurch relations, current Serbian Patriarch Mr Porphyry and Archbishop of Ohrid and Macedonia Mr Stefan established the highest level of interchurch relations between the SOC and MOC in the recent historical period. They have very positive sociopolitical consequences in the area of the 'Western Balkans', making the preconditions for the establishment of current economic and political cooperation between its countries under the name 'Open Balkans'. This initiative was recently launched by the President of the Republic of Serbia Mr Aleksandar Vučić and was supported by the state leadership of the Republic of North Macedonia. This Platform was also positively accepted and recognized by the European Union as precondition for Regions' integration in its membership. 'Open Balkans' would be difficult to imagine without the existence of good neighbourly relations between two states and peoples, which are largely conditioned and influenced by the quality of interchurch relations.

*179.* Finally, the *social activity* of the SOC stems from the balance with its primary 'spiritual, praying and saving' activity. Today, it deals with numerous problems of modern society – *care for* and *nutrition of the needy* (religious – charitable guardianship of the Archbishopric of Belgrade – Karlovac SOC), *free health care, treatment of addiction* (drug addiction, alcoholism, gambling), as well as many *other social issues and activities.* In accordance with the circumstances and needs of SOC, it educates individuals of various profiles who deal with issues of *abuse of modern technologies, personal dignity, ethics of birth, opposition to violence, ecology,* etc. She is of the general opinion that the solution to the threatening world problems can be found only in a *clear and unambiguous return to the basic Christian values* that civilization has forgotten over the centuries and from which it has deviated, with 'everything else being added by God himself'. In this context, she points out that the problems of a nation or state are manifested territorially, economically, demographically, etc., but that their *causes and solutions are always in the spiritual dimension.*

---

513. *Ibid.*

*180. Cooperative separation*, which characterizes the relationship between the SOC and the state, as well as their mostly harmonious cooperation in connection with many important social affairs, is interpreted in the atheistic part of the public inclined to exclusive secularism as the increased and undesirable influence of the Church on politics. Such influence, which would disrupt the secularity of society and the state, does not exist and cannot exist because the citizens of Serbia are mostly believers in the traditional sense, and political factors (parties) are not programmatically based on the system of religious values. The only factor that can collectively and psychologically bring the SOC to the position of a potential political reference, but not a political actor, on the moral and identity level is the feeling of national endangerment of the Serbian people. The same, in principle, applies to other churches and religious communities, with the proviso that, given the nature of the social teachings of Islam, the influence of this religion on the political organization and activities of members of the Bosnian/Muslim minority is more direct and pronounced.

## Chapter 2. Political Influence in Religion

*181*. Starting from *socialist atheistic goals and interests*, the 'religious potentials' of Christianity, Islam and Judaism were the subject of special interest of the Yugoslav state during the entire second half of the twentieth century. It sought *full control and direction* of the life and work of its religious entities in the *function of resolving a complex national issue* in a multi-confessional and multinational environment.[514] To this end, the state influenced the overcoming of existing antagonisms in the inherited relations of its religious entities,[515] wary of the possibility of creating their 'common front' against its ideological system. Because of that, the state relativized the undeniable historical facts. It should be borne in mind that the *central matrix and stronghold of then and present* interchurch ('ecumenical') relations in the countries of the region (Serbia, BiH, Croatia, Montenegro and also the Northern Republic of Macedonia) is a common interest and goal *related to evangelization.*

*182*. With the Socialist Constitution from 1946, the state clearly defined the *separation of the church from the state* and the *separation of the school from the church* as the *basic principles* in relation with religious communities. In fact, it opted for the conduct and implementation of a policy that in practice implied a *qualitative discontinuity* in relation to the Kingdom of Yugoslavia. Through *repressive policies* throughout the second half of the twentieth century, on a pronounced ideological basis, the state *largely managed to contro*l the social activities of its religious communities (SOC, ICS, Old Catholic Church and JC, but not the RCC in the long run), and to channel them in a direction favourable to itself through 'neutralizing the influence of their most reactionary elements'.[516] In her performance, she strived to achieve what was proclaimed primarily through informal (non-administrative) measures due to the political sensitivity of the whole issue while making it clear to her religious subjects that she would not tolerate any hostile political views.

*183*. With the laws on the nationalization of buildings and construction land and agrarian reform and colonization, the Yugoslav state largely reduced the material basis of religious entities. For example, on the basis of the Law on Agrarian Reform (1952), all 'land holdings of churches, monasteries, religious institutions and all types of endowments, secular and religious' were confiscated, with the exception of churches and monasteries of 'greater historical value', which were left with up to 30 hectares of land or forest.[517] The state did not show enough understanding of the vital interests of the SOC, focusing its activities on 'tidying up relations' with other

514. Izveštaj Komisije za verska pitanja NR BiH za 1962, Arhiv Jugoslavije, fond 144, fascikla 64, arhivska jedinica 495, 6.
515. Especially between the SOC and the RCC due to the painful historical legacy related to the participation of RCC priests in Nazi crimes against Serbs, Jews, and the Roma in the then fascist 'Independent State of Croatia'.
516. Recommendation of the Federal Executive Council (SIV), confidential, no. 12, 18 Jul. 1959.
517. Law on Agrarian Reform, Official Gazette of the SFRY, Belgrade, 28 Aug. 1945.

religious communities.[518] The difficult financial situation faced by religious entities in Serbia and the region for more than half a century was caused by the actions of the then state authorities.

*184.* During the war in the former Yugoslavia during the 1990s, there were examples of certain religious representatives being associated with interests, corruption, and exclusivity, as well as hatred and wars.[519] From this historical distance, it can be stated that the root cause, along with the existing spiritual and moral weakness of individuals, was also a largely inherited practice of *instrumentalizing religion for political purposes*. Despite this, political subjects today have a good understanding of the fact that religious communities have above all a positive *social-integrative potential*, which 'must not be neglected'.[520] The best examples of this are the countries of Eastern and Central Europe, including Serbia, where the religious factor played a significant role in the transition processes in the late 1980s and in the 1990s, primarily in the *value-civilizational critical-corrective and moral sense.*

*185.* At the international level, the Republic of Serbia is committed to improving understanding and strengthening the unity of the international community in the *processes of protection and promotion of religious freedoms based on universal values and standards*. Respect for religious rights and freedoms is 'one of the key indicators' for the human rights situation in the country and an indicator of the level of readiness of its society to 'harmonize different cultural, ethnic, and religious identities'.[521] Serbia supports all activities aimed at combating *religiously motivated bigotry, intolerance, discrimination, violence and hate speech, that is, the full and sustainable realization of human rights of each particular religious group*. At the domestic level, it *applies all international norms and standards in the field of religion*, solves all problems through *active dialogue with its religious entities* and, at the same time, encourages and supports *interreligious dialogue at all levels.*

*186.* In the province of KiM, which has been under the UN protectorate since 1999 on the basis of UN Security Council Resolution no. 1244, the Republic of Serbia is unable to influence the tragic situation on the ground in the field of religious rights and freedoms. In today's KiM, members of the Serbian people, the SOC, Christian culture and historical heritage are victims of what can be considered the

---

518. Material for the session of the Federal Commission on religious issues of SIV, confidential, no. 558, 25 Nov. 1963, Archives of Yugoslavia, fund 144, folder 67, 1963.
519. Đorđević Jelena, *'Interreligijski dijalog i svakodnevni život'*, in: *Interreligijski dijalog kao vid pomi renja u Jugoistočnoj Evropi*, Milan Vukomanović, Marinko Vučinić (prir.), BOŠ, Beograd, 2001, 199.
520. Vukomanović Milan, *'Religion, Conflict, Reconciliation'*, in: *Interreligijski dijalog kao vid pomir enja u Jugoistočnoj Evropi*, Milan Vukomanović, Marinko Vučinić (prir.), BOŠ, Beograd, 2001, 27.
521. Serbia's solidarity with messages against religiously motivated bigotry, intolerance and discrimination on all grounds – Speech by the First Deputy Prime Minister of the Government of Serbia and Minister of Foreign Affairs Ivica Dačić at the Ministerial Conference on Religious Freedom in Washington on 19 Jul. 2019, https://mfa.gov.rs/mediji/saopstenja/verska-tolerancija-i-medjureli gijski-dijalog-imaju-vodecu-ulogu-u-unapredjenju.

nationalist ideology of creating a homogeneous ethnic, cultural and religious space. The Serbian authorities have frequently denounced the problem that all traces of Slavism and Orthodoxy are being destroyed and devastated in the province, followed by verbal and physical attacks, as well as the murders of SOC priests.[522] Of the *four religious sites of exceptional importance that are on the UN Organization for Education, Science and Culture (UNESCO) List of World Heritage in Danger* (the Patriarchate of Peć, the monasteries of Visoki Dečani and Gračanica, and the Holy Virgin of Ljevisa in Prizren), three have survived, which were under the full physical protection of UN forces during the organized *Albanian ethnic pogroms in 2004*. Religious freedoms and rights of the Serbian people and the SOC in KiM (participation in prayers, baptisms, weddings, communions, funerals, etc.) exist only in churches and monasteries located in areas with a majority or predominantly Serbian population. At the same time, the facilities of the SOC there are not museums but the seats of a 'living church' to which autochthonous believers should be able to come unhindered. Finally, the SOC in KiM is experiencing threats concerning its *property rights,* which *mostly lead to thefts* which remain unpunished. Due to all the above, the Republic of Serbia appeals[523] to the international community to advocate and ensure the promotion and implementation of religious rights and freedoms in KiM, and to end the current practice of double standards, denial, minimization and relativization of continuing discrimination by the majority Albanian community and its institutions in KiM.

*187.* At the domestic level, the Republic of Serbia has been striving for several decades *to completely remove the historical injustice* inflicted on religious entities during the communist period. The proclaimed principles of its religious policy are an *affirmation of religious freedoms and position of religious entities in society, return of confiscated property, return of religious education to the state school system, improvement of dialogue and cooperation of the state with religious entities,* as well as *affirmation of interreligious dialogue at the domestic, regional and international level.* Competent state bodies *financially support the life and work of religious entities*, based on the criteria of their *percentual representation in society*, the *number of active believers and real needs in the field as presented by religious leaders*, as well as *positive discrimination of minority communities in affirmation of their position and influence in society.*

*188.* Since the change of attitude towards religion after the collapse of communism and the abandonment of the doctrine of 'scientific atheism', despite some hints of the existence of such ambitions, churches and religious communities have failed to occupy political space. However, segments of the political class have shown a

---

522. Serbia's solidarity with messages against religiously motivated bigotry, intolerance and discrimination on all grounds – Speech by the First Deputy Prime Minister of the Government of Serbia and Minister of Foreign Affairs Ivica Dačić at the Ministerial Conference on Religious Freedom in Washington on 19 Jul. 2019, https://mfa.rs/mediji/saopstenja/solidarnost-srbije-sa-porukama-protiv-verski-motivisane-netrpeljivosti.
523. MFA and other state officials, including President of Serbia, have been addressing for example to the UN Security Council many times during past several years, sending the appeals and presenting the facts from the ground on KiM.

tendency to reach for the moral authority of churches and religious communities in legitimizing and affirming their party programmes and goals. There were also unsuccessful attempts to create political parties which, following the example of some European ones, declared themselves to be value-based and ideologically inspired by religious social teachings (e.g., Christian Democrats). Politics has no direct influence on religion in Serbia, but social interaction between churches and religious communities, on the one hand, and political factors, on the other, creates situations in which it is difficult to discern to what extent there are attempts to place the religious hierarchy in a political function in specific situations or, politics in a religious function.

# Chapter 3. Interaction Between Religion and State on a Political and Legal Level

*189.* The permeation of spiritual (church) and secular (state) power is desirable, among other things, for the purpose of *curbing the aspiration of each of them to supremacy.*[524] This civilizational and state-building principle was neglected during the reign of communist ideology in Yugoslavia during the second half of the twentieth century. The hostile and manipulative policy of the state towards religious entities left negative consequences in the field of state-church law and the practical life of religious entities.

*190.* After the change of the state-political system in Yugoslavia and Serbia in 2000, part of the *FRY Government's Programme*, accepted by the Federal Assembly in November of the same year, referred to the *rejection of the previous practice of state control of religious entities* and the need to *settle and improve mutual relations.* It states that these relations are characterized by 'legal disorder' as a consequence of the 'legacy of the past'.[525] Therefore, the state should have drafted a 'legally civilized and tradition-based agreement on mutual relations and competencies'. On that basis, it was necessary to deal with the return of confiscated property to religious entities. It was emphasized that the *right to religion* must be a factual right and not just a constitutional proclamation, which will be guaranteed by the state as an *inherited good and personal need of every individual.* At the beginning of the twenty-first century, the importance of the contribution of the religious factor in the social and political life of the Republic of Serbia was recognized and acknowledged.

*191.* The Government entrusted the realization of the proclaimed task in the institutional sense to the *newly established Ministry (Secretariat) of Religions*, whose working principles were based on 'care for the welfare of all believers', as well as the fact of the historically proven positive role of religious entities in 'achieving the common good' for society and the state. The Secretariat defined the *adoption of legal regulations in the religious field* as a priority goal, primarily the Law on the Relations between the State and the Church/Religious Communities and the Law on Return of Confiscated Property, as well as undertaking concrete activities with the goal *of gradual integration of religious values and content in institutional and social life.*

*192.* During 2001–2004, no religious regulation existed. Educational institutions of religious entities were outside the state education system. Officials of religious entities (priests, imams, pastors, rabbis, etc.) did not have a regulated social

524. Archpriest Mateja Nenadović (1777–1854), one of the leaders of the First Serbian Uprising against the Turks, first President of the Ruling Council, and diplomat, more in: Radulović Milan, *Obnova srpskog državno-crkvenog prava*, Konrad Adenauer Stiftung, Christian Cultural Centre, 2009, p. 7.
525. Encounter of the State and the Church, Report of the Federal Ministry (Secretariat) of Religions, Federal Secretariat of Religions, Belgrade 2003, p. 5.

status (health care, PIO), pupils and students at religious schools were not entitled to state scholarships and financial assistance, etc.

*193.* During 2004–2007, the level of cooperation between the state and religious communities was raised to a higher level, which primarily resulted in the launch of a *broader debate on the principle of mutual relations* and then the *adoption of the necessary constitutional and legal regulations in the religious field.*

**Adoption of Constitutional and Legal Regulations**

*194.* The current Constitution defines the Republic of Serbia as a *secular state*[526] that guarantees all citizens *individual* and *collective freedom of religion*[527] and religious entities (churches and religious communities) *separate* and *autonomous status in relation to the state.* All legal entities are guaranteed equality and shall be *equal before the law.*[528]

*195.* The work on the adoption of the Law on Churches and Religious Communities lasted for more than ten years. The Federal Law (FRY) was adopted in 2002. Certain provisions of the text were included in the newly adopted Constitution in 2006. In consequence, religious entities (churches and religious communities) in Serbia became a *constitutional category.* Thus, began the process of *renewal of Serbian state-church law* as an integral factor in the development of the legal system of the modern Republic of Serbia.

*196.* On the occasion of the Preliminary Draft Law, experts from the Venice Commission of CoE, Head of the OSCE Mission to Serbia (Ambassador Maurizio Massari), advisors to the Synod of Bishops of SOC, Bishops' Conference of RCC SCG, Islamic Community of Serbia (ICofS) and the Meshihat Islamic Community of Sandžak, the Association of Jewish Communities of SCG, numerous Protestant churches in Serbia (Evangelical, Reformed, Adventist, Baptist, etc.), Ministry of Human and Minority Rights of the Republic of Serbia, Council of National Minorities in Serbia (Greek, Bulgarian, Bunjevak, Romanian), the Helsinki Committee for Human Rights in Serbia, as well as many others participated in a broad public debate and commentary in mid-2004. Based on its results, the Draft Law on Freedom of Religion, Churches and Religious Communities was drafted, which consisted of sixty-two articles. After consultations with high representatives of religious entities and experts from the Faculty of Law at the University of Belgrade, the draft was supplemented and reduced to forty-eight articles. Before sending it to the Government for an opinion, it received the consent of the Expert Commission of SOC, the Bishops' Conference of RCC of Serbia, traditional Protestant churches, as well as the Islamic and Jewish Communities. During the adoption of the Draft Law, a high level of agreement was reached by all mentioned entities on the issue of essential principles, which included – broad individual religious freedoms, guaranteed public status of religious entities and affirmation of their cooperation with the state

526. Constitution of the Republic of Serbia from 2006, *supra* n. 4, Art. 11.
527. Constitution of the Republic of Serbia from 2006, *supra* n. 4, Art. 43.
528. Constitution of the Republic of Serbia from 2006, *supra* n. 4, Art. 44.

in conditions of clear separation.[529] The general conclusion of all[530] was that the new Law met the highest criteria and standards of international and European law.

*197.* When it comes to remarks and criticisms, they were presented mainly by individual associations with a pronounced ideological (atheistic) profile. In fact, the phenomenon of state interventionism in the religious field 'permeated' them.[531]

*198.* In 2004, the Ministry of Religions started implementing *programmes of cooperation and state assistance to religious entities*. Two years later (2006), they received the legal basis of their existence by Article 28 of the Law on Churches and Religious Communities.

## Interaction Today

*199.* The relationship between the state and religious entities in the Republic of Serbia today can be defined as 'cooperative separation'. The highest representatives of state and religious entities hold *regular consultations and communicate on the most important issues* for the life of society, the state, and the church as a whole. Compared to the period at the end of the twentieth and the beginning of the twenty-first century, it can be stated that relations are characterized by *intensive cooperation.*

*200.* On the one hand, the SOC recognizes and provides unequivocal *prayerful, moral and public support* to the state's efforts in the dialogue with Albanian representatives from KiM, with the aim of preserving peace, stability and finding a just, sustainable and mutually acceptable solution. In the complex situation in international relations, the SOC has faith in God, history and the help of friends to reach such a solution and emphasizes that the most important thing is the existence of *understanding with the state*, which regularly demonstrates good intentions and effort. On the other hand, the highest political representatives of the Serbian people from the region point out that without a common position and unity of all important factors in Serbia and all Serbs, no important state and national issue can be resolved. The highest representatives of the state of Serbia believe and emphasize that it is their obligation to *fight and obtain the most* out of everything for the Serbian people while preserving peace and stability, but without agreeing to unjustified conditioning and giving what is not our right to give, nor should we give it.[532] Representatives of state bodies in this complex process accept the differences in the approach of the church, which they respect and believe that it works in the best interest of our

529. *Ibid.*, 25–27.
530. 'Meeting of the State and the Church', Report of the Federal Ministry (Secretariat) for Religions 2001–2002, Federal Secretariat for Religions, Belgrade, 2003, p. 5.
531. 'Meeting of the State and the Church', Report of the Federal Ministry (Secretariat) for Religions 2001–2002, *supra*, p. 6.
532. President of the Republic of Serbia, *'President of the Republic of Serbia Mr. Aleksandar Vučić met with His Holiness Serbian Patriarch Irinej on 2 December 2019.'* https://www.predsednik.rs/pres-centar/saopstenja/sastanak-sa-njegovom-svetoscu-patrijarhom-srpskim-gospodinom-irinejem, 7 Mar. 2024.

homeland, but they also *'point out that it was not always in full agreement with reality, and that it cost us dearly. That is exactly what should be avoided in the future'*. For the representatives of the state, the Church 'continues to be an important social factor which helps the Serbian people in all territories where they are endangered, especially in KiM', and one of the most important goals for everyone today is to work more in unity so as to achieve significant results.[533]

*201.* According to the SOC, the coexistence of Serbs and Albanians from KiM would undoubtedly be possible and achievable if only Serbs and Albanians discussed and agreed on peace. It supports the responsible approach of the state bodies of Serbia, which *preserve peace and stability*, and strive to protect both the Serbian and Albanian people from temptations and suffering. When it comes to the situation in Montenegro, the 'vital interest' for both the SOC and Serbia is the survival of the Serbian people there despite the 'fierce assimilation campaign', with neither the SOC nor Serbia intending to 'threaten the state's legal status'.[534] In the whole context, the highest representatives of the former Montenegrin government, including the current President of Montenegro, Mr Milo Đukanović, continued to promote the position that 'the Serbian Orthodox Church is the worst instrument of Greater Serbian nationalism to which we must respond with the strength of our state ... .'[535] The same official also announced in 2020 that *if the SOC rejects the agreement, we will form the Orthodox Church in Montenegro.*[536] In my view, this at least indicates the intention of certain structures in Montenegro to openly and violently interfere in the internal life and structure of the largest religious community in the country, which I consider as a practice inherited by totalitarian and authoritarian communist authorities in the former Yugoslavia during the second half of the twentieth century. In this case, I believe it cannot be said that certain representatives of political authorities in Montenegro are 'promoters of the European value system', as they present themselves.[537]

*202.* Although the Republic of Serbia is a *secular state*, the fact must be accepted that almost 95% of its citizens declare themselves as believers, who cannot be 'dual personalities'. As in all Orthodox countries, the local SOC in Serbia is 'historically connected to the people and the nation'. Therefore, it is logical that there is a 'greater degree of inclination' for the church and the state to 'jointly resolve issues of great state and national importance'.[538] A similar relationship can

533. Srpska Patrijaršija, *'Predsednik Republike Srbije g. Aleksandar Vučić sastao se 2. decembra 2019. sa Njegovom Svetošću Patrijarhom srpskom gospodinom Irinejom'*, https://mitropolija-zagrebacka.org/intervju-mitropolita-porfirija-za-politiku/, 02 Dec. 2019.

534. President of the Republic of Serbia, *'Objava predsednika Republike Srbije posle sustreta sa Patrijarhom srpskim g. Irinejom'*, https://www.predsednik.rs/lat/pres-centar/vesti/obracanje-predsednika-republike-srbije-nakon-susreta-sa-njegovom-svetosti-patrijarhom-srpskim-gospodinom-irinejom, 7 Mar. 2024.

535. Đukaković: SOC the worst instrument of Greater Serbian nationalism', newspaper 'Danas' from https://www.danas.rs/svet/djukanovic-spc-najopakiji-instrument-velikosrpskog-nacionalizma/.

536. https://www.slobodnaevropa.org/a/djukanovic-crna-gora-spc-pravoslavna-crkva-kriza/30619177.html.

537. www.danas.rs/svet/djukanovic-spc-najopakiji-instrument-velikosrpskog-nacionalizma.

538. Osetljiv trenutak, *Žasto je važan dolazak Vučića i Dodika na Sabor SPC? Interview with Professor*

be found in many countries in the world, where there is one universal RCC (also present in Serbia) with its state organization, the Holy See, in which there is constant and intensive cooperation between the two entities in numerous social areas and issues. This does not mean that the church directly influences political decision-making or participates in it in a formal sense. In the case of the Republic of Serbia, and especially on the issue of KiM, the SOC can and should express its opinion since her historical and deep essential connection with this province, Serbian people, and the state needs no further explanation. In resolving this issue, which has lasted for more than a century, as always throughout history, the 'action capacity' of Serbia today largely depends on the quality of its relationship with the SOC.

---

*Darko Tanaskovic*, Sputnjik, https://rs.sputniknews.com/analize/201905151119809946-srbi-predsednik-patrijarh-spc-analiza/, 16 May 2019.

# Part VI. Labour Law within Religious Communities

## Chapter 1. Scope of Application of Labour Law

*203.* The *Labour Law* of the Republic of Serbia from 2018,[539] among other things, further elaborates the *principles of prohibition of direct and indirect discrimination* – of persons seeking employment and all employees with respect to gender, origin, language, race, skin colour, age, pregnancy, health status (including disability), nationality, *religion,* marital status, family commitments, sexual orientation, political or other beliefs, social background, financial status, membership in political parties, syndicates and other.[540] *Direct discrimination* implies any action caused by some of the grounds referred to in Article 18 of this Law, which puts the job seeker or employee at a *disadvantage* to other persons in the same or similar situation. *Indirect discrimination* exists when a certain seemingly neutral provision, criterion or practice puts or would put the said persons at a disadvantage compared to other persons due to a certain quality, status, *orientation or belief* referred to in Article 18 of this Law.[541]

*204.* In accordance with the stated, pursuant to Article 179 of the Labour Law, the following *are not considered justified reasons for termination of the employment contract*: (1) temporary incapacity for work due to illness, injury at work or occupational disease; (2) use of maternity leave, leave from work for the purpose of childcare or special care of the child; (3) military service; (4) membership in a political organization, trade union, gender, language, ethnicity, social origin, *religion,* political or other belief or any other personal feature of the employee; (5) activity in the capacity of representative of employees pursuant to this Law; (6) filing a complaint to the trade union or competent bodies for protection of labour rights in accordance with the law, general document and employment contract.[542] Therefore, this Law prohibits discrimination against persons seeking employment and employees based on *religion, religious affiliation or belief. No one can have their employment contract terminated* because of them.

539. Labour Law, *supra* n. 97.
540. Labour Law, *supra* n. 97, Art. 18.
541. Labour Law, *supra* n. 97, Art. 19.
542. Labour Law, *supra* n. 97, Art. 183.

*205.* When it comes to the area of *application of Labour Law* within religious communities in Serbia, the best example is the *status and position of teachers of religion in public schools*. This will be discussed in more detail in the chapter 'Other Church Officials and Labour Law'.

## Chapter 2. Religious Ministers and Labour Law

*206.* Every citizen, as well as persons who have a permanent or temporary residence in the Republic of Serbia, are guaranteed numerous *social and labour rights* by law.

*207.* The *Law on Health Care from 2015*[543] not only guarantees every individual the right to *health care* but also prescribes the 'duty to protect and improve their own and other citizens' health', including 'living and working conditions'.[544] This also refers to *priests and religious officials.*

*208.* The *Law on Health Insurance from 2016* provides for 'mandatory and voluntary health insurance' for each individual,[545] whereby '*priests and religious officials who perform their duties as self-employed activities*' are also covered.[546] These include their 'children up to 18 years of age, wives for 12 months after birth, and monks and nuns',[547] as 'members of the family of the insured'.[548] Funds for the stated purposes are provided in the budget of the Republic of Serbia.[549]

*209.* The *Law on Payment of Contributions for PIO for certain categories of insured persons from 2005*[550] provided that every individual in Serbia, who in the period '1 January 1991 to 31 December 2003, was employed by and registered with an enterprise (company), institution, bank, organization and agricultural cooperative', and for whom the employer did not pay contributions, was *entitled to the possibility of paying the contribution for PIO.*[551] Article 38 of this Law defines that the basis for the payment of contributions is 'the lowest basis valid in the month in which the payment of contributions is made'. The *Law on PIO from 2004* stipulates that 'insured persons in self-employed activities' also includes 'priests and religious officials'.[552]

*210.* The issue of the amount, manner and dynamics of payment of contributions for health care, PIO for priests and religious officials from the budget of the Republic of Serbia is elaborated in detail and defined by the *Regulation on payment of contributions for pension and disability and health insurance for priests and religious officials from 2012.*[553] For the stated purposes, the state provides funds 'up to

543. Law on Health Care, *supra* n. 247.
544. Law on Health Care, *supra* n. 247, Art. 3.
545. Law on Health Care, *supra* n. 247, Art. 2.
546. Law on Health Insurance from 2016, *supra* n. 246, Art. 17, para. 20.
547. Law on Health Insurance from 2016, *supra* n. 246, Art. 22, paras 1, 2 and 6.
548. Law on Health Insurance from 2016, *supra* n. 246, Art. 24.
549. Law on Health Insurance from 2016, *supra* n. 246, Art. 204.
550. Law on Payment of Contributions for Pension and Disability Insurance (PIO) for Certain Categories of Insured Persons from 2005, Official Gazette of RS, no. 85/2005.
551. Law on Payment of Contributions for Pension and Disability Insurance (PIO) for Certain Categories of Insured Persons from 2005, *supra* n. 550, Art. 2.
552. Law on Pension and Disability Insurance (PIO), *supra* n. 248, Art. 13.
553. Regulation on payment of contributions for pension and disability and health insurance for priests and religious officials from 2012, Official Gazette of RS, no. 46/2012.

the amount of the lowest monthly contribution base' prescribed by Article 38 of the Law on Compulsory Social Insurance Contributions, and the *difference between the minimum monthly base and the determined contribution base is paid by the insured*, that is, the church or religious community. Budget funds up to the amount of the lowest monthly base are at the disposal of the state *body in charge of religious affairs*,[554] which transfers them to the *payment accounts of pension, disability and health insurance contributions of religious entities* no later than the 15th for the previous month.[555] The *competent organization for compulsory social insurance* submits data on religious insured persons to the Tax Administration within the legally prescribed deadlines, and the contribution base for each religious insured person is *jointly determined* by the religious entity (church or religious community) and the competent organization for compulsory social insurance. This organization submits the data to the Tax Administration, which then makes decisions on obligations based on contributions determined jointly by the two entities. A tax base defined in such a manner is determined for a certain insurant and cannot be changed during a calendar year.[556] The Tax Administration records the paid contributions of each insured person after the payment and submits the data to the competent organization for compulsory social insurance.[557] Finally, no later than the 5th of the month, it shall submit all relevant data on contributions for priests and religious officials to the body responsible for religious affairs.[558]

*211.* The Republic of Serbia fully guarantees the exercise of labour and social rights of members of its religious entities. Over 2,200 priests and religious officials of all religious entities in the country have received part of the funds for health care, pension, and disability insurance from the state budget monthly since 2012.[559]

554. Regulation on payment of contributions for pension and disability and health insurance for priests and religious officials from 2012, *supra* n. 553, Art. 2.
555. Regulation on payment of contributions for pension and disability and health insurance for priests and religious officials from 2012, *supra* n. 553, Art. 3.
556. Regulation on payment of contributions for pension and disability and health insurance for priests and religious officials from 2012, *supra* n. 553, Art. 4.
557. Regulation on payment of contributions for pension and disability and health insurance for priests and religious officials from 2012, *supra* n. 553, Art. 5.
558. Regulation on payment of contributions for pension and disability and health insurance for priests and religious officials from 2012, *supra* n. 553, Art. 6.
559. *Source*: Ministry of Justice.

## Chapter 3. Other Church Officials and Labour Law

*212.* The employment status and rights of all employees in the Republic of Serbia are regulated by a *collective* and *special agreement* in accordance with the Labour Law.[560]

*213.* In the case of teachers of religion (teachers and lecturers of religious education in elementary and secondary schools), they are signed with the competent *Ministry of Education, Science and Technological Development*. The mentioned category of lecturers has the *status of fixed-term* employees. In practice, at the suggestion of religious communities, teachers of religion have been signing (renewing) employment contracts with the Ministry since the introduction of religious education in schools in 2001, just prior to the beginning of each school year. Religious education is a *compulsory elective subject* in the Republic of Serbia. This will be discussed more in the part of the encyclopaedia dedicated to 'Education'.

*214.* Teachers of religion sign an individual fixed-term employment contract based on Article 192, paragraph 1, item 1 and Article 30, paragraphs 1–2 of the mentioned Labour Law, the Law on the Foundations of the Education System[561] and the provisions of the *statute of the school* in which they will be engaged. It is signed between the *school principal* and the *employee* for a period of twelve months, until the end of the school year. The religious teacher has all the rights and obligations in accordance with the *law and general acts of the school* and based on the *Decision* issued by the *religious entity* which appoints him. He initiates an employment relationship of 100% of the total working time. It can vary depending on the real needs on the ground. However, the school is obliged to *submit the prescribed applications for compulsory social insurance* immediately after the employee starts working and to pay contributions for health care, PIO in a timely manner. The salary of an employee is determined based on the *Regulation of the Government of Serbia on coefficients for calculation and payment of salaries of employees in public services*, which refers to the salaries of employees in secondary schools. A religious teacher is entitled to *allowances, salary compensation* and *other income* in accordance with the law and general acts of the school. He/she is obliged to adhere to all *prescribed safety measures at work* and is entitled to a *daily rest* of thirty minutes and a *weekly rest* of twenty-four hours continuously. The provisions of the *Law* and *general acts of the school* apply to the rights and obligations that are not determined by the employment contract.[562]

560. Labour Law, *supra* n. 97. Also, Official Gazette of RS, nos 61/2005, 54/2009, 32/2013, 75/2014 and 113/2017.
561. Law on Foundations of the Education System, Official Gazette of RS, nos 88/2017, 27/2018 and 10/2019.
562. Regulations, organization and functioning of religious communities in Serbia are under the jurisdiction of their regulation, whose autonomy and application are guaranteed by the state. In particular, teachers of religion for schools are appointed and dismissed by the religious communities themselves, on the basis of their internal decisions or the decisions of their competent courts. Thus,

religious communities decide whether and when their teachers of religion meet their own 'moral standards'. Finally, within the RCC, according to its internal regulations (canons), no second wedding is possible in the Church.

# Part VII. Religious Communities and Protections of the Individual

*215.* This part of the encyclopaedia contains a descriptive and 'practical' synthesis and interpretation of original theological positions and attitudes of religious entities in the Republic of Serbia (RCC, ICofS, IZinS, SECAV, Jewish Community of Serbia (JCS) and SOC), viewed from the angle of secular social sciences and existing universal and state regulations. When it comes to procedures, methodology, structure and content, the starting point is the authentic contributions of religious entities, who, on the basis of an official request, had full freedom to appoint authorized persons to write them.[563] A review of the views of the Reformed Christian Church in Serbia, which did not send its contribution, is missing. The thematic guidelines (Chapters) proposed by Kluwer for writing this part of the monograph were sent to the religious entities. Due to the pandemic circumstances during 2020, the contributions arrived in the period from March to October. On this occasion, it is expedient to remind that the current Law on Churches and Religious Communities[564] on the basis of previous laws in the Republic of Serbia recognized continuity with the legal entity of the SOC (Article 11) RCC (Article 12), Islamic Community (Article 15), SECAV, Reformed Christian Church and Evangelical Christian Church (Article 13), as well as JC (Article 14). Since there are two *registered Islamic communities in the country*, continuity with the legal entity is recognized by the ICofS and the ICinS. The First (ICofS) establishes continuity with the Islamic Religious Community from the Principality of Serbia, based on the Decree of Prince Mihailo Obrenović from 18 May 1868, which officially recognized the freedom of religion in the country for Islamic believers. At that time, Serbia was the first country in Europe to recognize the right of Islamic believers to freedom of religion. The headquarters of today's Rijaset ICofS is located in Belgrade. The second Islamic Community – Meshihat ICinS – with its headquarters in Novi Pazar, in organizational and territorial terms, belongs to the Riyaset of the Islamic Community of BiH, with its headquarters in Sarajevo. Both communities belong to the *Sunni denomination of Islam*.

563. Archbishop, Reis-ul-Ulema, mufti, priest, rabbi and professors of the OTF.
564. Official Gazette of the RS, no. 36/2006.

## Chapter 1. Protecting Privacy

*216.* The Second Vatican Council of the *RCC* (1962–1965) affirmed the thesis that the *protection of the rights and duties of the human person* is the central point and precondition for achieving *personal perfection* and, thus, the common good of the entire society. In that sense, the *human person* is the *principle, subject and goal of all social institutions*, which contains the 'engraved' image of God with *transcendent dignity and the heritage of the rights* of every human being. The special characteristics of a human person according to the RCC are *reason, freedom and personal and social responsibility*, which make him a *co-creator with a special dignity* that no one has the right to take away. It is this dignity that *religious communities are called upon to promote and protect.* Starting from the Aristotelian–Thomistic tradition, the RCC teaches that man is capable of *knowing good by reason*, which is in accordance with his nature, *natural moral law* and published Christian morality, which teaches him to do good and avoid evil. In this context, the promotion of the dignity of the human person and individual human rights necessarily implies the *right to a religious relationship with God*; *respect for religious beliefs and symbols*; *freedom of religious practice*, as well as to *leisure, rest and quality of life*. According to the RCC, every individual has the right *to just and benevolent policies, the right of children and parents to mutual support; the right to learning and socialization; the right to life (and birth) and respect for life from the moment of conception to natural death; to education; the right of parents to sexually educate their children; to encouragement and support from the state and society in general;* the *right to respect for civil liberties*, which include *physical integrity, choice of life and service*; *freedom of movement and expression; the right to a good reputation and the right to respect for private life* (defence of the right of every person to his or her own freedom and dignity*); the right to accurate and undistorted information; the right to private and professional security and peace*; *the right to free enterprise, private property and the transfer of material goods to others; as well as respect for the right to work and a fair wages.*[565] An individual (especially the poor and sick) has the right to *physical, social, political and economic security*; *the right to an apartment; the right to express oneself and appear before public, economic, social and cultural authorities, directly or through associations.* Finally, *minors have the right to legal protection from harmful drugs, pornography and alcoholism*, and the *elderly to a dignified life and a dignified death.*[566]

*217.* Islamic communities in the Republic of Serbia also pay great attention to issues of human rights and individual freedoms. *ICofS* emphasizes that starting from the principles of Sharia law and obligations, it fulfils its mission in society in *full accordance with the Constitution and the Law on Churches and Religious Communities*, and with the primary goal of preserving physical health and life, protection

565. 'Religious Communities and the Protection of the Individual', contribution by Archbishop of the Belgrade RCC, Monsignor Stanislav Hočevar, Administration for Religions of the Ministry of Justice, 2020.
566. *Ibid.*

of property and honour (dignity), as well as 'metaphysical health' (mind and reason) of its believers and all citizens of Serbia. She emphasizes that her believers, as well as all religious entities, are obliged to respect the Constitution and the state system of their country and apply their internal regulations *within the framework prescribed by state regulations*. In its laws and regulations, the ICofS has paid great attention to protecting the privacy of believers, referring to the text of the Qur'an: 'O believers! Do not let some "men" ridicule others, they may be better than them, nor let "some" women ridicule other women, they may be better than them. Do not defame one another, nor call each other by offensive nicknames. How evil it is to act rebelliously after having faith! And whoever does not repent, it is they who are the "true" wrongdoers.'[567] Based on the above, ICofS fully accepts and supports the provision of the Law on Churches and Religious Communities, which emphasizes that 'religious freedom must not be used in a way that endangers the right to life, the right to health, children's rights, the right to personal and family integrity and the right to property'.[568] For example, when conducting *probate proceedings*, the competent court asks the heirs whether they have a proposal on the division of property, and they are free to offer their agreement to the court stemming from *inherited Sharia law, which the state court will accept*. In this process, the ICS has an *advisory role*, in terms of giving suggestions to the heirs on how to properly distribute the inheritance in accordance with the principles of Sharia law.[569] ICofS was very pleased to accept the adoption of the *Law on Identity Card*[570] which allows a person who, according to nationality, religion or folk customs, wears a hat or scarf *to be photographed with the specified parts of clothing*, in accordance with the regulation on the manner of taking biometric data. Also, the current *Labour Law of the ICS is based on the principles of the state Labour Law*, whereby the community *reserves and uses the right to adjust the internal law to its needs for the benefit of both the community and society*. In particular, since the religious official (imam in the mosque) does not have exclusively eight-hour working days, the ICofS prescribed in a special way his rights and obligations during daily prayers: morning (before sunrise), noon (after his zenith), afternoon (when the shadow of the object reaches its two lengths), evening (when the sun's rays set) and night (night has fallen completely). Also, by internal regulations, it motivates imams to perform their regular service and rewards them for achieved results. Imams accept disciplinary measures and decisions on appointment by signing *employment contracts*, too. In case of the impossibility to resolve a possible dispute within the ICS between the employed person and the Community, and in connection with labour law, *the case is handed over to the competent state court whose decision the community accepts as final*.[571]

567. Al-Hujurāt, 11–13.
568. 'The Attitude of the ICS Towards the Issue of Protection of Individuals', contribution of the Reis-ul-Ulema of ICS Sead effendi Nasufović, Administration for Religions of the Ministry of Justice, 2020.
569. *Ibid.*
570. Official Gazette of RS no. 62/2006 and 36/2011.
571. 'The Attitude of the ICS Towards the Issue of Protection of Individuals', *supra* n. 568.

*218.* Also starting from the text of the Qur'an,[572] *ICinS* emphasizes and points to the *inherent nature and universal value of every human person, as a priori and God-given by virtue of birth.* The philosophy of Islamic law (*usūl al-fiqh*) articulated the idea of human law (*haqq al-'abd*), clearly defining the *concept of duality* with which God characterized the human being and state – on the one hand, man is a slave of God (*'abd al-lāh*), and on the other hand, God's representative on Earth (*Khalīfat al-lāh*) – which is the very essence of human existence and function on Earth. IZS points out that the Qur'an does *not support a radical spirit-body distinction,* which is why *the concept of realizing the ideals of human rights necessarily presupposes the incorporation of both mentioned aspects of existence* on the path to its realization. Also, human rights according to ICinS imply *constant human effort towards self-improvement,* as well as the inevitable existence of obstructions and difficulties on that path. The *protection of privacy is a fundamental human right,* and ICinS seeks to strengthen respect for human physical and mental integrity. In this context, the *mosque* and the *imam* have a central role in building and shaping a healthy community, that is *personality.* That is why they are in the centre of attention and action of the educational institutions of ICinS, which especially strives to engage in the field of *enlightenment* because God has endowed man with knowledge – with meaning and purpose. The ICinS considers the r*ight to education to be the right of members of both sexes, regardless of nationality and cultural affiliation.* In addition, the community pays great attention to *humanitarian work* because every person has the *right to a normal existence.* Therefore, the ICinS organizes the work of vakuf kitchens on a voluntary basis, in which the needy are fed on a daily basis.[573]

*219. SECAV,* which grew out of the roots of the Protestant Reformation in Germany in the sixteenth century, advocates that *secular law should be separated from religion,* defining consensus on the 'nature of moral values' as the primary goal of its mission in society. It is their *significance and influence that should be promoted in society.* SECAV believes that the *theory of human and individual rights is not inherited exclusively from the texts of Scripture and Christian science* but also from the 'natural ethos of humane world society' and 'the heart of ethical and social teachings'.[574] Since the *individual* today is under *double pressure* from the state and the market, which is why he becomes a 'producer and consumer of goods and government', *the ethical teaching* of SECAV emphasizes that man is *above all a being and an individual.*[575] The *protection of the individual* rests on the 'ethical path of the Christian tradition', for man was *created in the image of God,*[576] the individual

572. 'We have certainly honoured the sons of Adam!' (17:70).
573. 'The Attitude of Islam and IZinS Towards the Protection of Individuals', contribution of the President of the Meshihat of IZinS Mufti Prof. Dr Mevlud effendi Dudić, Administration for Religions of the Ministry of Justice, 2020.
574. 'Church and Protection of the Individual from the Perspective of SECAV', contribution of the SECAV Priest in Serbia Ana Petrović, MA, Administration for Religions of the Ministry of Justice, 2019.
575. *Ibid.*
576. Genesis 1:27.

has received an abundance of life from Christ as a gift,[577] and freedom versus slavery.[578] *Evangelical, Lutheran thinking about human rights*, which shaped SECAV's position on this issue, evolved from *Dr Martin Luther's doctrine of two kingdoms* (*spiritual* in the focus of the church and *temporal* in the domain of the state), whereby both church and state are *obliged to support the purpose and goals of the Kingdom of God*. SECAV, therefore, encourages *a theological critique of the existing order to stimulate political reform*, as opposed to 'indifference to political and social issues' (*Ibid.*). After the adoption of the Universal Declaration of Human Rights and support for the Study of the Lutheran World Federation 'Theological Perspectives on Human Rights' published in 1977, SECAV in Serbia began to point to the *inherent link between religious freedom and other basic human rights*. Starting from *Dr Martin Luther's Small Catechism*, it advocates *the security rights of individuals* that protect them from murder, torture, and genocide, as well as fair and public trials for those accused of crimes. It advocates *the protection of fundamental human freedoms in the field of religion*, the use of the *mother tongue*, the *right to association and movement, as well as equality before the law* and the *prohibition of discrimination against every individual*. SECAV's interest in human rights and individual protection issues has been further deepened thanks to the technical *advances of civilization*, the *development of biotechnological research*, and the *challenges of plastic surgery*, which can be *abused against the individual*. Today's *bioethical dilemmas* put the church in front of the need to take positions that cannot be based on previous traditions. SECAV in Serbia is dedicated to the *physical security and spiritual growth* of all children, youth, teachers, church members and clergy. *Sexual or emotional abuse, harassment and exploitation of children and adults occur in church communities*, as well as in all economic, cultural, and racial structures. Since such incidents have devastating consequences for children, families, local churches, clergy, and the church, SECAV in Serbia introduces *appropriate security measures when selecting candidates and introducing them to the service*, as well as *thorough operational procedures* for all programmes and events. It undertakes to *immediately respond, report and investigate all allegations* of sexual or any other form of harassment and abuse, focusing on the *needs and feelings of the abused and aggressors*. The *Decree on the Protection of Personal Data* partially established the legal relations between the individual and the church, but it also opened numerous issues and controversies within the community on this issue.[579]

*220.* The position and attitude of the *JCS* towards the issue of protection of privacy are based on the principles of the Torah, in which it is written: 'And lifted up his eyes and saw Israel standing among his tribes.' What did Bilam, a pagan sage, see in the Jews that inspired him so much? He saw that the entrances to their tents were not facing each other so that one family did not visually *endanger the privacy*

577. John 10:10.
578. Gal. 5:1.
579. 'Church and Protection of the Individual from the Perspective of SECAV', contribution of the SECAV Priest in Serbia Ana Petrović, MA, *supra* n. 574.

of another family. It is the commentary in the Talmud on the mentioned verse.[580] 'When your neighbour is indebted to you, do not go to his house to take his pledge, but stand outside, and let the man who is indebted to you bring his pledge outside.' 'Stand outside' is a biblical way of saying 'do not endanger the privacy of his home'. *Jewish law* distinguishes between *two forms of invasion of privacy – intrusion and disclosure.*[581] Intrusion into someone's privacy is described in the Torah when a creditor comes for a pledge at the debtor's home. The Talmud states two opinions as to whether the ban on entering the house applies only to citizens who act at their discretion or also to court officials. The *binding decision is that even a court clerk cannot enter the debtor's house to take a pledge*. This prohibition applies to the case of a lender who did not secure the pledge at the time of the loan and seeks it as collateral later before the loan expires. However, when the money owed is not a loan but a salary or rent, entry into the house is allowed. Disclosure includes the *return of a stolen item.* The difference is that a loan is something that the one who takes it should spend, and therefore a violent intrusion on someone's property is an *illegal invasion of the privacy of that home.* Otherwise, stolen items or salaries that have been withheld do not for a moment belong to the one who keeps them, and therefore *entry and confiscation in this case go beyond respect for privacy. Courts are therefore not allowed to violate privacy that is not allowed to private individuals.* The only difference between them is that the court may order that the lender's case may be forcibly confiscated outside the debtor's house.[582]

*221.* In the concluding document of the Third Prosynodal Pan-Orthodox Conference in 1986, the entire Orthodox Church, including the *SOC*, committed itself to attempt to make the abundance of God's gifts available to all people and to engage in eliminating the consequences of disease, poverty and hunger in the world. The Orthodox Church then proclaimed as its goal the establishment of justice and the elimination of all forms of repression and terror against individuals, groups and entire nations. This activity is based on faith in Christ, which can renew and build 'a new humaneness and a new humanity'.[583] The Orthodox Church points out that the concept of human rights in the anthropological sense is based on the Christian teaching according to which God created Adam in His own image and likeness. Therefore, the consequences of the mentioned creation extend to the whole of humanity, that is, every human being without exception because he possesses personal dignity. Since all people are children of God, humanity is existentially indivisible and unique; that is, One in Christ is manifested as a loving transformation of the biological existence of people into a community of persons.[584] However, there

580. 'Religious Communities and Protection of the Individual' contribution of Rabbi of the JC in Serbia Isak Asiel, Administration for Religions of the Ministry of Justice, 2020.
581. *Ibid.*
582. *Ibid.*
583. 'Religious Communities and Protection of the Individual,' contribution of archpriest-stavrophore Dr Zoran Krstić and presbyter Dr Zoran Devrnja, full and associate professor at the Orthodox Theological Faculty of the University of Belgrade, Administration for Religions of the Ministry of Justice, 2020.
584. Јанулатос Анастасиос Архиепископ Тиране, Глобализам и Православље, Хришћански културни центар, Београд, 2002, 65.

is a unity of people in the experience of sinfulness and distance from God. It causes the disease of all mankind and brings people to a dead-end of conflict, non-acceptance of diversity and social disharmony which are manifested in all segments of individual human experience and the history of all mankind.[585] The Orthodox Church therefore points to the existential need to respect the dignity, freedom and equality of every human being, regardless of sex, race, nationality, language, cultural identity, social or legal status. Reducing human dignity from divine and metaphysical grounds to the level of social justification and utility, restricting human freedom on any basis and for any purpose, as well as the manifestation of racial, sexual, legal, economic, and technological inequality among people, the Orthodox Church perceives as an obvious manifestation of injustice and sin.[586] Different political, economic and social ideologies today cause the alienation of modern man from God and other people, as well as people in relation to nature. Man's anthropocentric and egocentric use of nature as God's creation also leads to the danger of destroying the natural and social environment.[587] Because of all this, the Orthodox Church calls on all people to restore humanity as the highest gift of God's creation, criticizing at the same time the experience of disenfranchisement and systemic injustice over individuals and specific social groups, as well as the relentless exploitation and unjust distribution of natural and human resources. The real alternative and goals for it are social justice, basic respect for universal human rights, access to education, primary health care and clean drinking water for all people. The Orthodox Church therefore promoted 1 September as a day dedicated to prayer for the salvation of man's natural environment as God's creation.[588] Finally, it points to the necessary interdependence of individual rights with the rights of entire communities, that is, individual and collective human rights. That is why it strives to harmonize them and points out that only love for one's neighbour and his social and legal articulation can transform both the individual and society. The ideal and aspiration of the Orthodox Church imply the creation of an organically connected community of individuals, 'who freely sacrifice themselves out of love for the benefit of another', as opposed to the self-sufficient existence of a group of atomized individuals. Thus, every law and every declaration of human rights will be fulfilled.[589] The Orthodox Church considers a very important attempt to balance individual and collective rights in the UN Universal Declaration of Human Rights.[590]

*222.* Religious entities in the Republic of Serbia pay great attention to the universal (secular) concept of human rights and individual freedoms in different areas and with different intensities, unequivocally advocating its full application in practice. Evaluating it through the prism of their theological principles and goals, they

585. Mitropolit Pergama Jovan Zizjulas, *'Zajednica i drugačijnost'*, *'Svetigora'*, 31/1994, 22–24. i 32/1994, 31–33.
586. A. Јанупатос, *supra* n. 584, 67–68.
587. His All-Holiness the Ecumenical Patriarch Demetrios of Constantinople, The World Convocation on Justice, Peace and the Integrity of Creation, Seoul, 1990, www.ecupatria.org, 11 Feb. 2014.
588. *Ibid.*
589. A. Јанупатос, *supra* n. 584, 78–79.
590. Patriarch Kirill of Moscow, 127–130.

strive to *'enrich' the exclusively secular understanding of human rights* and advocate its *deepening, expansion and 'verticalization'*. In accordance with that, religious subjects in Serbia pay different attention to certain areas and aspects of human rights and freedoms and give various suggestions on how to improve the current situation in them. In this context, the internal regulations of religious entities have a greater or lesser degree of 'closeness' and compliance with state regulations. When it comes to the *protection of privacy*, all of them are fully committed to the acceptance of principles and goals, as well as the full implementation of the provisions of international conventions and the Constitution and laws of the Republic of Serbia in this area. However, from the point of view of state (secular) regulation, it is noticed that ICS, RCC, SECAV, and even JC have a more elaborate contour of 'social doctrine' and a more concrete relation and attitude towards the issue of privacy protection. It can be concluded that the content of internal regulations of religious entities and state regulations is permeated and coincides but is not identical. There is certainly room for improving cooperation in this area.

## Chapter 2. Freedom to Marry (The Right to a Family)

*223.* The *RCC* points out that all religious entities today have a special responsibility in *defending the rights of the family and freedom of marriage* in today's 'unbearable abuses' by society and the state.[591] For the RCC, marriage is a natural institution that has the exclusive *mission, duty and right to transfer life*, within its central institution of the family as a 'close community' in which *men and women complement each other*. Marriage is established by a *freely accepted and publicly recognized indissoluble marital bond*. The *Charter on the Rights of the Family of the Holy See* (1983) therefore promotes the right of *every person to freely choose his or her state of life*, that is, the *right to start a family and to support it by appropriate means*. Accordingly, the family *has the right to carry out the mission of transmitting life and raising children*, and *everyone has the right to freely choose and respect the spouse*, the *intimacy of married and family life*, and the *permanence of the marital relationship and institution of marriage*. Within marriage, he also has the *right to believe, confess and spread his faith* and to *raise his children in accordance with his own religious and cultural values and beliefs* and with the assistance and assistance of his religious community and state. According to the RCC, an individual has the *right to an appropriate and proper family life* and the *establishment of associations with other families and institutions with the aim of fulfilling their family task responsibly*. The individual and the family have the right to 'honourable entertainment' that promotes family values as well as *emigration in order to seek better living conditions*. Finally, *every child within the family has the right to emotional and financial stability and parental support*.[592]

*224.* In resolving open issues and misunderstandings in the field of family and marriage law in Serbia, in a practical, primarily *advisory sense*, *ICofS* is especially engaged. In many cases, it has managed to reach satisfactory agreements with its believers, having in mind both internal and state regulations.[593]

*225.* In valuing and dealing with the issue of marital rights of individuals, the *JCS* starts from the theological fact that in Judaism, the *freedom to marry is limited exclusively to persons who have the status of a Jew*. A Jew is allowed to marry a person who belongs to another religion *exclusively if that person converts to Judaism*.[594] Also, the Jews who have directly descended from Aaron, the brother of Moses, known as kohanim, are *forbidden to marry a woman who converted to Judaism after the age of 3 years and one day of her life*. Finally, the JC points out that, according to its teaching, *same-sex marriage is prohibited*.[595]

591. 'Religious Communities and the Protection of the Individual,' contribution by the Archbishop of the Belgrade RCC, Monsignor Stanislav Hočevar, *supra* n. 565.
592. *Ibid.*
593. 'The Attitude of the ICS Towards the Issue of Protection of Individuals', contribution of the Reis-ul-Ulema of ICS Sead effendi Nasufović, *supra* n. 568.
594. 'Religious Communities and Protection of the Individual' contribution of Rabbi of the JC in Serbia Isak Asiel, *supra* n. 580.
595. *Ibid.*

*226.* Religious entities in Serbia believe that marriage and the family are categories and institutions that do not have exclusively secular character, meaning and purpose but also represent 'individual and collective' rights and obligations that have an existential source and origin 'in Divine law'. For believers, marriage and the family are not only 'legal' based solely on contract and individual freedoms but also a union for which its 'members' have a special responsibility ('individual and collective') before God, who established and supported them. As in almost the whole world, religious entities in Serbia point out that marriage implies *exclusively the union of a man and a woman* because its primary goal is *to prolong life, that is, to have children.* According to them, this fact in no way relativizes the other, also existentially important functions of marriage and family, such as upbringing, educational, economic, or 'social-integrative' in the broadest sense of the word. However, guaranteeing all marital rights and obligations of individuals in accordance with international standards, the legislator in Serbia is increasingly expressing the 'potential' and intention towards a 'horizontal evolution' of this issue in terms of readiness for dialogue and decision-making on the question of 'expansion and recognition of rights of certain distinctly "minority" social groups' in this area as well.

## Chapter 3. Freedom of Expression

*227.* The *RCC* emphasizes that freedom of religious expression and freedom of conscience are among the basic human rights[596] that directly affect the respect and dignity of each individual. In this context, each individual has the right to freely explore the truth and the moral order on which 'the common good depends', to express and spread his opinion and beliefs, to develop his abilities and to be truthfully informed about all public events.[597] The RCC catechism emphasizes that every individual has the right to act according to the judgment of his own conscience, freely and without any coercion from the outside, in order to be able to make moral decisions and adhere to divine truth.[598] This right and freedom should also be enjoyed by those who 'do not live up to their obligation of seeking the truth and adhering to it'.[599] The RCC in Serbia highlights that all religious communities are 'called' to promote and protect the rights of personal conscience towards the truth, as long as they do not endanger the rights of others.[600] This also implies the right of others to respect the conscience of each individual, even if it is 'invincibly wrong'. The exception is the belief of an individual that harms another person or community.[601] Finally, the dignity of an individual's personal conscience implies that he 'seeks the truth' (nurtures his conscience) because 'true good improves him as a person'.[602]

*228.* Referring to its religious text and internal regulations, the *ICofS* urges believers to cultivate 'humility' above all and without 'sinful suspicion', as well as responsible and sincere relationships regardless of gender, race, nationality or any other personal or collective trait. According to it, God 'does not look at the appearance and property' of a man, but 'at his heart and deeds'.[603] ICofS fully accepts and supports the provision of the Law on Churches and Religious Communities in Serbia according to which 'religious freedom must not provoke and encourage religious, national or racial intolerance' because ICS itself 'condemns them, does not consider them an integral part of its faith, and strictly forbids them of its believers'.[604] For the full realization of constitutional and legal rights to freedom of religion, *ICofS cultivates good cooperation with the Serbian Army (VS).* In this state institution, *exclusively on a voluntary basis*, Muslims have the opportunity to participate in the performance of their religious rites, respecting the obligations arising from military service. For their needs, *military imams* perform religious activities in

596. Catechism of the RCC, PT 14.
597. 'Religious Communities and the Protection of the Individual', contribution of the Metropolitan and Archbishop of the Belgrade RCC, Monsignor Stanislav Hočevar, *supra* n. 561.
598. Catechism of the RCC, no. 1782.
599. Catechism of the RCC, no. 2106.
600. 'Religious Communities and the Protection of the Individual', contribution of Archbishop of the Belgrade RCC, Monsignor Stanislav Hočevar, *supra* n. 565.
601. Catechism of the RCC, DH 13.
602. 'Religious Communities and the Protection of the Individual', contribution of Archbishop of the Belgrade RCC, Monsignor Stanislav Hočevar, *supra* n. 565.
603. Al-Hujurāt; 11–13.
604. 'The Attitude of the ICS Towards the Protection of Individuals', contribution of Reis-ul-Ulema of ICS Sead effendi Nasufović, *supra* n. 568.

designated premises, as *professional military personnel with the status of officers*, in accordance with the *law and the concluded agreement between ICofS and VS*. During 2019, a prayer space for believers of the Muslim faith was opened at the Military Medical Academy in Belgrade.[605] The ICofS signed a *cooperation agreement with the Department for the Execution of Criminal Sanctions of the Ministry of Justice* for the same purpose. If necessary, ICofS sends *its religious officials for worship activities and conversations with persons of the Islamic faith who are executing criminal sanctions*. In both cases, the religious officer of the ICofS respects his internal rules and the rules of the Serbian Army and the Department for the Execution of Criminal Sanctions, between which there is no disagreement (*Ibid.*). They include, among other things, *confidentiality*. It is important to emphasize that the affiliation, activities, assistance in the work of ICofS of *each adult individual are based on voluntariness*, while he reserves the *right and freedom to cease at any time* to be an official or member of ICofS.[606]

*229. ICinS* also *emphasizes respecting and guaranteeing the freedom of expression and expression of each individual's own views* since freedom is a necessary precondition for building a 'quality individual, and thus a community'. Especially through *the education system*, it seeks to promote the view that freedom 'should not be understood indefinitely' since it is 'limited by the right of another'.[607] The presented understanding of freedom for IZS also represents the framework and limit for the freedom of expression of each individual.

*230.* Referring to their religious text,[608] *JCS* teaches and invites all leaders in Serbia to *promote the right to freedom of speech and to protect it*.[609]

*231.* Finally, the Orthodox Church points out that only through 'the unique experience of love by which each person reaches the full meaning of his own existence and the existence of another being', *each individual can see everything as it really is*, that is, as God wanted and created it.[610] Only in the *context of the existence of*

605. *Ibid.*
606. *Ibid.*
607. 'The Attitude of Islam and ICinS Towards the Protection of Individuals', Prof. Dr Mevlud effendi Dudić, *supra* n. 571.
608. 'And Moses went out, and spoke unto the people the word of the LORD; and he gathered together seventy men from among the elders of the people and set them round about the tabernacle. And the LORD came down in the cloud, and spoke unto him, and took of the spirit that was upon him, and put it upon the seventy elders; and when the spirit came upon them, they prophesied, but never again. And two men remained in the camp, one named Eldad, and the other Medad, to whom the spirit came, for they too were written, but they did not come to the tabernacle, and began to prophesy in the camp. And the lad ran, and told Moses, saying, Eldad and Medad are prophesying in the camp. And Joshua the son of Nun, Moses' servant, one of his servants, said, My LORD Moses, forbid them. And Moses said unto him, hast thou envy me? Let all the people of the LORD become prophets, and let the LORD send his spirit upon them! Joshua sees Eldad and Medad as a threat and asks Moses to forbid them to speak. However, Moses resisted him and did not forbid them to speak.'
609. 'Religious Communities and Protection of the Individual' contribution of Rabbi of the JC in Serbia Isak Asiel, *supra* n. 580.
610. А. Јанупатос, *supra* n. 584, 69.

*love* is Christian freedom 'free from all prejudices about the other, from his characteristics, beliefs, values or morals'.[611] Consequently, the *freedom of others*, manifested even in a negative manner as a commitment to sin, *cannot be an obstacle for Christian love* to affirm the freedom *given to each individual by his very existence*. Thus, from what has been said, it can be concluded that according to the Orthodox Church, the existence of freedom, even true freedom of expression, cannot exist without the existence of love within each community, that is, between its believers and members. Specifically and implicitly, *every true believer* necessarily respects the freedom of each individual and thus his *freedom of expression.*

*232.* All religious entities in the Republic of Serbia fully accept and advocate for the full application of the universally adopted right of each individual to freedom of expression, accepted by the Constitution and laws of the state, implying the principle that it should not jeopardize the same right of another individual or community.

611. 'Religious Communities and Protection of the Individual', contribution of archpriest-stavrophore Dr Zoran Krstić and presbyter Dr Zoran Devrnja, full and associate professor at the Orthodox Theological Faculty of the University of Belgrade, *supra* n. 583.

## Chapter 4. Professional Secrecy

*233.* In the 'moral-theological' sense, the *RCC* distinguishes between the natural secret (secretum naturale), the promised secret (secretum promissum), the contractual secret (secretum commisum, secretum officiale) and the medical secret.[612] The natural refers to facts that require discretion, silence and caution. The promised is bound by the force of the given promise, the breach of which signifies a breach of honour and sincerity. A contractual secret is based on a contract by which the two parties voluntarily prescribe that it will not be disclosed. Finally, medical secrecy obliges the doctor not to disclose anything he saw or heard during his professional relationship with the patient. It arises from the free entrustment of the patient to the physician and in principle implies his obligation of confidentiality.[613]

*234.* With its internal acts (Regulation on organization and work, Regulation on providing religious services, Regulation on civil servants, etc.), *ICinS* prescribed that all data received (personal and professional data from requests and requests of religious officials, believers, and civilians) regardless of whether it was obtained orally or in writing, it is *kept as a business secret that could violate someone's privacy*. The same applies to data of persons whose *employment has been terminated in the ICS*.[614]

*235.* *SECAV* pays special attention to the *careful and secure use of personal data* obtained in the work, considering them a professional secret. All information obtained through screening, forms, reference control, interview and eventual insight into criminal proceedings are *considered confidential unless otherwise prescribed by law*. They are archived, kept in a safe place, and their access is strictly limited.[615]

*236.* The *JCS* points out that the disclosure of confidential information concerning another person is *prohibited by Jewish law,* even if it is not expressed in confidence.[616] In that sense, *there is no time limit* on the disclosure of confidential information. However, the privileged nature of private communication is not absolute since respect for the privacy of communication cannot be above the protection

612. 'Religious Communities and Protection of the Individual', contribution by Archbishop of Belgrade of RCC Monsignor Stanislav Hočevar, *supra* n. 565.

613. *Ibid.*

614. 'The Attitude of the ICS Towards the Protection of Individuals', contribution of Reis-ul-Ulema of ICS Sead effendi Nasufović, *supra* n. 568.

615. 'The Church and Protection of the Individual from the Perspective of SECAV', contribution of the SECAV Priest in Serbia, Ana Petrović, MA, *supra* n. 575.

616. This prohibition is based on the verse: 'Thou shalt not be a gossip to thy people.' According to Maimonides' codification, the regulation is: 'Who is the gossip? One who carries information and goes from person to person' and says, 'This and that said it' or 'so and so I heard from this and that'. Even when he speaks the truth, the buzzer destroys the world. In 'Religious Communities and the Protection of the Individual', contribution by Rabbi of JC in Serbia Isak Asiel, *supra* n. 580.

of the lives and safety of others. For example, a doctor is obliged to inform the competent traffic authorities that his patient is an epileptic who should be denied a driver's licence. JCS emphasizes that *the protection of life is above all religious and personal obligations,* which is why the *failure to provide such information is a violation of the biblical command*: 'Do not stand idly by while your neighbour's blood is shed.'[617]

*237.* The internal regulations of religious entities in the Republic of Serbia 'deeply and vertically' elaborate the right that priests, religious officials and believers are guaranteed by Article 8, paragraph 7 of the Law on Churches and Religious Communities, which refers to *the secrecy of knowledge during confession.* Professional secrecy for all of them implies not only a professional but also an ethical and spiritual category closely related to the protection of privacy and the general concept of human rights.

617. *Ibid.*

## Chapter 5. Medical Deontology

*238*. Starting from the complete understanding of the human person (unity of mind and body) and his dignity, that is, the fundamental principle 'do no harm', the *RCC* points to several principles that define its attitude towards medical ethics, that is, bioethics. The first refers to the *inviolability of human life that only God has at his disposal*. Therefore, *under no circumstances can anyone appropriate the right to directly destroy an innocent human being* whose life must be respected from the very beginning of inception.[618] The second principle is the *right to life* because man was created in the image of God and therefore is endowed with dignity (freedom, mind and will). The right to life is given authority by God himself, and it springs from both divine natural law and divine positive law. The third principle is the *therapeutic principle* or the *principle of wholeness (totality)*, from which follows the position of the RCC that medical procedures on a part of the human body are possible only under the condition that they have the purpose of saving the whole body, that is the very life of an individual. In particular, the medical procedure should cover only the diseased part of the body or the one that is the cause of the disease, and with the exclusive goal of its removal. The community further explained the mentioned attitudes according to the principles according to which 'a part exists for the sake of the whole', 'the good of the part remains subordinated to the good of the whole', and 'the whole decides on the part and can dispose of it in its own interest'.[619] The fourth principle refers to the *application of regular and extraordinary means*. *Regular* includes all procedures and therapies that provide reasonable hope for the success of the treatment and can be applied without creating too much pain or other special discomfort for the patient. *Extraordinary means* refer to those that do not provide a great chance of success (often only prolonging the vegetative life without hope of recovery), where the proportionality of success and the pain caused is in favour of pain. Since the precise boundary between regular and extraordinary means cannot always be determined with certainty, the application of this principle should always imply a new assessment of the existing circumstances because a certain means may change its status and consequences. From the ethical point of view, the RCC points out that regular means must be used to treat illness, relieve pain, and prolong life, while extraordinary ones may or may not be used.[620] The fifth principle of the RCC in the field of deontology refers to the right *to natural death and giving up therapeutic persistence*. It implies the right to remove or discontinue treatment procedures which do not contribute to any improvement in the patient's condition while only delaying and prolonging death without just cause and purpose. In particular, medical procedures that do not correspond to the real condition of the patient are rejected because they are not proportional to the expected results or are unbearable for him or his family. In such conditions of imminent and impending

618. 'Religious Communities and the Protection of the Individual', contribution of Archbishop of Belgrade of the RCC Monsignor Stanislav Hočevar, *supra* n. 565.
619. *Ibid.*
620. *Ibid.*

death, procedures and means that would cause only an uncertain and painful prolongation of life can be rejected in conscience, but without interrupting the normal and justified treatment of the patient.[621]

*239.* Although it does not reject the use of genetic technology entirely, *SECAV* has taken an open and sharply negative stance on human cloning, germ cell donation, surrogacy, and direct euthanasia, while it has taken a positive stance on organ transplantation and somatic gene therapy.[622] It emphasizes that every life, born or unborn, is worthy of protection, which is why it fundamentally opposes termination of pregnancy, considering it a violation of God's commandments. Unjustified termination of pregnancy, as well as the termination of pregnancy motivated by egoistic reasons of an economic nature, is considered morally unacceptable. Knowing the value of life as a gift of God, it is not allowed to kill a human foetus that has its own identity and right to life. Because of all the above, SECAV opposes abortion as a means of solving the problem of unwanted pregnancy. In this context, the community recognizes and respects the possibility of unforeseen circumstances and situations in pregnancy which lead a woman to a hopeless situation. In particular, SECAV considers that abortion can be morally justified in extreme ethical or health cases.[623]

*240.* Referring to the Bible and God's commandments (mitzvah), the *JCS* points out the obligation to provide medical services to an individual,[624] emphasizing that a doctor has permission to treat. Ramban in the *Torat HaAdam* explains that 'permission' actually implies an *order or obligation to provide medical assistance.*[625] In the codification of the Jewish law,[626] it is pointed out that if the doctor *refuses his help, it is considered as if he has shed blood.*[627] However, the community openly poses the question 'is the patient obliged to seek medical help, does he deny God's Omnipresence by seeking it, and is the sickness a suffering from God that serves as a punishment for sins?' In response to the same, the JC points out that numerous Talmudic passages testify that patients are not only allowed *but also obliged to seek medical help*. Such a stance is justified by a literal interpretation of the biblical verse: 'Now, vigilantly guard your souls' and leads to the conclusion that people are *obliged to take care of their health and lives.*[628]

*241.* It is noticeable that RCC, SECAV and JC in the Republic of Serbia have a more elaborate relation and more concrete attitudes towards the issue of medical

621. *Ibid.*
622. 'The Church and the Protection of the Individual from the Perspective of SECAV', contribution of the Priest of SECAV in Serbia, Ana Petrović, MA, *supra* n. 578.
623. *Ibid.*
624. It is written in the Talmud: 'And get him a complete cure.'
625. 'Religious Communities and the Protection of the Individual', contribution by Rabbi of JC in Serbia Isak Asiel, *supra* n. 580.
626. In the Shulchan Aruch: 'The Torah gave permission to the doctor to heal, moreover, it is a mitzvah and is included in the category of saving lives.'
627. 'Religious Communities and the Protection of the Individual', contribution by Rabbi of JC in Serbia Isak Asiel, *supra* n. 580.
628. *Ibid.*

deontology, in conditions when it is not fully regulated by state regulations. Other religious entities obviously approach this issue primarily from a spiritual and ethical point of view, leaving its medical aspect to science and the competent authorities for consideration and decision-making.

## Chapter 6. Prohibition of Discrimination

*242.* Bearing in mind what has been said thus far, as well as the theological principles and goals of religious subjects in the Republic of Serbia, all of them *unequivocally advocate the prohibition of all forms of discrimination against individuals or groups, on any grounds*. In this sense, there is complete compatibility of their internal regulations and state regulations. For the sake of example, this is underlined by IZinS,[629] SECAV[630] and JC[631] referring to the comparison of the Mishnah between the Creator and man who mints coins[632] and a midrash on this subject.[633]

629. 'The Attitude of Islam and ICinS Towards the Protection of Individuals,' contribution of the President of the Meshihat of ICinS Mufti Prof. Dr Mevlud effendi Dudić, *supra* n. 581.
630. 'The Church and Protection of Individuals from the Perspective of SECAV', contribution of the Priest of SECAV in Serbia, Ana Petrović, MA, *supra* n. 583.
631. 'There shall be one standard for you; it shall be for the stranger as it is for the native, for I am the Lord your God.' And 'So, God created man in his own image … male and female he created them.'
632. 'Man was created alone to express the greatness of God. While a man forges many coins from one mould and they are all the same, the King of all kings, the Holy One, may he be blessed, imprinted in every man the image of Adam and none is similar to the other. Man was created alone to understand that he who destroys one human soul seems to have destroyed the whole world, and he who saves one human soul seems to have saved the whole world. And for the sake of peace among men, lest they should say to one another, "My father is greater than yours".'
633. 'I call Heaven and earth to witness that whether be Gentile or Jew, man or woman, slave or free, the divine spirit rests on each in accordance with his deeds' in: 'Religious Communities and the Protection of the Individual', contribution by Rabbi of JC in Serbia Isak Asiel, *supra* n. 580.

## Chapter 7. Criminal Law and Religion

*243.* Referring to his Text,[634] the *JC* points out that the current *Criminal Code of the Republic of Serbia is 'good'* and believes that its content should be supplemented, in the near future, by a provision concerning the Holocaust denial.[635] Other religious subjects in the Republic of Serbia leave the principle of sanctioning the violation of basic human and religious rights and freedoms primarily to the competent state bodies.

634. 'Upon three things the world rests: upon justice, upon truth, and upon peace, for when justice is done, truth prevails, and peace is established.' JT, Taanit 4.2; Megilla 3:5.
635. 'Religious Communities and the Protection of the Individual', contribution by Rabbi of JC in Serbia Isak Asiel, *supra* n. 580.

# Part VIII. Church Financing

## Chapter 1. Direct Financing of Religious Communities

*244.* In Yugoslavia, after the Second World War, a whole series of 'reforms' were adopted and implemented, which brought religious entities to the brink of material and financial ruin. The *Law on Agrarian Reform and Colonization of 1946* deprived them of a large portion of their property, agricultural land,[636] pastures, forests, buildings, facilities, and business premises. All of them *became the property of the state.* The law stipulated that 'certain places of worship, monasteries and religious institutions will have any excess of over ten hectares confiscated from the existing possessions of (fields, gardens, vineyards, orchards, meadows and forests), while religious institutions of greater cultural significance and historical value will be allowed to keep 'up to thirty hectares of arable land and up to thirty hectares of forest'.[637]

*245.* In the Republic of Serbia, the Constitution today stipulates that all legal entities have *equal legal status on the market,* on which *free competition and the prohibition of a monopolistic or dominant status are guaranteed.* In that context, the rights that entities gain through capital investments, in accordance with the Law, may not be curtailed by the Law.[638] The Constitution recognizes and guarantees *equality of all forms of assets* (private, cooperative, and public), which have equal legal protection.[639] Based on this, the necessary preconditions have been created for the elimination of historical injustice and the existence of equal treatment of religious entities in society – in terms of their property and financial status.

*246.* The third part of the *Law on Churches and Religious Communities (2006)* regulates and defines the *procedure related to property and financing* of religious entities. It emphasizes that churches and religious communities finance their activities with *income from their property, endowments, legacies, funds, inheritance, donations, and contributions, as well as other non-profit transactions and activities.*[640] Religious entities manage their property and financial assets *independently*

636. Law on Agrarian Reform and Colonization of 1946, Official Gazette of the FPRY, no. 24/46. Art. 3, para. c. states 'land holdings of churches, monasteries and religious institutions and all kinds of endowments, secular and religious'.
637. Law on Agrarian Reform and Colonization of 1946, *supra* n. 636, Art. 8, paras 1 and 2.
638. Constitution of the Republic of Serbia from 2006, *supra* n. 4, Art. 84.
639. Constitution of the Republic of Serbia from 2006, *supra* n. 4, Art. 86.
640. Law on Churches and Religious Communities, *supra* n. 92, Art. 26, para. 1.

*in accordance with their autonomous regulations*,[641] as well as *business and other activities* in accordance with relevant regulations.[642] Sacral and cultural heritage, including structures of cultural significance, belonging to Churches and religious communities, shall *not be subject to enforcement and bankruptcy proceedings or settlement*,[643] and the competent public or local self-administration authority may, in accordance with the Law, *cede without compensation the use of confiscated property* until the enactment of regulations on its return on the basis of the Law on Restitution.[644]

*247.* When it comes to *providing financial assistance to religious entities in Serbia*, the key legal basis and provision is Article 28 of the Law on Churches and Religious Communities, which stipulates that the state 'cooperates with churches and religious communities to promote religious freedom and accomplish common good and mutual interest'. For this reason, it *can and should help their life and work.* As stated, it also provides part of the funds for health care, PIO of priests and religious officials through the competent state body, based on the *principle of equality* and *positive discrimination* of 'minority' communities.[645] In this context, the law left the possibility for religious entities to establish independent health and pension funds in accordance with autonomous regulations.[646] The state also respects the right of religious entities to build *temples and other buildings* and in accordance with the Law and its budget *may assist in the restoration or construction.*[647] In the field of *education*, it accepts the establishment of *religious educational institutions* (pre-school, elementary and secondary schools, and faculties and universities), which if accredited (passing verification by a state body) also *acquire the right to funding from the budget.*[648] Finally, state and local authorities of the Republic of Serbia also *financially support the cultural activities of their religious entities*, that is, religious buildings and institutions of exceptional historical, national and cultural significance, professional and scientific institutions for their protection, as well as their informational, cultural, scientific and publishing activities and programmes.[649] In most cases, it provides support to them through the competent body for religious affairs.

*248.* At the end of 2016, the Republic of Serbia adopted, as far as is known, a unique law in the field of religion on a European and world scale – the *Law on Remedying Consequences of Seizure of Assets from Holocaust Victims with no*

641. Law on Churches and Religious Communities, *supra* n. 92, Art. 26, para. 2.
642. Law on Churches and Religious Communities, *supra* n. 92, Art. 26, para. 3.
643. Law on Churches and Religious Communities, *supra* n. 92, Art. 27, para. 1.
644. Law on Churches and Religious Communities, *supra* n. 92, Art. 27, para. 2.
645. Law on Churches and Religious Communities, *supra* n. 92, Art. 29 which is further elaborated Regulation on Payment of Contributions for Pension, Disability and Health Insurance of Priests and Religious Officials from 2012.
646. Law on Churches and Religious Communities, *supra* n. 92, Art. 29, para. 4.
647. Law on Churches and Religious Communities, *supra* n. 92, Art. 32.
648. Law on Churches and Religious Communities, *supra* n. 92, Arts 34 and 36.
649. Law on Churches and Religious Communities, *supra* n. 92, Arts 41–44.

*Legal Living Heirs.*[650] Its proclaimed goal is to *remedy the consequences of confiscation of property and assets* of Holocaust victims in the period from 6 April 1941 to 9 May 1945. Confiscated property is returned to organizations that were an integral part of the JC in Serbia during the occupation.[651] Pursuant to this Law, the Republic of Serbia today provides financial support from the budget to its JC, that is, the *Union of Jewish Municipalities of Serbia*, in the amount of EUR 950,000 per year, for a period of twenty-five years, starting from 1 January 2017.[652] Unlike the returned property, the mentioned financial support *is not subject to any type of tax*.[653] The restitution procedure is conducted by the Agency for Restitution,[654] which, based on a final decision, transfers the property to the ownership of the respective JC. If a living heir addresses the same, the JC is obliged to transfer the returned property to his ownership.[655] The Association and municipalities are obliged to direct financial support to the *study and documentation of the Holocaust, marking its significant dates* (at least 20% of funds in ten years), *scientific research projects, education and scholarships for students, support for surviving victims in Serbia, strengthening the Jewish Community in the country and its ties with compatriots from around the world, for humanitarian purposes, as well as paying their expenses during the calendar year.*[656] The management of funds is controlled by the *State Supervisory Board*, whose members are a representative of the Government, two representatives of the World Jewish Organization and two representatives of the Union of Jewish Municipalities of Serbia.[657] In that context, the Union is obliged to keep records of revenue management programme and records of former owners, repossession of property and total income.[658]

*249.* An internal act of the Administration for Religions from 2017 – *Directive on Procedures, Internal Controls and Internal Control Procedures* in this body – adopted on the basis of the Law on State Administration,[659] Budget System Law, Budget Law and Law on Ministries, Regulation on Payment of Contributions for Pension, Disability and Health Insurance for Priests and Religious Officials, Regulation on Issuance of Additional Postage Stamp 'Construction of Memorial Temple Sveti Sava',[660] as well as several Decisions and Resolutions of the Government and

---

650. Law on Remedying Consequences of Seizure of Assets from Holocaust Victims with no Legal Living Heirs, Official Gazette of RS, no. 13/2016 (further referred to as: Law on Remedying Consequences of Seizure).
651. Law on Remedying Consequences of Seizure, *supra* n. 650, Art. 3.
652. Law on Remedying Consequences of Seizure, *supra* n. 650, Art. 9, paras 1 and 2.
653. Law on Remedying Consequences of Seizure, *supra* n. 650, Art. 10.
654. Law on Remedying Consequences of Seizure, *supra* n. 650, Art. 12.
655. Law on Remedying Consequences of Seizure, *supra* n. 650, Art. 21.
656. Law on Remedying Consequences of Seizure, *supra* n. 650, Art. 22.
657. Law on Remedying Consequences of Seizure, *supra* n. 650, Art. 23.
658. Law on Remedying Consequences of Seizure, *supra* n. 650, Arts 24 and 25.
659. Law on State Administration, Official Gazette of RS, nos 79/2005, 101/2007, 95/2010 and 99/2014.
660. Regulation on Issuance of Additional Postage Stamp 'Construction of Memorial Temple Sveti Sava', Official Gazette of RS, no. 65/2019.

the National Assembly of the Republic of Serbia,[661] it was defined that the principal programme of the Administration for Religions is 'the cooperation of the state with churches and religious communities', and is implemented through the application of the following *programme activities: 'Support to the work of priests, monks and religious officials*' (economic classification 0001), '*Support to clergy and monks in Kosovo and Metohija*' (0002), '*Support to Secondary Theological Education*' (0003), '*Support to Higher Theological Education*' (0004), '*Protection of Religious, Cultural and National Identity' of the Serbian People and National Minorities* (0005), '*Support for the Construction and Reconstruction of Religious Buildings*' (0006), '*Promotion of Religious Culture, Religious Freedoms and Tolerance*' (0007), as well as '*Pension, Disability and Health Insurance for Priests and Religious Officials*' (0008).[662] It specified that the body may allocate budget funds to religious entities through *three types of open competitions*: *public competition* (0007), *invited competition* (0001, 0003, 0004, 0005, 0006 and 0007) and *competition according to a special procedure and criteria based on the request of leaders of religious communities in unexpected and urgent situations* (0001, 0002 and 0005).[663] The *key criteria for allocation of funds* are the most *underdeveloped parts* of religious entities in the country, the *percentage of their believers* according to the last census, *priorities and current needs* presented to the Administration by religious entities themselves, as well as the *application of the principle of positive discrimination* of those 'minorities' in the function of their survival and promotion in the society.[664] When it comes to the *allocation of funds procedure*, it implies *announcing a regular and extraordinary open competition, reviewing submitted applications and documentation*, drafting a *draft decision by the commission to the director*, making a *decision by the director on the allocation and distribution of funds*, as well as *signing an agreement between the director and the head of the religious entity*. The Administration for Religions collects and controls reports on earmarked funds, on the basis of which the *Annual Report of the Administration on the intended use of funds for each programme activity is compiled at the end of each budget year*, as well as the *Report on the work of the* Administration as a whole.[665]

*250.* The Directive on Procedures, Internal Controls and Internal Control Procedures is, *in essence and according to the envisaged procedures*, fully harmonized and compatible with the mentioned *Government Regulation on Funds for encouraging programmes or the missing funds for financing programmes of public interest implemented by associations.* In this manner, the legality, efficiency, control, and transparency of the procedure for allocating budget funds to religious entities in the Republic of Serbia are fully ensured.

661. For example, Decisions of the Government on annulment of illegal acts of temporary self-government bodies in Kosovo and Metohija from 9 Mar. 2010, Official Gazette of RS, no. 19/2010, Resolution of the National Assembly of the Republic of Serbia on Basic Principles for Political Talks with Provisional Institutions of Self-Government in Kosovo and Metohija, Official Gazette of RS, nos 4/2013, etc.
662. *Source*: Administration for Religions of the Ministry of Justice of the Republic of Serbia.
663. For example, due to natural disasters and force majeure.
664. *Source*: Ministry of Justice.
665. *Source*: Administration for Religions, Ministry of Justice.

## Financial Support and Assistance to Churches and Religious Communities in the Republic of Serbia

*251.* Religious entities in the Republic of Serbia today are mostly financed from their own income. According to the Constitution of the *majority SOC*,[666] it is financed from *donations from worshipers* and from *renting land and real estate*, of which, based on the Law on Restitution from 2006, *nearly 80%* had been returned by the end of 2020.[667] It is expected that the entire process of returning property to religious entities in Serbia will be completed in the next several years. The issue of *financing the RCC* as a universal church organization is legally regulated primarily by the *Codex iuris canonici* of 1983. Specifically, the material aspect of the functioning of the RCC is defined by the 5th book of the Codex entitled 'On the temporal goods of the Church' (*De bonis ecclesiae temporalibus*). It authorized the Episcopal Conferences in different countries to pass legal regulations and apply them in the field, depending on the specific needs of the life and work of the Local Church. In the Republic of Serbia, the RCC is also primarily financed by *donations from worshipers* and *renting land and real estate* and regularly receives assistance from its 'headquarters' – the Holy See and the Vatican.[668] The *Islamic Community* operates and is financed pursuant to the provisions of its Constitution,[669] which, in a broader context, has a foothold in Sharia law. It also collects the *donations of worshipers during their lifetime* (waqf goods), *rent from movable and real property, regular contributions, obligations of believers to give a certain amount of their property* (zakat), *income from travel organization* (hajj and umrah), those from their various institutions, bequeaths of believers left to the community after death, etc. Finally, especially since the beginning of 2017, the *JC* in the Republic of Serbia is mostly financed on the basis of the aforementioned Law on Removal of Consequences of Confiscation of Property for Holocaust Victims Who Do Not Have Living Legal Descendants.

*252.* The essence of the material and financial aspect of the religious policy of the Republic of Serbia today comes down to the fact that it *does not finance* its religious entities but only *provides them with assistance in eliminating the historical injustice* inflicted on them by the atheist regime in the second half of the twentieth century. It will remain so *until the moment of completion of the process of returning property to religious entities* based on the Law on Restitution of Property to Churches and Religious Communities.[670] In accordance with the Budget Law in 2016,[671] in 2017[672] and 2018,[673] the Administration for Religions of the Ministry of Justice had at its disposal financial resources in the amount of about EUR *8.5 million* annually, which it distributed to churches and religious communities through

666. Constitution of the Serbian Orthodox Church 1957, https://www.unifr.ch/orthodoxia/de/assets/public/files/Dokumentation/Synodality/Serbia_Statutes.pdf, 7 Mar. 2024.
667. *Source*: Agency for Restitution of the Republic of Serbia.
668. Believers' contributions are not taxed, and the rental of real estate is.
669. More on: https://www.rijaset.rs/, and www.mesihat.org, 20 Sep. 2019.
670. Law on Restitution of Property to Churches and Religious Communities, *supra* n. 93.
671. Budget Law 2016, Official Gazette of RS, no. 103/2015.
672. Budget Law 2017, Official Gazette of RS, no. 99/2016.
673. Budget Law 2018, Official Gazette of RS, no. 113/2017.

the aforementioned *Programme Activities*, based on the already presented criteria (percentage of believers of religious entities, real needs on the ground and priorities presented to the competent state body, and positive discrimination against 'minority' communities). On this basis, in 2016–2018, the Administration distributed budget funds to religious entities in the following manner:

(1) the *SOC*, represented by 85.12% of the population, received close to 78% of the funds;
(2) *RCC*, represented by 4.99% of the population, received about 6% of the funds;
(3) the *Islamic Community* with about 3% of the population received 5.75% of the funds;
(4) although the grant was not realized through the Administration for Religions but directly through the Ministry of Finance of Serbia, based on the aforementioned Law on Removal of Consequences of Confiscation of Property for Holocaust Victims Who Do Not Have Living Legal Descendants, the *Union of Jewish Municipalities of Serbia,* starting 1 January 2017 shall for the following twenty-five years receive funds in the amount of EUR 950,000 annually;
(5) funds in the amount of 11.82% of the total budget were allocated to other religious communities, primarily to the Reformed Christian Church, the Slovak Evangelical Church and other Protestant communities.[674]

*253.* The Administration for Religions of the Ministry of Justice performs regular *analysis, control, and evaluation* of earmarked and through competition budget allocated funds to religious entities and on that basis projects a distribution plan for the following period. In that sense, it applies a prescribed, foreseen, and multidimensional system of control procedures and processes. Pursuant to the *Law on Accounting and Auditing from 2006,*[675] as well as all legal entities in Serbia, the body submits *regular financial annual reports to the Treasury Administration of the Ministry of Finance and the National Bank of Serbia.*[676] They process and publish them.[677] Also, pursuant to Articles 81–83 of the *Budget System Law*[678] and after the amendments to the *Rulebook on Systematization of Work Positions in the Ministry of Justice* in 2016 and 2019, the process of introducing the newly proclaimed system of supervision of budget spending: *Financial Management and Control* was intensified in the Administration for Religions. The goal of this body is to make a planned *Risk Management Strategy* with the aim of dealing with them as efficiently as possible and avoiding risks when allocating funds. When it comes to the transparency of the distribution of funds, all data of the Administration related to the financing of religious entities are available to the public. There have been no substantive objections from religious entities and civil society representatives in the past few years. The existence of minor problems is mainly caused by passivity in

674. *Source*: Administration for Religions of the Ministry of Justice.
675. Law on Accounting and Auditing from 2006, Official Gazette of RS, no. 46/2006.
676. Law on Accounting and Auditing from 2006, *supra* n. 675, Art. 30.
677. Law on Accounting and Auditing from 2006, *supra* n. 675, Arts 31 and 33.
678. Budget System Law, Official Gazette of RS, no. 99/2016.

terms of appearing and participating in open competitions, as well as attempts at abuse by 'informal groups' to gain legal status (to register) in order to obtain material benefits and profits.

*254.* It should be emphasized that 'minority' religious entities in the Republic of Serbia (RCC with the GCC, Reformed Christian Church, Evangelical Christian Church, Slovak Evangelical Church, as well as parts of the Islamic and Jewish Communities), whose members mostly live in the north of Serbia, in AP Vojvodina, receive additional and regular financial support from its Provincial Budget, through the *Provincial Secretariat for Culture, Public Information and Relations with Religious Communities*. Those from the territory of AP Vojvodina received *close to 50% of the budget* of the mentioned Provincial Secretariat through open competitions during 2017–2019.[679]

*255.* In accordance with the conditions provided by special regulations, religious entities in the Republic of Serbia may receive financial assistance and support from the state through other ministries: construction, transport, and infrastructure; science, education and technological development; labour, employment and social issues; Administration for Enforcement of Penal Sanctions of the Ministry of Justice; Administration for Diaspora of the Ministry of Foreign Affairs, etc.

*256.* In exceptional situations, direct financing of religious entities in the Republic of Serbia can also be made from *budget reserves* based on special *Conclusions of the Government of the Republic of Serbia*. This practice is applied only in exceptional cases that require the *necessary allocation of a larger amount of financial resources*, which, for example, far exceeds the annual budget of the Administration for Religions. Such cases are serious damage caused by natural disasters, construction, or renovation of religious buildings of exceptional importance on great historical anniversaries, marking of important church and religious holidays and manifestations, etc. For example, the Government of Serbia helped continue the construction of the SOC Memorial Church of St. Sava in Belgrade, with the aim of finally completing it after more than a century, and in the context of the great anniversaries of eight hundred years since obtaining of autocephaly by the SOC and one hundred years since the renewal of the Pec Patriarchate (2020). Also, the National Council of the Croatian National Minority received a larger amount of funds from the Government of Serbia for the purchase and renovation of the house where Ban Jelačić was born in Novi Sad who symbolizes the presence and preservation of the identity of this minority in Serbia. Finally, the Islamic communities have received this type of assistance on several occasions as well.

*257.* Religious entities pay tax liabilities for their economic activity, as do all other legal persons in Serbia. The *Companies Law*[680] prescribed the procedure for

679. *Source*: Provincial Secretariat for Culture, Public Information and Relations with Religious Communities of AP Vojvodina.

680. Companies Law, Official Gazette of the RS, nos 99/2011, 83/2014 – other law, 5/2015, 95/2018, and 91/2019.

acquiring the status of a legal entity and *registration of their economic activities*, status changes and liquidation. This also applies to *companies whose founders are religious entities*. With the entry into force of the *Law on the Registration Procedure in the Serbian Business Registers Agency*,[681] certain provisions of the Law on Associations related to registration *ceased to be valid*. Since this Law does not mention religious associations, the conclusion is that the *general regime of registration in the Register maintained by the Serbian Business Registers Agency applies to them*, as well as to all other legal entities that have financial resources and are engaged in economic activities. Therefore, all *registered religious entities that have registered economic activities* (wine production, pilgrimages organized by religious travel agencies, etc.) in accordance with the thematic regulations *pay taxes like all other economic entities in the Republic of Serbia*.

**Renovation and Construction of Religious Buildings in the Republic of Serbia**

*258.* Pursuant to the Law on Churches and Religious Communities,[682] the Budget System Law,[683] and the Budget Law of the Republic of Serbia,[684] during 2015–2020, the Administration for Religions of the Ministry of Justice implemented the programme activity ‘Support for the Construction and Renovation of Religious Buildings’, as part of its programme ‘Cooperation of the State with Churches and Religious Communities’. For the stated purposes and needs of religious entities in Serbia, a budget in the amount of about EUR *2.15 million* on an annual level was approved and realized. The *criteria for allocating funds* were the *significance and degree of endangerment* of the respective religious facility (including the extent of the threat to the safety of believers), the *material position of the religious entity* to which it belongs, the *level of development of the region* where the religious facility is located, whether it represents a *priority for renovation for the religious entity*, as well as whether the building is *under the protection of the state as its cultural treasure* (opinion and consent on this is given by the competent Institute for the Protection of Cultural Monuments). The Administration has defined the *strengthening of the religious and cultural identity of religious entities* through the construction, reconstruction, and repair of their religious buildings, especially in *underdeveloped areas of Serbia*, as the *principal goals of this programme activity*. The *main indicator* on which the programme was evaluated was the number of *started, completed, or repaired* religious buildings on an annual basis.

*259.* Activities for the renovation and construction of religious buildings in Serbia are also based on the thematic *Planning and Building Act*,[685] which, among other things, affirms the *principle of preservation of customs and traditions*.[686] For the application of the mentioned principle, in addition to the Ministry of Culture and

681. Law on Registration Procedure in the Serbian Business Registers Agency, *supra* n. 105.
682. Law on Churches and Religious Communities, *supra* n. 92, Art. 28, para. 2.
683. Budget System Law, *supra* n. 678, Art. 71.
684. Budget Law, *supra* n. 102, Art. 8.
685. Planning and Building Act, Official Gazette of the RS, nos 81/2009 – corr., 64/2010 – Decision US, 24/2011, 121/2012, 98/2013 – Decision US, 145/2014, 83/2018 and 37/2019.
686. Planning and Building Act, *supra* n. 685, Art. 3, para. 11.

the Administration for Religions of the Ministry of Justice, the Ministry of Construction, Transport and Infrastructure of Serbia is also responsible, as well as the bodies of the provincial and local self-government. Local self-government bodies are obliged to determine an *organizational unit* to implement a unified procedure for issuance of *site conditions*, issuance of building permit, notice of works and attainment of conditions for design and connecting the facility to the infrastructure network, as well as to *obtain all documentation* kept in the register of procedures.[687] The Serbian Business Registers Agency keeps a single, central, public, and electronic database in which all the above data for the territory of the Republic of Serbia are listed.[688] The construction of a religious building must be in compliance with *planning documents* on all levels of the Republic of Serbia (general ones adopted by the Government, regional and local spatial and urban plans).[689] *General and detailed regulation plans* for measures for protection of cultural and historical monuments are applied in the process[690] as well as *building rules* that also apply to religious buildings.[691] The competent authorities shall also determine the *location conditions* (urban, technical, etc.) necessary for the development of conceptual designs, design for construction permits and construction, and then issue a *construction cadastral parcel*[692] and *building land* for construction and use of facilities.[693] In accordance with this act, the construction of religious facilities is carried out based on a *building permit* and *technical documentation.*[694] The *Ministry of Construction* shall issue a *building permit* for facilities of immovable heritage of exceptional importance and cultural assets entered in the World Cultural and Natural Heritage List, as well as those located in their protected surroundings.[695] The *investor* submits to the Ministry the building design project[696] and provides *expert supervision during construction* through its commission.[697] The body of the local self-government unit for construction affairs is responsible for the eventual removal of the facility once a *decision* is issued after determining that the facility was illegally used or built.[698]

687. Planning and Building Act, *supra* n. 685, Art. 8.
688. Planning and Building Act, *supra* n. 685, Art. 8g.
689. Planning and Building Act, *supra* n. 685, Arts 11–24.
690. Planning and Building Act, *supra* n. 685, Art. 26, para. 7 and Art. 28, para. 7.
691. Planning and Building Act, *supra* n. 685, Art. 31.
692. Planning and Building Act, *supra* n. 685, Art. 53a.
693. Planning and Building Act, *supra* n. 685, Art. 82.
694. Planning and Building Act, *supra* n. 685, Art. 110.
695. Planning and Building Act, *supra* n. 685, Art. 133, para. 9.
696. Planning and Building Act, *supra* n. 685, Art. 135.
697. Planning and Building Act, *supra* n. 685, Arts 153–155.
698. Planning and Building Act, *supra* n. 685, Art. 167.

## Chapter 2. Indirect Financing of Religious Communities

*260. Indirect financing* of religious communities in the Republic of Serbia primarily implies *tax relief* that they enjoy. The Law on Churches and Religious Communities stipulates that religious entities may be *entirely or partially exempt from tax obligations* provided by the regulations if they perform the activity foreseen by this Law. This also applies to *legal and natural persons who give contributions to them.*[699]

*261. The Property Tax Law*[700] exempted all registered traditional churches and religious communities in the Republic of Serbia from paying property tax if the real estate is 'intended and exclusively used for the performance of religious ceremonies'. In particular, this applies to land, buildings and property that has been proclaimed *a cultural or historical monument*[701] as well *as heritage, gifts, endowments and registered associations dealing with public community work.*[702]

*262.* The *VAT Law*[703] prescribes *exemption from VAT for the supply of goods and services without the right to deduct the previous tax* in the case of 'rendering services of religious character by registered churches and religious communities and the directly related supply of goods and services'.[704]

*263.* The Rulebook on Procedure for Exercising the Right to VAT Refund[705] stipulates that VAT refunds to religious entities may be realized on the basis of requests submitted to the Central Office of the Tax Administration in the Ministry of Finance by authorized administrative bodies of the SOC, RCC, ICS, SECAV, JC, Reformed Christian Church and Evangelical Christian Church. Religious entities are also obliged to submit to the Central Office paid invoices for the procurement of goods and services (customs documents) and a written notice on the appointment of the administrative body authorized to submit a request for refund.[706] An invoice that has not been issued in accordance with the mentioned Law[707] and the Rulebook cannot be used in the procedure of VAT refund.[708] After ascertaining that all the necessary conditions for tax reimbursement have been met, the Central Office passes a decision on the request.[709]

---

699. Law on Churches and Religious Communities, *supra* n. 92, Art. 30, paras 1 and 2.
700. Property Tax Law, Official Gazette of RS, nos 26/2001, no. 80/2002, 135/2004, 61/2007, 5/2009, 101/2010, 78/2011, 57/2012.
701. Property Tax Law, *supra* n. 700, Arts 2 and 12, paras 1–3.
702. Property Tax Law, *supra* n. 700, Art. 21, para. 5a.
703. Law on Value Added Tax, *supra* n. 103.
704. Law on Value Added Tax, *supra* n. 103, Art. 25, para. 16.
705. Rulebook on Procedure for Exercising the Right to VAT Refund, Official Gazette of the RS, no. 67/2005.
706. Rulebook on Procedure for Exercising the Right to VAT Refund, *supra* n. 705, Art. 30, paras 3 and 4.
707. Rulebook on Procedure for Exercising the Right to VAT Refund, *supra* n. 705, Art. 42.
708. Rulebook on Procedure for Exercising the Right to VAT Refund, *supra* n. 705, Art. 3.
709. Rulebook on Procedure for Exercising the Right to VAT Refund, *supra* n. 705, Art. 4.

*264.* The Rulebook on Procedure for Exercising the Right to VAT Refund and on Method and Procedure of VAT Refund and Reimbursement[710] stipulates the right of the SOC, RCC, ICS, SECAV, JC, Reformed Christian Church and Evangelical Christian Church to VAT refund. Along with the request, the applicant also submits originals and copies of paid invoices for purchased goods and used services in the Republic of Serbia or abroad, as well as proof that VAT has been previously paid by the person entitled to a refund. After checking the conditions, the Central Office decides on the request. The Rulebook on Refund precisely defines that goods and services directly related to the performance of religious services include candles, incense, briquettes, oil, wine, flour and unleavened bread for ritual purposes, holy dishes and ritual symbols, vestments for priests and religious officials and materials used for their production, construction services and construction material for construction, refurbishing, conservation and restoration work and maintenance of places of worship and other facilities related to the missionary activity of religious entities, material for the production of iconostases and iconography, liturgical books, religious calendars, other religious editions, paper for printing of these editions, as well as the organ.[711]

*265.* Finally, pursuant to the Law on Republic Administrative Fees[712] all registered religious entities in Serbia are also exempt from paying this type of tax.[713]

710. Rulebook on Procedure for Exercising the Right to VAT Refund and on Method and Procedure of VAT Refund and Reimbursement, Official Gazette of RS, nos 107/2004, 65/2005, 63/2007 and 120/2012.
711. Rulebook on Procedure for Exercising the Right to VAT Refund and on Method and Procedure of VAT Refund and Reimbursement, *supra* n. 710, Art. 6a.
712. Law on Republic Administrative Fees, *supra* n. 252.
713. Law on Republic Administrative Fees, *supra* n. 252, Art. 18, para. 4a.

# Part IX. Education

*266.* The Law on the Education System[714] in the Republic of Serbia specifies that every citizen has an equal right to education, regardless of his religious affiliation.[715] It also prohibits discrimination on religious grounds.[716] In accordance with the law, the process of education in Serbia is conducted in the Serbian language and the languages of all national minorities.[717]

*267.* The *Law on Elementary Education*[718] stipulates that the school principal or the Minister of Education will 'remove a teacher from teaching until a decision is made in disciplinary proceedings *if he incites religious intolerance*' in the performance of his duty.[719]

*268.* The Law on Secondary Education[720] stipulates that the curriculum for religious instruction is adopted by agreement between the Minister of Education and the Minister of Religion, based on the agreed proposal of traditional churches and religious communities.[721] In that context, the Government of Serbia has formed a Commission for harmonization of proposals for religious education programmes, with the task of giving opinions and proposals to the Minister of Education for the development of textbooks and teaching aids, selection of advisors for religious education, as well as monitoring, organizing and implementing the curriculum.[722] Textbooks and teaching aids are approved by the Minister of Education on the agreed proposal of traditional churches and religious communities,[723] and religious instruction is an elective subject that the student chooses during enrolment in each subsequent grade.[724] The success of the student is assessed descriptively and does not affect the general Grade Point Average (GPA). Criteria and method of assessment, as well as the type and level of education of teachers of religion, are determined by

714. Law on the Education System, Official Gazette of the RS, nos 55/2013, 88/2017, 27/2018 and 6/2020.
715. Law on the Education System, *supra* n. 714, Art. 6.
716. Law on the Education System, *supra* n. 714, Art. 44.
717. Law on the Education System, *supra* n. 714, Art. 9.
718. Law on Elementary Education, *supra* n. 99.
719. Law on Elementary Education, *supra* n. 99, Art. 73.
720. Law on Secondary Education, *supra* n. 100.
721. Law on Secondary Education, *supra* n. 100, Art. 24, para. 2.
722. Law on Secondary Education, *supra* n. 100, Art. 24, para. 3.
723. Law on Secondary Education, *supra* n. 100, Art. 25.
724. Law on Secondary Education, *supra* n. 100, Art. 27.

the Minister of Education on a joint proposal of the Ministry of Religion and traditional churches and religious communities.[725] Finally, the list of teachers of religion is determined by the Minister of Education at the proposal of traditional religious entities in Serbia, from which they are selected and sent to duty in schools.[726] Religious entities, in accordance with autonomous internal regulations, appoint and dismiss teachers of religion themselves, starting from their legal principles and missionary goals and interests. The competent Minister of Education makes a decision based on their guidelines and requirements. Specifically, at the beginning of each school year, religious entities in Serbia send their lists and proposals with the names of teachers of religion, which they can change themselves from year to year for a certain position. The state authorities do not enter into the consideration of the issue of correctness and 'moral' grounding of the decisions of religious entities in this case, and as a rule, accept them if the person has not violated state regulations and procedures on any grounds.

*269.* The *Law on Higher Education*[727] stipulates that all persons who have passed the general, professional, or artistic graduation exam have the right to higher education in Serbia.[728] The National Council for Higher Education determines the standards and procedure for accreditation of higher education institutions[729] which may be established by the Republic of Serbia and *other legal or natural persons*.[730] At its own request, and after obtaining a work permit from the Ministry of Education, a higher education institution may begin its activities,[731] while *no religious organizations and their activities are allowed in a higher education institution*.[732]

*270.* The state education system in Serbia and its institutions have a *secular character*.

725. Law on Secondary Education, *supra* n. 100, Art. 48.
726. Law on Secondary Education, *supra* n. 100, Art. 70.
727. Law on Higher Education, *supra* n. 101.
728. Law on Higher Education, *supra* n. 101, Art. 9.
729. Law on Higher Education, *supra* n. 101, Art. 12.
730. Law on Higher Education, *supra* n. 101, Art. 51.
731. Law on Higher Education, *supra* n. 101, Art. 52.
732. Law on Higher Education, *supra* n. 101, Art. 43.

## Chapter 1. Religious Education in Public and Private Schools

*271.* The second part of the Third Chapter of the Law on Churches and Religious Communities regulates the issue of educational activities of religious communities in the Republic of Serbia. The law stipulates that they may also establish appropriate educational institutions with the aim of educating future priests and religious officials and improving spiritual and theological culture in the country.[733] Religious entities may establish preschool institutions, elementary schools, grammar schools, technical and artistic secondary and high schools, faculties and universities.[734] General regulations on education in Serbia give religious educational institutions the opportunity to be incorporated into the state education system, that is, to obtain accreditation with the competent authorities, after which they acquire the right to financing from the state budget in proportion to the number of believers according to the last census. The Law on Churches and Religious Communities provides for the possibility of allocating state financial assistance to religious educational institutions that are not included in the general education system if it is assessed that their work is of common interest.[735] In accordance with constitutional and legal principles, religious educational institutions have organizational and curricular autonomy, which means autonomously determining the curriculum, textbooks and reference literature, appointing and dismissing teaching and other staff, as well as supervising their own work. Those incorporated in the state educational system are obliged to observe conditions and standards of its general regulations.[736] Certificates and diplomas of verified and accredited religious educational institutions are equal and have the same legal effect as those from state institutions, while certificates and diplomas acquired in other religious educational institutions may have, upon determining equivalence before the competent state authority, the same legal effect as corresponding certificates and diplomas acquired in state educational institutions.[737] Full-time pupils and students of religious educational institutions are entitled to health care and social insurance, students' standard and delay of military service, while their parents have the right to child support under the same conditions that apply to pupils and students of state educational institutions.[738] The Law on Churches and Religious Communities guarantees all students in Serbia the right to attend religious instruction in all state (public) and private elementary and secondary schools.[739]

*272.* The Regulation on the Organization and Realization of Religious Instruction and Teaching of Alternative Subjects in Elementary and Secondary Schools

733. Law on Churches and Religious Communities, *supra* n. 92, Art. 34.
734. Law on Churches and Religious Communities, *supra* n. 92, Art. 35.
735. Law on Churches and Religious Communities, *supra* n. 92, Art. 36.
736. Law on Churches and Religious Communities, *supra* n. 92, Art. 37.
737. Law on Churches and Religious Communities, *supra* n. 92, Art. 38.
738. Law on Churches and Religious Communities, *supra* n. 92, Art. 39.
739. Law on Churches and Religious Communities, *supra* n. 92, Art. 40.

from 2001[740] enabled the organization and implementation of religious instruction of traditional churches and religious communities and civic education in all elementary and secondary schools in Serbia, as mandatory elective alternative subjects.[741] In the case of elementary school, the parent or guardian decides which of them the child will attend, while in secondary school, the decision is made by the pupil, and the parent or guardian is informed of the decision.[742] When a student opts for religious instruction, it becomes a compulsory subject for him in that school year,[743] and it is implemented for all traditional religious subjects in the country, regardless of a number of worshipers in the particular milieu.[744] The curriculum of religious instruction forms part of the prescribed curriculum for elementary and secondary school, and it is adopted by agreement of the Ministers of Education and Religion with agreement from the religious community.[745] Textbooks and teaching aids are approved by the Minister of Education in agreement with the religious community.[746] Religious instruction may be conducted by a person with at least higher education for students up to the fourth grade of elementary school and with a university degree for students from fourth to eighth grade of elementary and all secondary schools. The decision on the type and level of professional education of teachers is determined by the Minister of Education in a joint proposal with the body responsible for religion and religious communities. At their proposal, the Minister of Education determines the list of teachers of religion from which they are chosen during each school year.[747] The Ministry of Education provides each religious teacher with a gross fee from the budget for the hired number of hours, which it pays through the religious entity that hired him, their number of hours being one hour per week. The regulation stipulates that the success of students in both alternative subjects is assessed descriptively and does not affect their general GPA. The criteria and method of assessment are determined by the Minister of Education on a joint proposal of the Ministry of Religion and religious communities,[748] and the Ministry of Education supervises the implementation of the curriculum.[749]

---

740. Regulation on the Organization and Realization of Religious Instruction and Teaching of Alternative Subjects in Elementary and Secondary Schools from 2001, Official Gazette of RS, no. 46/2001.
741. Regulation on the Organization and Realization of Religious Instruction and Teaching, *supra* n. 740, Art. 1.
742. Regulation on the Organization and Realization of Religious Instruction and Teaching, *supra* n. 740, Art. 2.
743. Regulation on the Organization and Realization of Religious Instruction and Teaching, *supra* n. 740, Art. 3.
744. Regulation on the Organization and Realization of Religious Instruction and Teaching, *supra* n. 740, Art. 4.
745. Regulation on the Organization and Realization of Religious Instruction and Teaching, *supra* n. 740, Art. 5.
746. Regulation on the Organization and Realization of Religious Instruction and Teaching, *supra* n. 740, Art. 7.
747. Regulation on the Organization and Realization of Religious Instruction and Teaching, *supra* n. 740, Art. 8.
748. Regulation on the Organization and Realization of Religious Instruction and Teaching, *supra* n. 740, Art. 11.
749. Regulation on the Organization and Realization of Religious Instruction and Teaching, *supra* n. 740, Art. 12.

*273.* The teaching of religious and civic education in the first grade of elementary and secondary school in the Republic of Serbia began in the school year 2001/2002.[750] Their organization and implementation are monitored and coordinated by the mentioned *Government Commission for Religious Education*, which is elected for six years. It consists of one representative (mostly heads or bishops) of traditional churches and religious communities (SOC, RCC, ICS, SECAV, Evangelical Christian Church and Reformed Christian Church, as well as the JC), and three representatives each of the Ministry of Education and the Ministry of Religion (now the Ministry of Justice).[751] The Ministry of Education of the Republic of Serbia is responsible for *supervising the implementation of the Regulation.*

*274.* Children of members of traditional churches have been attending religious education regularly and in increasing numbers in elementary and secondary schools in Serbia since 2001. When *creating the modalities of religious instruction*, the competent state bodies (Ministry of Education and Ministry of Religion) annually consult primarily the religious entities themselves (the heads and their professional associates) but also members of the professional public (professors in the field of law, psychology, political science, etc.) and the students themselves. During the introduction of religious education in the state education system, they all reached a very high level of agreement on the issue of the model that should be introduced, which was subsequently accepted by the Government of the Republic of Serbia. It is on these grounds that the mentioned Regulation was passed in 2001. In the second decade of the twenty-first century, the adopted principles are applied in accordance with the needs of each school year. If they want, the children of members of traditional Protestant churches (SECAV, Evangelical Christian and Reformed Christian churches) and JC have the opportunity to attend religious education in schools. In practice, it is organized in such a way that during the annual sessions of the Government Commission for Religious Education, a teacher is appointed by the head or authorized representative of the respective religious entity for a *minimum of five students who have expressed interest in attending it.* At the same time, for organizational and technical reasons, it is desirable that the mentioned five students live relatively close to each other to be able to attend this subject in the same place once a week. During the sessions of the mentioned Commission before each school year, this issue is jointly considered, harmonized, and precisely determined.

*275.* After the introduction of religious education in the state education system in the Republic of Serbia, several expert analyses and evaluations of its results were performed at the ministerial and educational levels. They were mostly positive, with a constant increase of interest in religious education among elementary and secondary school students, as well as the strengthening of the reputation and influence of teachers of religion themselves within the entire academic community in Serbia.

---

750. Regulation on the Organization and Realization of Religious Instruction and Teaching, *supra* n. 740, Art. 13.

751. Regulation on the Organization and Realization of Religious Instruction and Teaching, *supra* n. 740, Art. 14.

*276.* During the two decades of religious education, a great contribution to the preservation and development of the *religious, historical, national and cultural identity* of the Serbian people and all national minorities in Serbia has been made, as important strongholds and preconditions for its social development and European integration process.

## Chapter 2. Religious Schools in Serbia

*277.* In parallel with the process of returning religious education as an optional and then compulsory elective subject in elementary and secondary schools in the Republic of Serbia since 2001, the *Orthodox Theological Faculty, University of Belgrade (OTF) of the SOC was restored to Belgrade University*, from which it was excluded in 1952.

*278.* In the first decade of the twenty-first century, over 2100 students (graduate theologians) graduated from OTF. While preparing, among other things, for the *vocation of a religious teacher*, students were obliged to hold three to five hours of *practical classes in public schools*. In addition, they were given the opportunity to attend up to ten hours of professional practice in public schools instead of writing a graduate thesis. Within today's OTF, along with several other specialized ones, there is also the Catechetic Pedagogical Institute, which deals with *teaching issues* in the Republic of Serbia and the diaspora. It also publishes the magazine 'Religious Teacher at School'. Central seminars are also held at the faculty during the school year, in which *teachers of religion* also participate. They discuss current and practical issues and problems of religious education. In the second decade of the twenty-first century, compared to the first, the number of OTF graduates has doubled. To date, close to 4,000 of them have participated in religious instruction in Serbia, after which one part was ordained and transferred to other jobs in the country and abroad in accordance with the guidelines and needs of the Church. The *Higher School of Art and Conservation* from Belgrade is a *higher education institution of the SOC* in Serbia, which educates and profiles professional staff for several disciplines of sacred art. After graduation, they mostly deal with icon painting and artistic decoration of religious buildings (churches, monasteries, chapels, auxiliary religious buildings, etc.), especially for the SOC, but also, if necessary, other religious entities in Serbia and abroad. The *Faculty of 'St. Vasilije Ostroški' in Foča* is also a higher education institution of the SOC.

*279.* When it comes to *high school institutions* of the SOC, there are five: Theological Seminary 'St. Sava' in Belgrade, 'St. Arsenije Sremac' in Sremski Karlovci, 'St. John Chrysostom' in Kragujevac, as well as two with the same name, 'Saints Cyril and Methodius' in Prizren and Nis.[752] 'Sveta tri Jeraha' in the Monastery of Krk (Dalmatia, Republic of Croatia), 'Kantakuzina Branković' (Zagreb, Republic of Croatia) and 'Sveti Petar Cetinjski' (Cetinje, Republic of Montenegro) represent theological schools of SOC outside the borders of Serbia. All of them have existed for centuries, and they are symbols of survival and life for the Serbian population there.

752. In fact, they represent one institution, the famous Prizren seminary, whose division is due to the expulsion of professors and students from this city in Kosovo and Metohija in 1999. Most of them today live, teach and work in Niš. Some of the bravest, despite extremely difficult living conditions, remained in Prizren seminary, which was damaged during the ethnically motivated violence against Serbs in Kosovo and Metohija in 2004 and were only recently renovated.

**Religious Education of Members of National Minorities**

*280.* Members of national minorities in Serbia fully exercise their freedom of religion in the field of *education.* If they want, the children of members of national minorities have had the opportunity to attend religious education of the community to which they belong in elementary and secondary schools for nearly twenty years. Most *children belonging to national minorities* today *attend religious classes* in the Republic of Serbia. This also includes public schools. The RCC participates together with the GCC (*for Hungarians, Croats, Bunjevaks, Sokci, Czechs, Germans, Slovaks, Ukrainians and Ruthenians*), ICofS and ICinS (for *Bosniaks, Albanians, Roma, Egyptians, Ashkali and Gorani*), SECAV (*Slovaks*), the Reformed Christian Church (for *Hungarians*), JC (for *Jews*), and the Diocese of the RPC 'Dacia Felix' (for *Romanians*). It is important to emphasize that the SOC, at the request of parents and students, organizes religious education for the majority of Orthodox believers in Serbia who are not Serbs, such as *Roma, Vlachs, Bulgarians, Macedonians and Montenegrins*. Members of the mentioned national minorities of the Orthodox faith have long declared themselves as members of the SOC, in which they are baptized, married, and buried.

*281.* The school system of the RCC in Serbia consists of the *Theological and Catechetical Institute of the Diocese of Subotica* as a higher education institution, established by the decision of the Bishop of Subotica in 1993. Its classes are conducted in *Hungarian and Croatian*, educating and preparing candidates for teachers of religion and other services in the RCC. The institute is attended by about 140 full-time students from Serbia and the surrounding countries. The RCC plans for it to grow into a faculty and join the University of Novi Sad over the next few years. Of the secondary schools in Serbia, the RCC has the *Episcopal Classical Gymnasium 'Paulinum' in Subotica*, founded in 1962. It also has bilingual classes, with sixteen professors and about eighty students from Serbia, the Republic of Hungary and Slavonia (Croatia). Since February 2004, the high school has been *accredited* and included in the state education system in Serbia. Finally, the RCC also owns the *Theological Seminary 'Augustinianum' in Subotica*, which was founded in 2003.

*282.* The *ICofS school system* consists of the *Faculty of Islamic Studies in Novi Pazar* as a higher education institution. It traditionally has good cooperation with several Islamic educational institutions from around the world, primarily from North Africa and the Middle East. ICofS has four madrassas as secondary schools. *The Belgrade Islamic Madrasa* was founded in 2001, and the fifth generation of students will soon complete their education. Over twenty professors of various professional profiles make up its teaching staff, and the students are young Islamic theologians from all over Serbia. The well-known *'Sinan – beg' Madrasa in Novi Pazar, 'Tutin Madrasa' in Tutin*, as well as the women's *'Bakija Hanume' Madrasa in Prijepolje* also operate within the ICofS.

*283.* The ICinS school system consists of the *Faculty of Islamic Studies*, which has been operating within the International University of Novi Pazar since 2005. It arose on the foundations of the previous Islamic Pedagogical Academy. The faculty is attended by a relatively small number of students, and its teaching staff consists of professors and lecturers hired from other faculties, including those from BiH. ICinS has two secondary schools: *Gazi Isabeg Madrasa* and the *Women's Madrasa* in Novi Pazar. The Women's Madrasa has existed since 1996 and has had a department in Rožaje (Republic of Montenegro) since 2002.

*284*. Traditional Protestant churches (SECAV, Evangelical Christian and Reformed Christian churches) and JCS do not have their own educational institutions in the Republic of Serbia because they have few members, which is why they never submitted a request for their establishment.

# Part X. Matrimonial and Family Law

*285.* The *Family Law* in the Republic of Serbia from 2015[753] prescribed the right and duty of parents to provide the child with elementary education, as well as education that is in accordance with their *religious and ethical beliefs*.[754]

753. Family Law 2015, *supra* n. 107.
754. Family Law 2015, *supra* n. 107, Art. 71.

## Chapter 1. The Legal Position of Religious Marriage

*286.* The Byzantine emperors passed laws that regulated marriage issues,[755] and the *Nomocanon of St. Sava* and the *Law of the pious Emperor Stefan* contain many regulations on marriage for Serbs.[756] In the period of communist Yugoslavia in the second half of the twentieth century, the institution of marriage was completely secularized, which, as it turned out, had negative consequences for both the state and the Church.

*287.* On the *issue of marriage*, the Resolution of the Sixth Congress of Yugoslav Lawyers in Zagreb in 1934 proposed that material and personal property marriage law be 'urgently' regulated by state law as equal for all, that *compulsory civil marriage* be introduced, that registries be run by state authorities, and marital disputes resolved exclusively by state courts.[757] According to the Constitution of the FPRY from January 1946, *marriage became the responsibility of the state*,[758] whereby the *Marriage Act* of April 1946 recognized all marriages entered into in the Church by the beginning of May of that year. This law *left all citizens the possibility of marriage in the Church, but only after a civil marriage.*[759] *This rule is still valid in the Republic of Serbia.*

755. Перић Димшо, Црквено право, Правни факултет Универзитета у Београду, 2006.
756. *Nomocanon* or *Krmčmija*, is another name for the most famous work of Saint Sava 'Zakonopravilo' – the first source of both church and state law in today's Serbia.
757. V. Bakić, Family Law in SFRY, Belgrade, 1982, p. 71, quoted in: Перић, *supra* n. 755, 277.
758. Constitution of the Federal People's Republic of Yugoslavia, Art. 26, https://bs.wikisource.org/wiki/Ustav_Federativne_Narodne_Republike_Jugoslavije_(1946), 20 Feb. 2019.
759. Law on Marriage and Family Relations, Official Gazette of SR Serbia, nos 22/1980, 24/1984, 11/1988, 25/1993, 35/1994, 46/1995, 29/2001.

## Chapter 2. Legal Position of Religious Family Law

*288.* The current Family Law in the Republic of Serbia,[760] after the conclusion of a civil marriage, respects and acknowledges all the conditions and provisions of the SOC on the occasion and for the purpose of concluding a church marriage. Citizens in Serbia can get married in the Church (religious community) and/or before a state body (registrar in the Municipality), depending on their own will and decision. According to the valid Family Law, the state recognizes as a marriage only the one concluded before the state body (registrar), which, at the same time, the spouses can conclude in the Church subsequently. Thus, there are separate ceremonies for civil and ecclesiastical marriage. However, for the Church, only the marriage concluded in the Church is recognized as 'valid and sanctified' – a covenant before God. The Marriage Rules of the Serbian Orthodox Church[761] define church marriage as a holy mystery by which 'two persons of different gender are united in spirit and body for the purpose of a life union and having children'.[762] Unlike civil marriage, the spouses express their will before the priest in the temple, in the presence of witnesses and parents. In addition, unlike civil, church marriage cannot be concluded during fasts and fasting days[763] as well as passing the premarital exam in order to better and more responsibly prepare the spouses for the wedding. During such an examination, the priest checks and determines whether they understand the essence and meaning of church marriage, whether they enter it freely, whether they have basic knowledge about the teachings of the Church, as well as whether there are certain obstacles or prohibitions for marriage. Witnesses at the wedding must be of legal age, baptized and persons of the Orthodox faith.[764]

*289.* According to the teachings of the SOC, *obstacles to church marriage* can be *irremovable* (as in state law, persons under the age of 18 cannot marry, in the case of *blood kinship all provisions of the state Family Law are also accepted by the Marriage Rules of the Serbian Orthodox Church*, kinship by adoption, existing marriage, previous four marriages of one person, etc.) and *removable* (under eighteen for male and sixteen for female, collateral blood relation from five to seven degrees, double relationship from four to six degrees, triple relationship up to three degrees, spiritual kinship and kinship by adoption from three to seven degrees, annulled marriage until it is terminated by a court, previous three marriages of the same person, *different religion with decision brought by the Bishop*, adultery after one year from the final judgment, age over 70 for a male and over 60 for a female, as well as the difference in the age of the spouse over fifteen).[765]

760. Family Law 2015, *supra* n. 107.
761. Marriage Rules of the Serbian Orthodox Church, http://www.rastko.rs/bogoslovlje/bracna-pravila/index.html, 25 Feb. 2018.
762. Marriage Rules of the Serbian Orthodox Church, *supra* n. 761, Art. 1.
763. Marriage Rules of the Serbian Orthodox Church, *supra* n. 761, Art. 65 lists the periods of fasting during Christmas, Easter, Peter and Paul fast as well as Dormition of the Mother of God fast, certain daily church holidays, as well as Wednesday and Friday.
764. Marriage Rules of the Serbian Orthodox Church, *supra* n. 761, Art. 67.
765. More in: Перић, *supra* n. 755, 281–288.

290. *Marital prohibitions* on church marriage, as insignificant shortcomings, *can be removed or resolved.* Examples are the prohibition of marriage for a widow one year after the death of the husband, lack of parental consent, marriage without passing a proper premarital examination, marriage within six months after the premarital examination, blessing (consent) of the Bishop or priest, marriage at a time that prohibits Church, etc.[766]

291. The *rights and duties of the spouses in the case of a church marriage are almost the same as in a civil marriage* and relate to the obligation to cultivate mutual love, fidelity and help to overcome all difficulties in the marriage. The differences are the provisions of the Marriage Rules of the Serbian Orthodox Church, which define the husband as 'the *head of the family* who has the right and duty to manage the marital union', as well as to 'maintain it'. In accordance with the above, the wife is 'obliged to live with her husband in the place he chooses if it is not contrary to law and moral obligations', to 'assist the husband in running the house and household chores', and especially to '*dedicate herself to childbirth, care and upbringing*'.[767] In this context, *spouses cannot demand from each other not to have children.* When it comes to the duties and rights of spouses towards children, *everything that is prescribed by the state legislation is also valid in the church marriage law.* The difference relates to the task of parents who have a church marriage to *baptize their children in the Orthodox faith within one month after birth,* to *educate them in the spirit of Orthodox morality,* as well as to *teach them to perform all the duties of SOC believers from an early age.*[768]

292. There are *two groups of reasons for the termination of a church marriage: without a verdict* (on the day when the state authorities declare the spouse dead and at the ordination of the husband to the rank of Bishop) and *with a verdict of the Church Court* (in the case of adultery, abortion, malicious abandonment and disappearance of a spouse, physical and mental illness, moral depravity, as well as apostasy from the Orthodox faith).[769] A divorced person cannot marry during the temporary exclusion from the church community for the stated reasons. It is important to emphasize that according to the Marriage Rules of the Serbian Orthodox Church, an *Orthodox believer can enter into a mixed marriage* provided that the spouse of another faith declares in writing that they will not deter the spouse from the Orthodox faith and request conversion to another religion and that the children from the marriage can be brought up in the Orthodox faith. Such a marriage must be concluded in an Orthodox Church by an Orthodox priest and according to an

766. More in: Перић, *supra* n. 755, 288–290.
767. Marriage Rules of the Serbian Orthodox Church, *supra* n. 761, Art. 69. This provision is not opposed but more precisely elaborated in accordance with the 'vertical and moral' nature and goals of church marriage, and refers, of course, exclusively to cases that do not jeopardize the dignity and the whole set of human rights of the spouse (right to life, health, freedom of movement, employment, etc.).
768. Marriage Rules of the Serbian Orthodox Church, *supra* n. 761, Art. 74.
769. More in: Перић, *supra* n. 755, 292–296.

Orthodox rite. Children from a mixed marriage must be baptized in the Orthodox faith if one of the parents is an Orthodox believer.[770]

*293.* For Orthodox people who live in an extramarital relationship (concubinage), the Church is obliged to ensure that they get married in it over time, and if they cannot, they should separate. Children from the mentioned relationship, if they are not legalized according to state laws, are considered illegal, and the Church has an obligation to try to baptize and educate them in the Orthodox faith. In a church marriage, children can be from *marital* (whose parents married in the temple), *civil marriage* (whose parents entered into a civil marriage), *extramarital* (parents are not in any type of marriage) and *adopted* (in accordance with the conditions of the state and church laws). The marriage of parents in the Church results in the *recognition of the community and children as married based on a decision of the Church Court.*[771]

*294.* An Orthodox believer who initiates divorce proceedings before the Church Court *must first be divorced before a civil court* and submit the ruling. However, in the whole process, according to the Constitution of the SOC, the parish priest is obliged to try to reconcile the spouses and inform the Church Court, which tries to do the same regardless of the civil court ruling.[772] Only if the mentioned efforts do not bear fruit, the Church Court divorces the spouses in terms of church law. It is obvious that ecclesiastical law more intensively defends the institution of marriage than civil law. The provisions of Church law are not automatically recognized in the state-legal (civil) system of the Republic of Serbia. In the case of a specific issue, in practice, divorce is incomparably easier (in terms of time) to obtain before a civil court since the Church always gives 'extra time' to spouses to attempt to smooth relations and keep the 'sacred secret' to which they themselves 'forever vowed' in the Church, before God. This, however, hypothetically, does not mean that the civil court would automatically accept the decision on the divorce of the Church Court, but it would have to make its own decision. As a rule, a marriage can only be divorced before the body before which it was concluded. Thus, there are separate procedures for the divorce of civil and church marriages, and they are applied on a case-by-case basis.

770. More in: Перић, *supra* n. 755, 296–298.
771. More in: Перић, *supra* n. 755, 298–299.
772. Serbian Orthodox Church Constitution, Art. 176, item 12, https://sr.m.wikisource.org/sr-ec/Ustav_Srpske_pravoslavne_crkve, 09 Jan. 2017.

# Part XI. Religion and Culture

*295.* Starting with the constitutional principle of respecting and nurturing various aspects of the identity of its citizens,[773] the Republic of Serbia undertakes numerous measures, programmes, and projects in the field of culture. Their realization should contribute to becoming acquainted, building trust and enhancing the cooperation of all citizens of Serbia, including those who belong to *different religions.*

*296.* The *Law on Cultural Property*[774] defined that cultural properties of Serbia are also 'creations of *spiritual culture of general interest* that enjoy special protection established by law'. In that sense, depending on their importance, cultural property in Serbia is classified as *cultural property, cultural property of great importance and cultural property of exceptional importance.*[775] The National Assembly of Serbia determines those of exceptional importance, the Government of great importance, and the National Museum in Belgrade, the Archives of Serbia, the National Library of Serbia and the Yugoslav Film Archive on *movable cultural property* of great importance.[776] All goods are entered in the *public register of cultural property*[777] which are managed by competent protection institutions according to their *type*[778] and based on requests.[779] Competent state bodies and organizations are obliged to keep, classify, and archive registration material.[780] Cultural properties may change their appearance, features, or purpose only with approval from said institutions.[781] Their protection is performed by *institutions established specially for that purpose,*[782] that is by institutes for the *protection of cultural monuments, museums, archives, and film archives.*[783]

*297. Institutes for the Protection of Cultural Monuments* protect cultural monuments, archaeological sites, and significant places; *museums* conserve artistic-historic works; *archives* conserve archive and registry material, while the *film*

773. Constitution of the Republic of Serbia from 2006, *supra* n. 4, Art. 48.
774. Law on Cultural Property, Official Gazette of the RS, nos 71/1994 and 99/2011.
775. Law on Cultural Property, *supra* n. 774, Art. 2, para. 3.
776. Law on Cultural Property, *supra* n. 774, Art. 56.
777. Law on Cultural Property, *supra* n. 774, Art. 6.
778. Law on Cultural Property, *supra* n. 774, Art. 60.
779. Law on Cultural Property, *supra* n. 774, Art. 59.
780. Law on Cultural Property, *supra* n. 774, Art. 37.
781. Law on Cultural Property, *supra* n. 774, Art. 7.
782. Law on Cultural Property, *supra* n. 774, Arts 10 and 102.
783. Law on Cultural Property, *supra* n. 774, Art. 70.

*archive* preserves all film material.[784] In addition, institutes for the protection of cultural monuments prepare studies on cultural properties, participate in the process of preparing spatial and urban plans in which they are located, and publish material on implemented works and reconstruction.[785] The *owner of cultural property* is obliged to keep and maintain it, implement the prescribed protection measures, report to the competent institution on changes to the property, allow scientific and professional research, promote the property to the public, and bear the expense for all mentioned obligations up to the sum of income he receives from it.[786] The *Government of Serbia* shall, by an act on the respective cultural property, systematize the data related to the border of its protected environment (cadastral and land), and compile a list of *movable cultural property of special and historical significance* that the mentioned property possesses.[787]

*298.* *Measures of technical protection of cultural properties* include works on their conservation, restoration, reconstruction, revitalization, and presentation, as well as the change of form which is possible only based on prescribed conditions and obtained the consent of competent authorities.[788] Undertaking protective measures on *immovable heritage* and *those of great importance* are determined and permitted by the *competent institute for the protection of cultural monuments*, while the *Republic Institute for the Protection of Cultural Monuments* prepares projects and gives consent for their implementation in the case of *cultural properties of exceptional importance*.[789] The *Ministry of Culture* establishes conditions for protection of cultural property of *exceptional importance*.[790] For entities that damage or destroy a cultural property that enjoys the protection of the state, or those that do not preserve and implement the established protection measures, numerous fines are prescribed.[791]

*299.* Statistical data shows that today in the Republic of Serbia, the *SOC* has 106 religious buildings that belong to the category of immovable heritage of exceptional importance (of which thirty-one are in KiM), 235 of great importance and 316 cultural properties. *RCC* owns two religious buildings of exceptional cultural significance (in Čoka and Subotica), thirty-three of great importance and sixteen cultural properties. *ICS* has four of exceptional importance (three are in KiM), two of great importance and four cultural properties. *Protestant churches* (SECAV and the Reformed Christian Church) have two buildings of great importance and eleven cultural properties. JC owns one synagogue of exceptional importance (in Belgrade) and one cultural property.[792] Finally, the ROC 'Dacia Felix' has one building of

784. Law on Cultural Property, *supra* n. 774, Art. 74.
785. Law on Cultural Property, *supra* n. 774, Art. 75.
786. Law on Cultural Property, *supra* n. 774, Art. 31.
787. Law on Cultural Property, *supra* n. 774, Art. 47.
788. Law on Cultural Property, *supra* n. 774, Art. 99.
789. Law on Cultural Property, *supra* n. 774, Art. 100.
790. Law on Cultural Property, *supra* n. 774, Art. 101.
791. Law on Cultural Property, *supra* n. 774, Arts 130–134.
792. In addition, the Subotica Synagogue, built in 1902, was placed on the list of most endangered buildings by the UNESCO World Heritage Centre towards the end of the twentieth century. Also, the

exceptional importance (in Kovačica), three of great importance (in Zrenjanin, Bela Crkva and Vršac) and one cultural property in Serbia.[793]

*300.* The third part of the Third Chapter of the Law on Churches and Religious Communities regulates the issue of *cultural activities* of religious entities in Serbia. Bearers of cultural and scientific activities of churches and religious communities are *monasteries, treasuries, museums, archives, scientific-research institutions, libraries, specialized schools, artistic conservation and restoration workshops, cultural-artistic clubs, choirs* and other institutions and associations.[794] Religious buildings and institutions of special historical, national, and cultural significance enjoy special *protection, care, and financial* support by the state and local self-administration authorities.[795] In order to contribute to the *protection and development of sacral heritage* within a uniform system of protection, religious entities may establish both *professional and scientific institutions*. After the accreditation (verification) process, they have the opportunity to enjoy financial subsidies from the state or local self-administrative budget.[796] In accordance with the Constitution and the law, cultural institutions of religious entities have the right to *organize independent informative and publishing activities and use of public broadcasting services*, especially if their activity serves to promote religious freedoms in Serbia and freedom of information of religious entities. Religious entities are obliged to inform the public about their informative and publishing activities and inform them about their content.[797] Cultural and scientific institutions and programmes of churches and religious communities may also be financed and subsidized by the competent state and local authorities,[798] through the mentioned open competitions and under the same conditions as for all other legal and natural persons.[799]

*301.* Along with the competent Ministry of Culture and Information, local self-administration authorities and other institutions, part of the programmes and activities related to the protection and promotion of *spiritual cultural properties* in the Republic of Serbia are also implemented by the Administration for Religions of the Ministry of Justice. It also finances activities that stimulate religious entities to engage in the field of *cultural, social, scientific, informative and publishing activities*. Thus, the highest representatives of religious entities from the country participated recently in the work of numerous scientific symposia and round tables, which discussed the development of religious rights and freedoms and their application in

organizations 'Evropa Nostra' and the European Investment Bank put this building on the list of seven most endangered buildings of exceptional cultural importance in 2014. The reconstruction of the building, which was put into operation again in 2015, was assisted by the Governments of Serbia and Hungary, UNESCO World Heritage Centre, AP Vojvodina and the city of Subotica.

793. *Source*: Ministry of Culture and Information of the Republic of Serbia.
794. Law on Churches and Religious Communities, *supra* n. 92, Art. 41.
795. Law on Churches and Religious Communities, *supra* n. 92, Art. 41, para. 2.
796. Law on Churches and Religious Communities, *supra* n. 92, Art. 42.
797. Law on Churches and Religious Communities, *supra* n. 92, Art. 43.
798. Law on Churches and Religious Communities, *supra* n. 92, Art. 44, para. 1.
799. Law on Churches and Religious Communities, *supra* n. 92, Art. 44, para. 2.

Serbia. Collections of papers have been published by many as a testimony and contribution to the realization of the above. During 2015–2020, the Administration for Religions implemented the Programme Activity 'Protection of Religious, Cultural and National Identity' as part of its Programme 'Cooperation of the State with Churches and Religious Communities'. The annual budget averaged about EUR *1.6 million for these cultural activities* of religious entities in Serbia in the mentioned period.[800] The realization was based on *respecting and implementing the following criteria* – the need to protect the religious content of the national identity of the Serbian people and all national minorities in Serbia, the improvement of their spiritual culture as a stronghold and a cohesive social factor, as well as the development of part of the material base (books and professional literature) of educational institutions of religious entities. As *proclaimed goals* which should have been achieved, it defined the *encouragement of religious cultural activities* of the SOC, RCC, ICS, Protestant churches and JC (holding various programmes, professional and scientific gatherings and symposiums, publishing professional monographs, etc.) and *improving working and living condition in their higher and secondary education institutions* (procurement of teaching aids, equipment for faculties and in seminaries, madrasas, high schools, scholarships for the best students, etc.) The *main success indicator* of this programme activity was the number of cultural events held by religious entities on an annual basis, as well as the number of their secondary schools in which the procurement of equipment was financially supported.[801]

## Cooperation of the Republic of Serbia with UNESCO

*302*. Cooperation of the Republic of Serbia with the UN specialized agency for education, science, and culture (UNESCO) is important for the religious dimension of the social being and the attitude of the state towards churches and religious communities. Yugoslavia became a member of UNESCO in 1950, and the Republic of Serbia, as its successor state, has been a full member of this organization since 2013. Yugoslavia was a member of the Executive Council of UNESCO from 2005 to 2009, and the Republic of Serbia has been a member of the Executive Council since 2015. Its membership was renewed in 2019. In the Republic of Serbia, the National Commission, an inter-ministerial governmental body with an operational seat in the Ministry of Foreign Affairs, oversees cooperation with UNESCO. Although UNESCO gives priority in principle to universal values and goals of education, science and culture, this organization pays considerable attention to specific religious and identity-important aspects of culture and civilization, both globally and locally. The Republic of Serbia actively participates in many UNESCO programmes and projects that presuppose and imply appreciation, preservation and affirmation of religious equality through educational, scientific and, especially, cultural activities, both regular (within the UN educational agenda) and separately designed and conducted, independently or in collaboration with other members of the organization. The Republic of Serbia has the most comprehensive and intensive cooperation with

800. *Source*: Ministry of Justice.
801. *Source*: Administration for Religions of the Ministry of Justice.

UNESCO, and the World Heritage Centre, in the field of *cultural heritage protection*. The *UNESCO World Heritage List* includes the historical complex *Stari Ras and Sopoćani* monasteries (inscribed in 1979), *Studenica* Monastery (1986), Medieval Monuments in KiM – *Dečani Monastery* (2004), *Patriarchate of Peć Monastery, Gračanica Monastery, and the Church of the Holy Virgin of Ljevisa* (2006), then the *ancient site Gamzigrad – Romulijana* (2007) and *Medieval tombstones – stećci* (2016), as a joint nomination with BiH, Croatia and Montenegro. All inscribed monuments contain a fundamental religious component, and the most important ones in KiM are *sacral monuments of exceptional universal value*, as well as living centres of spiritual life and worship of the SOC. Four protected cultural and spiritual properties in KiM were inscribed on the *List of World Heritage in Danger in 2006* because they were threatened with physical destruction by radical Albanian nationalists. Since the end of the conflict in KiM and the placing of the southern Serbian province under the UN protectorate (1999), *150 Orthodox Churches and monasteries have been destroyed or severely damaged on its territory, sixty-one of which had the status of cultural monuments*. This difficult situation requires the active cooperation of the Republic of Serbia, which does not control the territory of KiM, with UNESCO, in order to protect Serbian churches, monasteries and other religious buildings from further destruction, and to rebuild and restore the damaged ones. The Permanent Delegation of the Republic of Serbia, headed by the Permanent Representative in the rank of Ambassador, operates at UNESCO. Serbia is active as a member of the UNESCO Executive Council (in the current mandate from 2019 to 2023), in specialized committees and other working bodies, as well as in a number of UNESCO programmes. Serbia's cooperation with UNESCO also takes place through the activities of the interdepartmental National Commission for Cooperation with UNESCO, whose headquarters are in the Ministry of Foreign Affairs of the Republic of Serbia.[802] In this regard, the state maintains close cooperation with the SOC, as the titular of the respective shrines.

802. Jović-Lazić, Ana, Marko Nikolić, '*Cooperation of the Republic of Serbia with the Organization for Education, Science and Culture (UNESCO)*', in: *Serbia and International Organizations*, Belgrade, 2011, pp. 294–316.

## Chapter 1. Religion and Art[803]

*303.* Religious and ecclesiastical art is a form of witnessing and promoting God's truth and presence in this world. As in the entire universal Orthodox Church, spiritual creators and God-inspired artists of the SOC express the deepest truths about God, man and the world through a living word, melody, colour, or construction. There are different means for the primary goal *to express faith in God.*

*304.* In *architecture*, it is achieved through the use of *space* and *light*. The Orthodox Church is always turned to the East, that is, to the Second Coming of Christ, since the Lord Christ will come from the East. The organization of the space inside the church has an identical meaning. The altar represents Heaven, that is, the Kingdom of God, the central part represents the earth, and the church as a whole is Heaven on earth. And just as Christ sits in the Kingdom of God on a throne surrounded by the Apostles sitting on co-thrones, so in the church, there is a throne on which a bishop sits surrounded by priests, thus depicting the Second Coming of the Lord.

### Visoki Dečani Monastery

*305.* In 2004, UNESCO declared the monastery of the SOC in Visoki Dečani in KiM a *World Heritage Site*. In the explanation, it is stated that the frescoes of Visoki Dečani are one of the most valuable examples of the Palaiologian Renaissance in *Byzantine painting* and a valuable record of life in the fourteenth century. The monastery itself represents the embodiment of *medieval church architecture* and the endowment of the Serbian King Stefan Dečanski. Its construction was completed in 1335 and the frescoes around 1348. It is dedicated to the church holiday of the Ascension of the Lord. The main builder was Master Vito Kotoranin. The monastery church is a five-nave building and belongs to the *Raška style* of the then church architecture. It is located in the valley of the river Dečanska Bistrica southwest of Peć, below the mountain massif of Prokletije in KiM. The relics of Holy King Stefan of Dečani and Saint Helena of Dečani rest in the monastery. The Turks intended to turn the Dečani Monastery into a mosque in 1692, but a miracle occurred that prevented them from realizing that intention.[804] The monastery belongs to the Eparchy of Raška and Prizren of the SOC and represents an immovable heritage as a *cultural monument of exceptional importance* of the Republic of Serbia. The monastery church is thirty-six meters long and thirty meters high, completely unusual for that time, which is why the monastery was named *Visoki Dečani*.[805] Today, it represents an undeniable testimony of the history and existence of the Serbian people and the SOC in KiM in the Middle Ages, as well as an invaluable and universal artistic and cultural property that was confirmed by UNESCO.

---

803. Editor-in-Chief of the newspaper of the Serbian Patriarchate 'Orthodoxy' and the religious – scientific journal of the Holy Synod of Bishops of the SOC 'Theological Views' Archdeacon Dr Damjan S. Božić.
804. http://www.zaduzbine-nemanjica.rs/Decani/index.htm, 15 Jul. 2020.
805. In Serbian it means tall Dečani.

### White Angel Fresco

*306.* The interior of the Orthodox Church has always been filled with frescoes and icons whose essence is the intention to bring the believer closer to the events from the life of Christ and His followers, as well as the truth about the future Kingdom of God. Guided by God's grace, the *icon masters* paint saints and events from the life of the Church in complete harmony with the Church's Tradition. The *icon* has the simplicity of the gospel language that describes the events in the Holy Scriptures.

*307.* In the southwestern part of the Republic of Serbia, there is a medieval monastery of the SOC *Mileševa,* with the Church of the Holy Christ the Saviour. The monastery is the endowment of the Serbian king Vladislav from the *Nemanjić* dynasty and was built between 1218 and 1219, exactly at the time when the SOC was gaining autocephaly. The relics of Saint Sava also rested in it for a while. On a global scale, the monastery is also known for the fresco of the *White Angel*, which is part of the composition of the Myrrh-bearers on Christ's tomb. It is one of the most famous frescoes in the Republic of Serbia and is one of the highest achievements of *Serbian and European medieval painting*. The picture shows an angel dressed in a white-golden gown sitting on a stone and indicating with his hand the place of Christ's resurrection, that is, his empty tomb. The first satellite transmission of video signals between Europe and North America in 1963 contained an image of the White Angel from Mileševa, in the first frames that represented the greeting of Europeans to Americans. This monastery is under the protection of UNESCO as part of the *world cultural heritage.*

## Chapter 2. Religion and Media[806]

*308.* Radio and TV shows of a religious character became more prevalent in the second half of the 1980s in the public media in Serbia. One of the first examples of the presence of church content in the state media was related to the commemoration of the 600th anniversary of the Battle of Kosovo on 28 June 1989. The solemn commemoration of the event was held on Kosovo field near Priština, where the then Patriarch of the SOC German served a memorial service for the fallen soldiers with numerous bishops, and the entire service was broadcast on *state television* (*Serbian Broadcasting Corporation* (*RTS*)). The church and religious people are familiar with new *forms of information transmission, different from the traditional ones.* With the improvement of information technology, both the SOC and other religious entities in the Republic of Serbia have accepted the widespread use of the Internet. Today, nearly everyone has internet presentations. Almost all SOC eparchies in the country and the diaspora are connected to the official website of the Serbian Patriarchate in Belgrade. The same applies to other religious entities in the country.

*309.* The first church *radio station* in RS, '*Glas Crkve*', started operating in 1996. The shows of this radio are broadcast in Western Serbia and can also be heard in Belgrade.[807] The SOC received permits to open local stations in eight municipalities and cities in 2008. After that, following the example of the radio station 'Glas Crkve', she founded several new ones.

*310.* Radio '*Slovo ljubve*' is a radio station of the SOC Archdiocese of Belgrade – Karlovac, which received a broadcasting licence in August 2009. Then the following radio stations were established: Radio '*Slavoslovlje*' (in Subotica), '*Beseda*' (Novi Sad), '*Tavor*' (Bačka Palanka), '*Blagovesnik*' (in Sombor), '*Istočnik'* (in Valjevo), '*Glas*' (in Nis), *'Mileševa*' (in the monastery of the same name near Prijepolje), '*Zlatousti*' (in Kragujevac) and '*Srpski Zion*' (in Ruma). The radio station '*Svetigora*' was established in the SOC Metropolitanate of Montenegro and the Littoral in 1998, with its headquarters in Cetinje.

*311.* The first *TV station* owned by the SOC, '*TV Hram*', started operating in 2015 and is managed by the Archdiocese of Belgrade and Karlovac. Its programme is broadcast on the territory of the city of Belgrade. The Serbian Patriarchate publishes the official magazines of the SOC '*Pravoslavlje*', '*Glasnik Srpske Patrijaršije*' and '*Teološki pogled*', and almost all eparchies of the SOC have their own magazines.

*312.* Other religious entities in the Republic of Serbia also have their own radio stations. Also, in addition to the existence of the minority desks and newsrooms of Radio Television of Vojvodina (RTV), the contents of the RCC and traditional

806. Editor-in-Chief of the newspaper of the Serbian Patriarchate 'Orthodoxy' and the religious – scientific journal of the Holy Synod of Bishops of the SOC 'Theological Views' Archdeacon Dr Damjan S. Božić.
807. http://www.ceir.co.rs/images/stories/rit_13/rit_13_mediji_crkava.pdf, 15 Jul. 2020.

churches of the Reformation are promoted. Within the RCC in the Republic of Serbia, the programme '*Radio Marija*' is broadcast, which belongs to the world radio network 'Radio Maria'. It also publishes the magazines '*Blagovesti*' (Belgrade Archdiocese), '*Zvonik i hirvivo*' (Subotica diocese), '*Nada*' (Srem diocese) and '*Dzvoni*' (Greek Catholic Diocese of 'St. Nicholas Ruski Krstur'). The traditional churches of the Reformation in the Republic of Serbia publish the magazines '*Evangelički glasnik*' (Slovak Evangelical Church) and '*Reformatuš elet*' (Reformed Christian Church). Within the ICS, the programme is broadcast by the radio '*Glas Muslimana Srbije*'. The Islamic Community also publishes the magazines '*Vakat*' and '*Glas Islama*', and the JC (Association of Jewish Communities of Serbia) '*Jevrejski Pregled*'.

*313.* Every year for Christmas and Easter, the state media with the national frequency broadcast live the Holy Liturgy served by the head of the SOC, as well as the heads of other churches in Serbia (especially the RCC). Also, every day, and prior to the morning programme, the television with a national frequency broadcasts a religious programme entitled 'Religious Calendar'. In it, the most important daily lessons and messages of the SOC, RCC, ICS and JC are presented to the believers.

*314.* The *biggest problems and challenges* that radio stations and television of the SOC in Serbia face today are related to the *lack of professional and experienced staff*, which is a prerequisite for their better work. At the Faculty of Philosophy in Novi Sad, in the Department of Media Studies, students are offered the elective course 'Media and Religious Communities'. During the course, they are acquainted with the basics of teaching religious subjects and media issues, learn to analyse media reports, and prepare a multi-confessional radio show. The issue of interaction between the church and media spheres, as well as the affirmation of religious contents and values through the media, is also represented in the curricula of multidisciplinary master studies 'Religion in Society, Culture and European Integration' at the University of Belgrade, which was launched in 2013.

## Chapter 3. Religion and Civil Society[808]

*315.* In the period of socialist Yugoslavia, religious entities were pushed to the margins of social and public life. In difficult circumstances, they tried to testify to their faith mainly through the written word, in thematic publications and magazines whose publication was allowed by the state authorities. The leadership of the Yugoslav Communist Party '... admitted that the Balkan Peninsula could not be communized until the backbone of the Serbs and the Orthodox Church was broken, since it is known that these two factors always prevented the penetration of the Ottomans into the West and communism and Austria towards the East'. Because of that, it was 'harmonious in preparing a common ground for the communization of Yugoslavia and the Balkan Peninsula and for the destruction of everything that is Serbian and Orthodox'.[809]

*316.* After the disappearance of ideological frameworks and coercion, the SOC and other religious entities in Serbia began to provide and offer believers and other citizens an 'old/new value perspective' and a philosophy of life. In accordance with their mission and competencies, they began to gradually integrate into the work of state institutions. As stated, since the beginning of the twenty-first century, religious communities have been present in the *Serbian Army*, *the education system* (through religious instruction), *hospitals and prisons*, as well as in many other areas of public life. In that manner, they began to fill a *great existing ideological and spiritual vacuum in the lives of most of their citizens*. However, in the post-communist transition period, there is an increased activity of civil society actors, primarily non-governmental organizations of atheistic-liberal orientation, who, declaratively concerned about the alleged de-secularization and clericalization of society, oppose wider public space for participation of churches and religious communities.

808. Editor-in-Chief of the newspaper of the Serbian Patriarchate 'Orthodoxy' and the religious–scientific journal of the Holy Synod of Bishops of the SOC 'Theological Views' Archdeacon Dr Damjan S. Božić.

809. For more information, *see*: Velibor V. Džomić, *Stradanje srbske crkve od komunizma*, 'Svetigora', Mitropolija Crnogorsko-primorska SPC, 2000.

## Chapter 4. Religion and Public Debate

*317.* The participation of churches and religious communities in public life in Serbia intensified at the beginning of the twenty-first century. As it was said, their highest representatives actively participated in the process of adopting the Law on Churches and Religious Communities. They participate in all television and radio shows, not only on religious media but also on those with a state frequency (RTS, RTV, TV Pink, Radio Belgrade, Radio Novi Sad, etc.), where religious issues are discussed with representatives of various social groups. In addition to their pastoral and missionary activities, many high-ranking and qualified representatives of religious communities in the Republic of Serbia are participants and bearers of their educational activities in secondary and higher religious educational institutions (deans, professors, teachers and lecturers). They are also promoters of a culture of dialogue, tolerance, and the establishment of cooperation of all factors that bring together a common social interest.

*318.* In the field of science and education, representatives of religious communities in RS are active participants at numerous scientific conferences, symposia, and round tables, which not only discuss issues of a principled relationship between science and religion, the contribution of religion to integration processes and social progress, but also those dedicated to interstate relations at the bilateral, regional and international level. For example, this refers to the Scientific Conference of the PBF SOC 'Serbian Theology in the Twentieth Century' (2015), the International Conference of PBF 'Christ – Priest of Narratives' (2015), the International Ecumenical Symposium on the Twentieth Anniversary of the Death of RCC Cardinal Ivo Kongar (2016), Scientific Meeting of the SOC Eparchy of Srem 'Patriarch Josif Rajačić and his time' (2017), Third International Conference of the University 'Singidunum' dedicated to religious tourism (2017), International Scientific Conference of PBF SOC 'Eight Centuries of SOC' (2018), Ecumenical RCC Conference 'Role and responsibility of traditional Christian churches in Europe in preserving the value of Christian cultural identity' (2018), General Assembly of the Conference of European Churches in Novi Sad (2018), Scientific Meeting of the SOC Eparchy of Bač 'Eparchy of Bač in eight centuries of SOC history' (2019), Scientific Conference IZS 'Religious Media and Contemporary Challenges' (2019), Round Table entitled 'Mission of Churches and Religious Communities and Work Experiences on Building Religious Tolerance and Coexistence in Serbia' on the occasion of visit of the Secretary General of the Muslim World League to Serbia, Sheikh Dr Mohammed bin Abdul Karim Al-Issa in 2020, etc.

*319.* Since 2011, the Republic of Serbia and the SOC have been holding a bilateral international *interfaith dialogue* with the Republic of Indonesia. So far, four sessions have been held, alternately in both countries (2011, 2013, 2015 and 2019). The most important representatives and participants of the two-state delegations are religious leaders, who present dialogues on various topics, such as those concerning the position, role and responsibilities of young people in society, the role and influence of media and education, etc. Based on the positive experience, the Republic of Serbia is the initiator of establishing this type of dialogue with other countries in the world, primarily in Southeast Europe but also in all those who remain committed to the values of peace, cooperation and overall progress.

# Selected Bibliography

## Books

Đorđević Jelena. *Interreligijski dijalog i svakodnevni život, u: Interreligijski dijalog kao vid pomirenja u Jugoistočnoj Evropi.* Milan Vukomanović, Marinko Vučinić (prir.), BOŠ, Beograd, 2001.

Džomić Velibor V. *Stradanje srbske crkve od komunizma.* Svetigora, Mitropolija Crnogorsko-primorska SPC, 2000.

*Istorija Srpskog naroda – Od prvog ustanka do Belinskog kongresa 1804–1878, 5.* knjiga, drugo izdanje, Sprska književna zadruga, Beograd, 1994.

Jović-Lazić, Ana & Marko Nikolić. *'Cooperation of the Republic of Serbia with the Organization for Education, Science and Culture (UNESCO)'.* In *Serbia and International Organizations*, Belgrade, 2011.

Mercier Jacques. *Povijest Vatikana.* Barbat, Zagreb, 2001.

Nikolić Marko & Ana Jović Lazić. *'Religious transition' and/or 'transition of religiosity' in Serbia.* In *Religiosity in Serbia 2010*, Christian Cultural Centre, Konrad Adenauer, Centre for European Studies, Belgrade, Brussels.

Nikolić Marko. *Aktuelna međureligijska saradnja na Balkanu.* u: *Srbija u Jugoistočnoj Evropi*, Dragan Đukanović, Vladimir Trapara (ur.), Institut za me unarodnu politiku i privredu, Beograd, 2012, str. 552–568.

Nikolić Marko. *Ekumenski odnosi SPC i RKC od 1962–2000.* godine, Službeni glasnik, Beograd, 2011.

Radulović Milan. *Obnova srpskog državno-crkvenog prava.* Konrad Adenauer Stiftung, Christian Cultural Centre, 2009.

Robbers Gerhard. *State and Church in the European Union.* In *State and Church in the European Union*, Gerhard Robbers & Bogoljub Sijaković (ed.), Orthodox Theological Faculty, Institute for Theological Research, Belgrade, 2012.

Sava Nemanjić, Sveti Sava & Istorija i predanje, (Akademik Vojislav Djurić (ed.)) *Predsedništvo*, knjiga 1, Srpska akademija nauka i umetnosti (SANU), Beograd, 1979.

Stefan Nemanja, Sveti Simeon Mirotočivi & Istorija i predanje, (Jovanka Kalić (ed.)) *Odeljenje istorijskih nauka*, knjiga 26, Srpska akademija nauka i umetnosti (SANU), Beograd, 2000.

Vukomanović Milan. *Religion, Conflict, Reconciliation*, u: *Interreligijski dijalog kao vid pomirenja u Jugoistočnoj Evropi*, Milan Vukomanović, Marinko Vučinić (prir.), BOŠ, Beograd, 2001.

## Selected Bibliography


Зиројевић Фатић Мина, Марко Николић, *'Тероризам и религија', Супротстављање савременом организованом криминалу и тероризму*, књига 2., Криминалистичко–полицијска академија (КПА), Београд, стр. 219–228.

Јанулатос Анастасиос Архиепископ Тиране, *Глобализам и Православље*, Хришћански културни центар, Београд, 2002.

Јовић Лазић Ана, Марко Николић, Сарадња Републике Србије са организацијом Уједињених нација за образовање, науку и културу (УНЕСКО), у: *Србија и међународне организације*, Институз за међународну политику и привреду, Београд, стр. 296–318.

Мандзаридис Георгије М., *Социологија хришћанства*, Хришћански културни центар, Београд, 2004.

Николић Марко, Актуелни односи Римокатоличке и Српске православне цркве, *Зборник Матице српске за друштвене науке*, Матица Српска, Нови Сад, VIII, 133, стр. 19–38.

Перић Димшо, *Црквено право*, Правни факултет Универзитета у Београду, 2006.


## Periodicals


Comparative-legal analysis of the position of religious communities in the surrounding countries of the EU Member States – Slovenia, Croatia, Hungary, Romania, Bulgaria and Greece, Ministry of Justice of the Republic of Serbia, 2016.

Cooperation of State with Churches and Religious Communities in Europe in 21st Century Case of Serbia, иизлагање помоћника директора Управе за вере Министарства правде Републике Србије др Марка Николића на Међународној конференцији. The Positive Side of Religious Freedom: How Governments Can Engage with Religious Organizations, Државни секретаријат за верске послове Републике Румуније, Букурешт, 6–7 јун 2019. Године.

FNRJ, Savezno izvršno veće (SIV), Dokument Komisije za verska pitanja, poverljivo, br. 01–243/1, 14. septembar 1959, Arhiv Jugoslavije, broj fonda 144, fascikla 65, Arhivska jedinica 495.

Izveštaj Komisije za verska pitanja NR BiH za 1962. godinu, Arhiv Jugoslavije, broj fonda 144, fascikla 64, Arhivska jedinica 495.

Materijali za sednicu Savezne komisije za verska pitanja, poverljivo, broj 558, 25. novembar 1963. godine, Arhiv Jugoslavije, fond 144, fascikla 67, 1963. Godina.

Medić Mile, Sveti Simeon Mirotočivi, Nemanjino zaveštanje i Nebesna liturgija, Srpska pravoslavna crkvena opština Linc, Austrija i manastir Velika Remeta, 1996.

Mitropolit Pergama Jovan Zizjulas. *'Zajednica i drugačijnost'*, 'Svetigora', 31/1994, 22–24. i 32/1994, 31–33.

Nikolić Marko. *The Role of Religion in Serbian Society and Politics*. In *Religion in the Post–Yugoslav Context*, Lexington Books, Lanham, Boulder, New York, London, pp. 155–171.

Nikolić Marko. Central–Eastern European Countries (CEEC) and Serbia's Perspective and Position towards Chinese 'One belt, One Road' Initiative – A Geopolitical Overview, Review International Affairs, Institute of International Politics and Economics, Belgrade, LXVII, 1161, pp. 45–64.

Nikolić Marko. *Strategic Potentials of Contemporary Religion in Serbia in the Context of European Integration*, Review International Affairs, Institute for International Politics and Economics, Belgrade, LXIV, 1152, pp. 71–85.

Nikolić Marko. *Ekumenizam, Ekumenski pokret i Svetski savet crkava, Religija i tolerancija*, Centar za empirijska istraživanja religije (CEIR) Filozofskog fakulteta u Novom Sadu, VIII, 14, str. 311–337.

Nikolić Marko. *Paradoks nužnosti i nemogućnosti dijaloga istine*, Pravoslavlje, 15. oktobar 2012. godine, str. 12–15.

Nikolić Marko. *Pozicija i uloga SPC u konfliktnoj i postkonfliktnoj Bosni i Hercegovini*, u: Republika Srbija i Republika Srpskastari i novi politički izazovi, Institut za međunarodnu politiku i privredu, Fakultet političkih nauka u Banjaluci, Predstavništvo republike Srpske u Srbiji, Beograd, str. 233–248.

Nikolić Marko. *Saradnja Republike Srbije sa svojim crkvama i verskim zajednicama*, izlaganje na Okruglom stolu Misija crkava i verskih zajednica i iskustva rada na izgradnji verske tolerancije i suživota u Srbiji, poseta generalnog sekretara Muslimanske svetske lige (MWL) dr Muhameda bin Abdul–Kerim Al Ise Srbiji, Beograd, 6. februar 2020. Godine.

Nikolić Marko. *Savremeni odnosi države i crkve u Evropskoj uniji*, Evropsko zakonodavstvo, Institut za međunarodnu politiku i privredu, Beograd, XIV, 51, str. 295–307.

Nikolić Marko. *Unapređenje saradnje države i crkve/verskih zajednica u Republici Srbiji*, Institut za međunarodnu politiku i privredu, Beograd, 2014.

Nikolić Marko. *Legal Framework and Religious Politics in the Republic of Serbia*, Presentation at the International Conference the Unifying Human Brotherhood, Oslo, 21. novembar 2019. Godine.

Nikolić Marko & Ana Jović Lazić. *Institutional Forms of Contemporary Ecumenical Dialogue*, Review International Affairs, Institute of International Politics and Economics, Belgrade, LXIII, 1146, pp. 50–69.

Nikolić Marko & Ana Jović Lazić. *Relations of Roman Catholic (RCC) and Serbian Orthodox Church (SOC) after the Second Vatican Council*, Studia Europaea, Faculty of European Studies, Romania, LVII, 1, pp. 101–128.

Nikolić Marko & Duško Dimitrijević. *Macedonian Orthodox Church in Former Yugoslav State*, Politikologija religije, Centar za proučavanje religije i versku toleranciju, Beograd, VII, 1, str. 193–215.

Osnovi učenja RPC o dostojanstvu, slobodi i pravima čoveka, Sveti Arhijerejski sabor Ruske Pravoslavne Crkve, Moskva, 2008, Hrišćanski kulturni centar, Beograd 2009.

Patrijarh Moskovski Kiril, Konferencija Ljudska prava i nacionalna samobitnost, Odeljenje za spoljne crkvene veze Moskovske patrijaršije, Konrad Adenauer, Moskva, 2007, u: Sloboda i odgovornost, ITI UBPBF, Beograd 2010.

**Selected Bibliography**

Patrijarh srpski Pavle, Izlaganje na skupu Hrišćanstvo i evropske integracije, Hrišćanstvo i evropske integracije, Hrišćanski kulturni centar, Beograd, 2003, str. 17.

Petković Petar & Marko Nikolić, *Princip supsidijarnosti u proučavanju evropskih integracija,* Evropsko zakonodavstvo, Institut za međunarodnu politiku i privredu, Beograd, X, 37–38, str. 9–19.

Pisma Patrijarha Pavla Preuzvišenom Mustafi Ceriću i Beogradskom Muftiji, Preuzvišenom Hamdiji Efendiji Jusufspahiću, Glasnik Srpske Patrijaršije, 2001.

Preporuka SIV–a, poverljivo, br. 12, 18. jul 1959, Arhiv Jugoslavije, broj fonda 144, fascikla 65, Arhivska jedinica 495.

Religioznost u Srbiji 2010, Hrišćanski kulturni centar, Konrad Adenauer, Centar za Evropske studije, Beograd, Brisel, 2010.

Sarajevski Prepis Zakonopravila Svetog Save iz XIV vijeka, Dabar, Mitropolija dabrobosanska SPC, 2016.

Socijalna koncepcija Ruske Pravoslavne Crkve, Sveti Arhijerejski sabor RPC, Moskva, 2000, Beseda, Novi Sad, 2007.

Susret države i Crkve, Izveštaj Saveznog ministarstva (Sekretarijata) za vere 2001–2002, Savezni sekretarijat za vere, Beograd, 2003.

Todić Dragoljub & Marko Nikolić, *Status nacionalnih i drugih manjina i proces evropskih integracija Srbije*, Evropsko zakonodavstvo, Institut za međunarodnu politiku i privredu, Beograd, XIII, 49–50, str. 445–467.

**Internet**

Address by the President of the Republic of Serbia after the meeting with the Serbian Patriarch Mr Irinej, https://www.predsednik.rs/lat/pres-centar/vesti/obracanje-predsednika-republike-srbije-nakon-susreta-sa-njegovom-svetosti-patrijarhom-srpskim-gospodinom-irinejom, 7 March 2024.

Address to the Holy Synod of Bishops of the Serbian Orthodox Church – Sopoćanska Poslanica, Sopoćani Monastery, 21 February 2001.

Christmas Epistle of the Serbian Orthodox Church, Serbian Orthodox Church to its spiritual children on Christmas 2019, http://spc.rs, 8 January 2020.

*Consultation on 'Church and Service'*, Chania, Crete, 20 to 25 November 1978, www.ecupatria.org, 11 February 2014.

European Court of Human Rights, *Case of Metropolitan Church of Bessarabia and Others v. Moldova*, no. 45701/99, https://hudoc.echr.coe.int/eng#{%22itemid%22:[%22001-59985%22]}, 15 February 2020.

His All-Holiness Ecumenical Patriarch Bartholemeos, *The Conference on Peace and Tolerance*, Istanbul, 1994, www.ecupatria.org, 11 February 2014.

His All-Holiness the Ecumenical Patriarch Demetrios of Constantinople, *The World Convocation on Justice, Peace and the Integrity of Creation*, Seoul, 1990, www.ecupatria.org, 11 February 2014.

Interview of Porfirije Metropolitan of Zagreb and Ljubljana SOC for Tanjug, https://mitropolija-zagrebacka.org/intervju-mitropolita-porfirija-za-politiku/, https://vidovdan.org/info/intervju-mitropolita-porfirija-za-tanjug-sta-god-da-ucinite-za-odredjene-ljude-u-cije-ciljeve-i-projekte-se-ne-uklapate-a-priori-ste-krivi/, 12 March 2024.

Irinej Episkop Bački, 'Ne mogu oteti Kosovo bez našeg pristanka, a mi ga ne damo', https://rtv.rs/sk/drustvo/irinej-backi-kosovo-i-metohiju-nam-ne-mogu-oteti-i-necemo-ga-dati_1054440.html, 6 March 2024.

Leaders of the Serbian people in the Patriarchate – Statement to the media of the Serbian Patriarch Irinej, https://www.eparhijazt.com/sr/news/vijesti-iz-crkve/-/1542.lideri-srpskog-naroda-u-patrijarsiji.html, 12 March 2024.

Leaders of the Serbian people in the Patriarchate – Statement to the media of the President of the Presidency of BiH Mr Milorad Dodik, https://www.eparhijazt.com/sr/news/vijesti-iz-crkve/-/1542.lideri-srpskog-naroda-u-patrijarsiji.html, 12 March 2024.

Leaders of the Serbian people in the Patriarchate – Statement to the media of the President of the Republic of Serbia, Mr Aleksandar Vučić, https://www.eparhijazt.com/sr/news/vijesti-iz-crkve/-/1542.lideri-srpskog-naroda-u-patrijarsiji.html, 12 March 2024.

Osetljiv trenutak: Žasto je važan dolazak Vučića i Dodika na Sabor SPC? Interview with Professor Darko Tanaskovic, Sputnjik, https://rs.sputniknews.com/analize/201905151119809946-srbi-predsednik-patrijarh-spc-analiza/, 16 May 2019.

Population – religion, mother tongue and ethnicity – data by municipalities and cities, Republic Statistical Office of the Republic of Serbia, Belgrade, 2013, www.stat.gov.rs, 19 October 2017.

Press release of the Holy Synod of Bishops of the Serbian Orthodox Church, http://arhiva.spc.rs/eng/statements_holy_synod_statement%3Fpage=2.html, 12 March 2024.

Press release of the Serbian Orthodox Church.

Religious Tolerance and Interfaith Dialogue have the leading Role in Promoting Human Rights and Building harmonized Societies – Speech by the First Deputy Prime Minister of the Government of Serbia and Minister of Foreign Affairs Ivica Dačić at the Ministerial Conference on Religious Freedom in Washington on 26 July 2018, https://mfa.gov.rs/mediji/saopstenja/verska-tolerancija-i-medjureligijski-dijalog-imaju-vodecu-ulogu-u-unapredjenju.

Serbian Patriarch Irinej, 'We have preserved religion, language, culture and state', Politika, https://www.politika.rs/scc/clanak/438810/Sacuvali-smo-veru-jezik-kulturu-i-drzavu, 12 March 2024.

The Conference 'Decade to Overcome Violence (2001–2010.) – Churches Seeking Reconciliation and Peace', www.ecupatria.org, 11 February 2014.

*The inter–orthodox consultations on The Place of the Woman in the Orthodox Church and the Question of the Ordination of Women*, Rhodos, Greece, 30 October till 7 November 1988, www.ecupatria.org, 11 February 2014.

The President of the Republic of Serbia, Mr Aleksandar Vučić met on 2 December 2019 with His Holiness the Serbian Patriarch Irinej, http://arhiva.spc.rs/eng/meeting_serbian_patriarch_president_republic_serbia.html, 12 March 2024.

*The Third Prosynodal Pan–Orthodox Consultation 1986*, www.ecupatria.org, 11 February 2014.

## Selected Bibliography

### Legislation


African Charter on Human and Peoples' Rights, 1981, https://au.int/sites/default/files/treaties/36390-treaty-0011_-_african_charter_on_human_and_peoples_rights_e.pdf, 12 March 2024.

American Convention on Human Rights 1969, http://www.oas.org/dil/treaties_B-32_American_Convention_on_Human_Rights.htm, 17 January 2019.

Budget Law in 2016, Official Gazette of RS, no. 103/2015-3.

Budget Law in 2017, Official Gazette of RS, no. 99/2016-3.

Budget Law in 2018, Official Gazette of RS, no. 113/2017.

Budget Law, Official Gazette of RS, nos 113/2017, 95/2018, 84/2019.

Budget System Law, Official Gazette of RS, nos 101/2010, 101/2011, 93/2012, 108/2013, 142/2014, 103/2015 and 99/2016.

CoE Framework Convention for the Protection of National Minorities, Official Gazette of the FRY no. 6/1998.

Constitution of Serbia from 1990, https://www.worldstatesmen.org/Serbia_const_1990.htm, 12 March 2024.

Constitution of the Federal People's Republic of Yugoslavia from 1946, https://en.wikisource.org/wiki/Constitution_of_Yugoslavia_(1946), 12 March 2024.

Constitution of the FRY in 1992, https://www.montenet.org/law/fryconst.htm, 12 March 2024.

Constitution of the Kingdom of Serbia 1903, https://sr.wikisource.org/sr-el/Ustav_Kraljevine_Srbije_(1903)#Deo_I._Oblik_vladavine,_državna_vera_i_državna_oblast, 20 September 2019.

Constitution of the Kingdom of Yugoslavia 1931, https://royalfamily.org/wp-content/uploads/2014/01/constitution.pdf, 12 March 2024.

Constitution of the Kingdom Serbs, Croats, and Slovenes 1921, https://www.uzzpro.gov.rs/doc/biblioteka/digitalna-biblioteka/Ustav%20Kraljevine%20Srba,%20Hrvata%20i%20Slovenaca.pdf, 12 March 2024.

Constitution of the Republic of Serbia from 2006, Official Gazette of RS, no. 98/2006.

Constitution of the Serbian Orthodox Church, https://sr.m.wikisource.org/sr-ec/Ustav_Srpske_pravoslavne_crkve, 9 January 2017.

Constitution of the SFRY in 1974, https://en.wikipedia.org/wiki/1974_Yugoslav_Constitution, 12 March 2024.

Constitution of the Socialist Federal Republic of Yugoslavia 1963, https://www.arhivyu.rs/en/leksikon-jugoslavije/konstitutivni_akti_jugoslavije, 12 March 2024.

Constitutional Charter of the State Union of Serbia and Montenegro from 2003, https://en.wikisource.org/wiki/Constitutional_Charter_of_Serbia_and_Montenegro, 12 March 2024.

Criminal Code of the Republic of Serbia, Official Gazette of RS, no. 35/2019.

Decision of the Government on annulment of illegal acts of temporary bodies of self-government in Kosovo and Metohija of 9 March 2010, Official Gazette of RS, no. 19/2010.

Decree on Religious Service in the Serbian Army, Official Gazette of RS, no. 22/2012.

Directive 89/552/EEC, https://eur-lex.europa.eu/legal-content/EN/TXT/?uri=CELEX%3A31989L0552, и Directive 2000/78/EC, https://eur-lex.europa.eu/legal-content/EN/TXT/PDF/?uri=CELEX:32000L0078, 20 February 2019.

EU Charter of Fundamental Rights (2016/c 202/02), Ministry of European Integration of the Republic of Serbia, https://www.mei.gov.rs/upload/documents/eu_dokumenta/povelja_osnovna_prava_jul_20.pdf, 25 December 2019.

European Convention on Human Rights and Fundamental Freedoms 1950, https://www.echr.coe.int/Documents/Convention_SRP.pdf, 15 July 2019.

Family Law 2015, Official Gazette of RS, nos 18/2005, 72/2011 and 6/2015.

Government of the Republic of Serbia, Albanian Terrorism and Organised Crime in Kosovo and Metohija, White Book, 2003, https://www.srbija.gov.rs/kosovo-metohija/19991, https://www.media.srbija.gov.rs/medsrp/dokumenti/bela_knjiga1.pdf, 7 March 2023.

Labour Law, Official Gazette of RS, no. 95/2018.

Law on Accounting and Auditing from 2006, Official Gazette of RS, nos 46/2006, 62/2013.

Law on Agrarian Reform and Colonization of 1946, Official Gazette of the Federal People's Republic of Yugoslavia, no. 24/46.

Law on Associations, Official Gazette of RS, no. 44/2018.

Law on Business Organizations, Official Gazette of RS, no. 99/2011, 83/2014 – dr. law, 5/2015, 95/2018, and 91/2019.

Law on Churches and Religious Communities, Official Gazette of RS, no. 36/2006.

Law on Contributions for Compulsory Social Insurance, Official Gazette of RS, nos 84/2004, 61/2005, 62/2006, 5/2009, 101/2011, 7/2012, 108/2013, 68/2014, 112/2015 and 5/2016.

Law on Cultural Heritage, Official Gazette of RS, nos 71/1994 and 99/2011.

Law on Determining the Jurisdiction of the Autonomous Province of Vojvodina, Official Gazette of RS, nos 99/2009 and 67/2012 US decision.

Law on Education, Official Gazette of RS, nos 55/2013, 88/2017, 27/2018 and 6/2020.

Law on Elementary Education, Official Gazette of RS, nos 55/2013, 101/2017, 27/2018 and 10/2019.

Law on Execution of Criminal Sanctions, Official Gazette of RS, nos 85/2005, 72/2009 and 31/2011.

Law on Government, Official Gazette of RS, nos 71/2005, 101/2007, 65/2008, 16/2011, 74/2012 and 44/2014.

Law on Granting of Identity Card, Official Gazette of RS, nos 62/2006 and 36/2011.

Law on Health Care, Official Gazette of RS, nos 107/2005, 2/2009, 99/2010, 57/2011, 119/2012, 45/2013, 93/2014 and 106/2015.

Law on Health Insurance, Official Gazette of RS, nos 109/2005, 110/2012, 119/2012, 123/2014, 126/2014, 106/2015 and 10/2016.

Law on Higher Education, Official Gazette of RS, nos 88/2017 and 73/2018.

Law on Local Self-Government, Official Gazette of RS, nos 129/2007, 83/2014-dr. law, 101/2016-dr. law, and 47/2018.

Law on Marriage and Family Relations, Official Gazette of SR Serbia, nos 22/1980, 24/1984, 11/1988, 25/1993, 35/1994, 46/1995, 29/2001.

Law on Ministries, Official Gazette of RS, nos 44/2014, 96/2015 and 62/2017.

Law on Official Use of Languages and Scripts, Official Gazette of RS, nos 45/1991 to 48/2018.
Law on Patients' Rights from 2013, Official Gazette of RS, no. 45/2013.
Law on Payment of Contributions for Pension and Disability Insurance (PIO) for Certain Categories of Insured Persons from 2005, Official Gazette of RS, no. 85/2005.
Law on Pension and Disability Insurance (PIO), Official Gazette of RS, nos 34/2003, 84/2004, 101/2005, 63/2006, 107/2009, 101/2010, 93/2012, 108/2013 and 142/2014.
Law on Planning and Construction, Official Gazette of RS, nos 81/2009 – corr., 64/2010 – decision US, 24/2011, 121/2012, 98/2013 – decision US, 145/2014, 83/2018 and 37/2019 – dr. The law.
Law on Police, Official Gazette of RS, no. 87/2018.
Law on Prohibition of Discrimination, Official Gazette of RS, no. 22/2009.
Law on Property Taxes, Official Gazette of RS, nos 26/2001, 80/2002, 135/2004, 61/2007, 5/2009, 101/2010, 78/2011, 57/2012.
Law on Public Procurement, Official Gazette of RS, no. 91/2019.
Law on Ratification of the European Convention for the Protection of Human Rights and Fundamental Freedoms of 1950, Official Gazette of Serbia and Montenegro – International Agreements, nos 9/2003, 5/2005 and 7/2005 – corr.
Law on Remedying Consequences of Seizure of Assets from Holocaust Victims with no Legal Living Heirs, Official Gazette of RS, no. 13/2016.
Law on Republic Administrative Fees, Official Gazette of RS, nos 51/2003, 101/2005, 54/2009, 70/2011, 93/2012, 65/2013, 57/2014, and 112/2015.
Law on Restitution of Confiscated Property and Compensation, Official Gazette of RS, nos 72/2011, 108/2013, 142/2014 and 88/2015 – US.
Law on Restitution of Property to Churches and Religious Communities, Official Gazette of RS, no. 46/2006.
Law on Secondary Education, Official Gazette of RS, no. 55/2013.
Law on State Administration, Official Gazette of RS, nos 79/2005, 101/2007, 95/2010 and 99/2014.
Law on State and Other Holidays, Official Gazette of RS, no. 4/2001.
Law on the Fundamentals of the Education System, Official Gazette of RS, nos 88/2017, 27/2018 and 10/2019.
Law on the Registration Procedure with the Serbian Business Registers Agency, Official Gazette of RS, nos 99/2011. and 31/2019.
Law on the Serbian Army, Official Gazette of RS, no. 36/2018.
Law on Value Added Tax (VAT), Official Gazette of RS, nos 84/2004 to 83/2015, 61/2005, 61/2007 and 93/2012.
Marriage Rules of the Serbian Orthodox Church, http://www.rastko.rs/bogoslovlje/bracna-pravila/index.html, 25 February 2018.
OSCE Helsinki Final Act from 1975, https://fer.org.rs/wp-content/uploads/2018/11/helsinski_zavrsni_akt.pdf, 15 January 2019.
OSCE Istanbul Document of 1999, https://www.osce.org/mc/39569?download=true, 15 January 2019.

OSCE Paris Charter of 1990, https://www.osce.org/mc/39516?download=true, 15 January 2019.

Regulation on the Organization and Realization of Religious Instruction and Teaching of Alternative Subjects in Elementary and Secondary Schools from 2001, Official Gazette of RS, no. 46/2001.

Regulation on Funds for encouraging programmes or the missing portion of funds for financing programmes of public interest implemented by associations from 2018, Official Gazette of RS, no. 16/2018.

Regulation on Issuance of Additional Postage Stamp 'Construction of Memorial Temple Saint Sava', Official Gazette of RS, no. 65/2019.

Regulation on payment of contributions for pension and disability and health insurance for priests and religious officials from 2012, Official Gazette of RS, no. 46/2012.

Republic of Serbia, Framework Convention for the protection of national minorities–*The Third Periodical Report submitted to the Secretary General of the Council of Europe in accordance with Article 25 of the Framework Convention, 2012*, https://www.ljudskaprava.gov.rs/sr/node/133, 20 December 2019.

Republic of Serbia, Framework Convention for the protection of national minorities–*The Fourth Periodical Report Submitted to the General Secretary of the Council of Europe in accordance with Article 25 of the Framework Convention, 2018*, https://ljudskaprava.gov.rs/sr/node/22332, 20 December 2019.

Resolution of the National Assembly of the Republic of Serbia on the basic principles for political talks with the provisional institutions of self-government in Kosovo and Metohija, Official Gazette of the RS, no. 4/2013.

Rulebook on the Content and Method of Keeping the Register of Churches and Religious Communities, Official Gazette of RS, no. 64/2006.

Rulebook on the procedure for exercising the right to VAT refund and the manner and procedure of VAT refund and refund, Official Gazette of RS, nos 107/2004, 65/2005, 63/2007 and 120/2012.

Screening Report for Serbia – Chapter 23 – Justice and Fundamental Rights 2013, Ministry of European Integration of the Republic of Serbia, https://www.mei.gov.rs/upload/documents/skrining/izvestaj_pg_23_16.pdf, 19 December 2019.

Stabilization and Association Agreement between the European Communities and their Member States and the Republic of Serbia, Official Gazette of RS, no. 103/2007.

Treaty establishing a Constitution for Europe, http://publications.europa.eu/resource/cellar/7ae3fd7e-8820-413e-8350-b85f9daaab0c.0005.02/DOC_1, 13 May 2019.

Treaty Establishing the European Community, https://eur-lex.europa.eu/legal-content/EN/TXT/?uri=CELEX%3A12002E%2FTXT, 20 February 2019.

Treaty of Amsterdam 1997, https://eur-lex.europa.eu/legal-content/EN/TXT/?uri=CELEX:11997D/TXT, 12 March 2024.

UN Declaration on the Elimination of All Forms of Intolerance and of Discrimination Based on Religion or Belief in 1981, https://www.ohchr.org/EN/ProfessionalInterest/Pages/ReligionOrBelief.aspx, 21 February 2019.

UN International Covenant on Civil and Political Rights in 1966, Official Gazette of the SFRY, no. 7/1971.

## Selected Bibliography

UN Security Council Resolution no. 1244 of 10 June 1999, https://unmik.unmissions.org/united-nations-resolution-1244, 12 March 2024.

UN Universal Declaration of Human Rights 1948, www.ohchr.org, 20 February 2020.

# Index

*The numbers here refer to paragraph numbers.*


Budget Law, 35, 249, 252, 258
Budget System Law, 249, 253, 258

CoE Framework Convention for the Protection of National Minorities, 157, 160
Comparative – legal analysis of the position of religious communities in the surrounding EU Member States, Slovenia, Croatia, Hungary, Romania, Bulgaria and Greece, 52, 148
Constitution of the Republic of Serbia (2006), 2, 9, 31, 34, 74–77, 91, 93, 97, 100, 101, 105, 119
Criminal Code, 25, 35, 36, 62–64, 243

Decree on Payment of Contributions for Pension and Disability and Health Insurance for Priests and Religious Officials, 71, 210
Decree on Religious Service in the Serbian Army, 79–84
Draft European Constitution, 140–143

EU Charter of Fundamental Rights, 146
European Convention on Human Rights and Fundamental Freedoms, 156
Evangelical Christian Church, 26, 41, 51, 102, 161, 215, 254, 263, 264, 273

Family Law, 35, 285, 288–294

Greek Catholic Church (GCC), 160, 161, 254, 280

Helsinki Final Act, 129, 130

Islamic Community in Serbia (ICinS), 218, 229, 318
Islamic Community of Serbia (ICofS), 196, 215, 217, 224, 228, 280, 282
Istanbul Documents OSCE, 129, 132

Jewish Community (JC), 21, 26, 41, 48, 51, 80, 95, 102, 126, 161, 162, 182, 215, 222, 225, 240, 241, 243, 248, 251, 263, 264, 273, 274, 280, 299, 301, 312, 313

Labour Law, 35, 36, 61, 203–214, 217
Law on Accounting and Auditing, 72, 253
Law on Associations, 35, 59, 257
Law on Churches and Religious Communities, 35–44, 50, 51, 53, 60, 70, 77, 92, 98, 102–106, 127, 150, 162, 195, 198, 215, 217, 228, 237, 246, 247, 258, 260, 268, 271, 300, 317
Law on Companies, 35
Law on Contributions for Compulsory Social Insurance, 71
Law on Cultural Heritage, 35
Law on Elementary Education, 35, 267
Law on Execution of Criminal Sanctions, 87
Law on Health Care, 71, 207
Law on Health Insurance, 71, 208
Law on Higher Education, 35, 269
Law on Marriage and Family Relations, 287
Law on Ministries, 35, 36, 52, 135, 249
Law on Patients' Rights, 88
Law on Pension and Disability Insurance (PIO), 71, 209
Law on Police, 35, 86
Law on Prohibition of Discrimination, 35, 60, 61, 94

## Index


Law on Public Procurement, 35
Law on Ratification of the European Convention for the Protection of Human Rights and Fundamental Freedoms, 155
Law on Registration Procedure in the Serbian Business Registers Agency, 35, 257
Law on Republic Administrative Fees, 72, 265
Law on Restitution of Confiscated Property and Compensation, 58
Law on Restitution of Property to Churches and Religious Communities, 35, 36, 53–58, 72, 252
Law on Secondary Education, 35, 268
Law on State and Other Holidays, 35, 96, 99
Law on the Serbian Army, 35, 78, 79, 99
Law on Value Added Tax (VAT), 35, 72

Marriage Rules of the Serbian Orthodox Church, 288, 289, 291, 292

Paris Charter of the OSCE, 129, 131

Reformed Christian Church, 20, 41, 51, 102, 128, 160, 161, 215, 252, 254, 263, 264, 273, 274, 280, 284, 299, 312
Regulation on Funds for encouraging programmes or the missing portion of funds for financing programmes of public interest implemented by associations, 109–116
Regulation on the Organization and Realization of Religious Instruction and Teaching of Alternative Subjects in Elementary and Secondary Schools, 272
Roman Catholic Church (RCC), 26, 41, 46, 51, 80, 95, 99, 102, 126, 161, 162, 167, 173, 174, 182, 196, 202, 215, 216, 222, 223, 227, 233, 238, 241, 251, 252, 254, 263, 264, 273, 280, 281, 299, 301, 312, 313, 318
Romanian Orthodox Church (ROC), 45, 51, 160, 161, 299
Rulebook on Procedure for Exercising the Right to VAT Refund, 263, 264
Rulebook on the Content and Method of Keeping the Register of Churches and Religious Communities, 44–51

Screening Report for Serbia – Chapter 23, 135, 147
Serbian Orthodox Church (SOC), 25, 26, 41, 45, 51, 52, 80, 99, 102, 126, 160, 161, 170–180, 182, 183, 186, 196, 200–202, 215, 221, 251, 252, 256, 263, 264, 273, 277–280, 288, 289, 291, 292, 294, 299, 301–303, 305, 307–311, 313, 314, 316, 318, 319
Slovak Evangelical Church a.v. (SECAV), 41, 51, 102, 126, 128, 160, 161, 215, 219, 222, 235, 239, 241, 242, 252, 254, 263, 264, 273, 274, 280, 284, 299,
Stabilization and Association Agreement between the Republic of Serbia and the EU, 134

Treaty of Amsterdam, 141

UN Declaration on the Elimination of All Forms of Intolerance and of Discrimination Based on Religion or Belief, 122
UN International Covenant on Civil and Political Rights, 121, 124, 127
UN Universal Declaration of Human Rights, 120, 219, 221

www.ingramcontent.com/pod-product-compliance
Lightning Source LLC
Chambersburg PA
CBHW071446230926
51846CB00001B/359
* 9 7 8 9 4 0 3 5 1 6 9 8 1 *